Spotting Dyslexia Warning Signs

A dyslexic person struggles long-term with written (and sometimes spoken) words, even though he's bright (or extra bright) in other areas. A whole bunch of symptoms tells a psychologist that your child has dyslexia, but warning signs include the following:

- Lack of interest in letters and words at a young age.

- Inability to identify rhyming words (like *hat, pat,* and *fat*) and word patterns (like *Bill, bear, bun, bed,* and *ball,* all beginning with "buh") at an early age.

- Difficulty remembering names of familiar objects, numbers, colors, and shapes at an early age.

- Inability to remember sequences of numbers (like 911 in an emergency) or letters (like the alphabet) or fast facts (like multiplication tables).

- Extreme difficulty with reading. A dyslexic child may leave out little words (like *of*), misread small everyday words (like *they*) even though he reads some harder words, read similar-looking words instead of actual words (like *was* for *saw* and *horse* for *house*), read words that are similar in meaning instead of actual words (reading *little* for *small* or *lovely* for *pretty*), and read words that make no sense but have one or two letters that are in the actual word (like *tall* instead of *lot* because both words have *l* and *t* in them). A dyslexic child might, for example, read "There were a lot of roses growing all around Jane's house" as "There was a tall flowers growing around Jane's horse."

- Extreme difficulty with spelling. A dyslexic child may transpose letters (*aleiv* instead of *alive*), leave out letters *(aliv)*, add letters *(alieve)*, and reverse letters (typically *b* and *d*). He may also write words phonetically (exactly as he hears them), producing spellings like *becuz, wur,* and *thay.*

Chapter 3 has more information about the general signs of dyslexia seen in people of all ages.

Engaging in Memorizing, Visualizing, and Rhyming

A dyslexic child struggles to remember how words are put together in print, but rhyming and visualization strategies can help him. When he turns letters into lively, more concrete characters, he can fix them better in his mind:

- Help your child with short-vowel sounds by having him draw images into the vowels while saying their short sounds. For example, he can create an apple out of *a;* draw an egg inside the top part of *e;* convert a pen with a blob of ink on top into *i;* change *o* into an octopus; and draw an arrowhead on each of the two top ends of *u* so it represents *up.*

- Help your child read and spell words like *late, hole,* and *cute* by showing him the *Bossy e* rule: When *e* is on the end of a short word, it bosses the earlier vowel into saying its name (but stays silent itself).

- Help your child read and spell long-vowel words like *meet, neat, nail,* and *boat* by teaching him this rule: "When two vowels go walking, the first one does the talking (and says its name)."

You can read the full account of these and other memory-jogging strategies in Chapter 11.

For Dummies: Bestselling Book Series for Beginners

Overcoming Dyslexia For Dummies®

Cheat Sheet

Picking Up Phonics

Phonics is the teaching method in which you show your child that letters and groups of letters represent speech sounds. Your dyslexic child needs to get a firm grip on phonics so that she discovers order in words that otherwise seem to her like an arbitrary mix of letters. You can read the complete ins and outs of phonics in Chapter 12, but right here are four simple strategies to help you guide your child through phonics in the systematic, sequential way that experts recommend:

- Emphasize single-letter sounds (rather than names) to your child. Play games like "I spy with my little eye something beginning with 'buh' or 'cuh'." Ask your child to tell you words to continue a word pattern like *Bill, bear, bun, bed,* and *ball* (all beginning with "buh").

- Read rhymes and rhyming stories to your child, and sing rhyming songs so you prime her for identifying word families like *pan, fan, man, can,* and *tan.*

- When you introduce written words to your child, start with a simple two-letter word like *at* and show her how she can add letters to *at* to build a whole *at* word family *(bat, mat, cat, sat, fat).* Make this activity more fun, and easy to repeat, by having your child use a book-sized whiteboard and marker pens. Even better, have two sets of boards and markers so you can do the same activity and you don't interfere with your child's board!

- Any time your child learns a word from which she could build a word family, build that family with her. Start her off with three-letter word families like *big, pig, fig,* and *wig;* build up to middle-level families like *chop, stop, flop,* and *shop;* and help her really think about tricky word families like *would, should,* and *could,* and *fight, might, fright, tight, sight,* and *flight.*

Having Some Multisensory Fun

Multisensory learning is the kind of learning method that suits dyslexics best. In simple terms, *multisensory learning* is hands-on learning that engages a few of your child's senses (typically, seeing, hearing, saying, and doing) together at about the same time.

You can help your child with multisensory learning at home by having her play a lot of hands-on and physical games, say out loud the words she reads and writes, and fit drawing and model building into homework assignments whenever she can. Additionally, when she first learns letters and words, have her

- draw their shapes in different mediums, like sugar and pudding
- trace over them on unusual textures, like sandpaper
- construct 3D models of letters out of modeling clay

Chapter 14 has the full scoop on multisensory learning.

Wiley, the Wiley Publishing logo, For Dummies, the Dummies Man logo, the For Dummies Bestselling Book Series logo and all related trade dress are trademarks or registered trademarks of John Wiley & Sons, Inc. and/or its affiliates. All other trademarks are property of their respective owners.

For Dummies: Bestselling Book Series for Beginners

Overcoming Dyslexia

FOR

DUMMIES®

Overcoming Dyslexia

FOR DUMMIES®

by Tracey Wood, MEd

Wiley Publishing, Inc.

Overcoming Dyslexia For Dummies®

Published by
Wiley Publishing, Inc.
111 River St.
Hoboken, NJ 07030-5774
www.wiley.com

Copyright © 2006 by Wiley Publishing, Inc., Indianapolis, Indiana

Published simultaneously in Canada

For general information on our other products and services, please contact our Customer Care Department within the U.S. at 800-762-2974, outside the U.S. at 317-572-3993, or fax 317-572-4002.

For technical support, please visit www.wiley.com/techsupport.

Wiley also publishes its books in a variety of electronic formats. Some content that appears in print may not be available in electronic books.

Library of Congress Control Number: 2005935149

ISBN-13: 978-0-471-75285-1

ISBN-10: 0-471-75285-1

Manufactured in the United States of America

10 9 8 7 6 5 4 3 2

1B/QY/RS/QV/IN

WILEY

About the Author

Tracey Wood was born in England. She went to teachers college in Leeds and graduated with an honors degree in psychology and education. She taught in a special school for four years and loved it. But sunnier climes called, and she left England for a backpacking vacation in Australia. Twelve years later she was still enjoying the warmth of Australia but had traded her backpack for a husband and two kids.

In Australia, Tracey earned a diploma in special education and a master's degree in education. For several years she ran a high school special education unit and then started her own reading clinic. In the 1990s Tracey moved (with her husband's job) to the San Francisco Bay area. She ran a reading and writing clinic; helped in her kids' school; led two scouting troops; instructed for the Red Cross; created her Web site, ReadingPains.com; and wrote her first book, *See Johnny Read! The 5 Most Effective Ways To End Your Son's Reading Problems*.

Still on the move, Tracey relocated to Toronto and wrote her second and third books, *Teaching Kids to Read For Dummies* and *Teaching Kids to Spell For Dummies*. While writing *Overcoming Dyslexia For Dummies*, she relocated again, to Boston.

Tracey is a literacy consultant and public speaker. She writes articles for magazines like *Big Apple Parent* and *Teachers of Vision*, has appeared on Access *Help TV* and national radio shows like *Parent's Journal* and *The Parent's Report*, and is committed to steering (albeit unsteadily) her two children through childhood with all their limbs and faculties intact.

Dedication

My gorgeous girls: I know you didn't get a choice, but thanks anyway for putting up with the moods that I blame on artistic temperament, the stories that I tell with artistic license, and my unreliable cooking. Pretty much everything I do feels better because of you and is dedicated to you (both of you, *equally!*).

Author's Acknowledgments

They say it takes a village to raise a child, and in my opinion, much the same is true of bringing a book into being. My village is small, but the hearts and talent in it are big:

David Futterman, a university instructor, high school teacher, educational therapist, and active member of the International Dyslexia Association, has experience and qualifications galore in dyslexia. He's also very nice. Thank you a zillionfold, David, for being my right-hand man with this book. Hope you enjoyed the view.

As well as answering every one of my questions and finding plenty of my mistakes, David introduced me to Kathy Futterman, who took time out of her busy teaching and parenting schedule to road-test some products for me. Kathy, I so appreciated your help!

As I wrote this book, several things happened: School vacation came around, landing me with two noisy, easily bored, and frequently hungry kids; I painted, plastered, scrubbed, and finally sold a house; and I bought a new house a whole ten-hour drive away. Over those months, a few stalwart friends painted and scraped with me, lured me from my computer to party and gamble (now I've exposed you to the world!) and whisked my children off at opportune times when I didn't care where or for how long. Valarie Cowton, Kelly Borden, and Phyllis Perry, you're the best!

And last but never least, Therese Hughes, Frances Faflik, and Liam O'Connor. Thanks for always being on the sidelines.

Publisher's Acknowledgments

We're proud of this book; please send us your comments through our Dummies online registration form located at www.dummies.com/register/.

Some of the people who helped bring this book to market include the following:

Acquisitions, Editorial, and Media Development

Project Editor: Georgette Beatty

Acquisitions Editor: Tracy Boggier

Senior Copy Editor: Tina Sims

Technical Editor: Susan Tarascio, Dyslexia Institutes of America

Editorial Manager: Michelle Hacker

Editorial Assistants: Hanna Scott, Nadine Bell

Cover Photo: © Emilio Ereza/Age Fotostock

Cartoons: Rich Tennant (www.the5thwave.com)

Composition Services

Project Coordinator: Kathryn Shanks

Layout and Graphics: Denny Hager, Joyce Haughey, Stephanie D. Jumper, Barry Offringa, Heather Ryan

Proofreaders: Leeann Harney, Charles Spencer, TECHBOOKS Production Services

Indexer: TECHBOOKS Production Services

Publishing and Editorial for Consumer Dummies

> **Diane Graves Steele,** Vice President and Publisher, Consumer Dummies

> **Joyce Pepple,** Acquisitions Director, Consumer Dummies

> **Kristin A. Cocks,** Product Development Director, Consumer Dummies

> **Michael Spring,** Vice President and Publisher, Travel

> **Kelly Regan,** Editorial Director, Travel

Publishing for Technology Dummies

> **Andy Cummings,** Vice President and Publisher, Dummies Technology/General User

Composition Services

> **Gerry Fahey,** Vice President of Production Services

> **Debbie Stailey,** Director of Composition Services

Contents at a Glance

Table of Contents

Introduction

You've picked up this book because you're concerned about your child. He isn't keeping up in class, hates to read, and makes spelling errors even in simple words. Is he dyslexic? Should you be asking for an assessment? What can you do to help him at home?

Or maybe you're flicking through these pages for yourself. When you were at school, you felt dumb, and now you avoid reading and hate to write. You're wondering whether you should call yourself "dyslexic" and, if you do, whether it will make much difference in your life. I hear you! You need straightforward, practical, upbeat advice.

I spend my (happy and ever-so-rewarding) working life helping dyslexic children and adults. I know I change lives. Sincerely, warmly, and rather proudly, I offer you this book so you too can make a difference.

About This Book

In this book, I give you all the relevant information and cut the rest. I don't bury you under a mound of theories, lose you in terminology, or wear you out with alternatives. I don't preach, prattle, or pretend there's always one definitive answer. Instead, I give you honest information about the stuff that matters. And I move you quickly from theory to practice.

You get hands-on activities your child can start straight away, strategies that are good for his whole lifetime, and handy tips for dealing with daily problems (like how to help him get organized and keep his *b*'s and *d*'s facing the right way once and for all). For teens and adults, I give the scoop on things like note taking, applying to college, and succeeding in the workforce. And to keep you on the ball with current research, you get news about brain mapping, dyslexia therapies, and the reading programs most educators prefer.

Whether you're just beginning to consider the term *dyslexia* or you've already done some research; whether you've got your child's IEP underway or you've never heard of an IEP; whether you want reassurance, practical strategies, or legal details made easy, this book is for you. Surf through it or immerse yourself chapter by chapter, as you need. The chapters in this book let you pick and choose, but they also follow a logical progression. There's so much information in here that you're sure to get the guidance you're looking for. And whatever your needs and interests, you'll love the Part of Tens, where you get quick lists, each of ten items, of really handy stuff.

Conventions Used in This Book

To *he* or not to *he?* In this book, I clean up that sticky dilemma by using *he* and *she* in alternate chapters. You can be sure this book is for everyone, and once you're used to the idea of switching between *he* and *she,* you'll probably end up thinking all other books should do the same.

In this book, I give you a lot of current prices for materials, therapy, tutoring, and more. These prices can change over time, so use them as your guide rather than as set-in-stone facts.

I feature a few other conventions to help you work your way through this book:

- *Italic* points out defined terms or emphasizes a word.
- **Boldface** text indicates keywords in bulleted lists and the action part of numbered steps.
- Monofont highlights Web addresses.

When this book was printed, some Web addresses may have needed to break across two lines of text. If that happened, rest assured that we haven't put in any extra characters (such as hyphens) to indicate the break. So, when using one of these Web addresses, just type in exactly what you see in this book, pretending that the line break doesn't exist.

And here's one more fact that you should know before you fully dive into this book: A lot of the information about testing and all the information on Individualized Education Programs (see Chapters 6 and 8, respectively) apply only to public (federally funded) schools.

What You're Not to Read

A lot of books about dyslexia seem to revel in technical jargon. This book doesn't. It gives you the jargon, sparingly, and warns you in advance with the Technical Stuff icon so that you don't have to read it if you don't want to. Don't let the jargon scare you though; it's there in case you need to assert yourself or write smart requests, applications, and other formal stuff. The Technical Stuff icon also highlights info that's interesting but not crucial to your understanding of dyslexia.

As well as bits of jargon, you're going to see sidebars in this book (they're in the shaded gray boxes). Sidebars offer bonus or additional information that you don't *have* to read but may enjoy all the same.

Foolish Assumptions

Because you're reading this book, I'm assuming the following about you:

- You'd like to help a child, or yourself, better understand dyslexia. You may be the parent of a child or a young adult who's having difficulty reading and may be dyslexic, or you may be a teacher looking for information so you can help dyslexic students and their parents. You may even be an adult looking for tips for yourself.

- You need plain-talking, down-to-earth guidance about things like your rights and the kinds of strategies that can make your life easier.

- You'd like pointers of how to get things right but not reams of jargon.

How This Book Is Organized

This book has six parts, all filled to the brim with information about dyslexia.

Part 1: Figuring Out What Dyslexia Is All About

In this part, I establish exactly what dyslexia does and doesn't mean. The "doesn't" part is important because, as many educators point out, the term dyslexia gets so overused that its meaning can be obscured. I also talk about the causes and types of dyslexia and give you an overview of the symptoms to watch out for at any age.

Part II: Determining When to Get a Diagnosis

In this part, it's time to look more closely at the signs of dyslexia. I examine your child's behavior in the preschool and school years and show you when and how to get an assessment.

Part III: Exploring Your Options for Schools and Programs

Your child struggles every day in class, but would he do any better in another class or even another school? How much does private tutoring cost, and are some learning centers better for your child than others? How can you make sure that your dyslexic child has a good Individualized Education Program (IEP), and what can you do to make schoolwork easier for him if he doesn't have an IEP? And how can you work effectively with your child's teacher? In this part, I answer your big questions.

Part IV: Taking Part in Your Child's Treatment

Most treatment for dyslexia involves structured multisensory and phonics-based instruction. Not sure what I'm talking about? That's fine. This part of the book explains it all in simple, straightforward terms that you can feel completely comfortable with. I also tell you about methods of memorizing, visualizing, and rhyming to help your child read more fluently; show you how to establish a happy reading routine; and give you tips to help your child accomplish everyday tasks easily.

Part V: Moving beyond the Childhood Years

Anyone who's been through high school in the last few decades has heard (at least a little) about stuff like portfolios, community service, and college entrance exams. In this part I tell you what dyslexics do to make these kinds of things less formidable during the college application process. I also give you the lowdown on helping your dyslexic child adjust to the teen years and show adult dyslexics how to be more successful in the real world.

Part VI: The Part of Tens

The Part of Tens is where a whole bunch of useful information gets boiled down to wonderfully easy lists. Here you get ten tools for making a dyslexic's life easier and ten dyslexia treatments and programs.

Part VII: Appendixes

In Part VII, I leave you with a battery of tests so you can determine your child's grasp on phonics skills, and I also include a handy reference guide to a variety of dyslexia resources.

Icons Used in This Book

The following icons highlight noteworthy information throughout the book.

This icon tells you that a piece of advice or an activity is good for adults as well as (or instead of) younger little beings.

You'll see this icon when I offer information that's really worth hanging onto.

Here's your alert to interesting but nonessential information (such as jargon). Skip ahead or brace yourself!

This icon means I'm offering a golden nugget of handy advice, probably learned firsthand.

Here's something you *don't* want to do. This icon warns you of the land mines that you may encounter.

Where to Go from Here

If you're not sure whether your child needs an assessment for dyslexia, you've come to the right place. Go to Chapter 3 to learn about general indicators of dyslexia, Chapter 4 for specific signs you may see during the preschool and kindergarten years, or Chapter 5 for signs of dyslexia that surface (or don't go away) later in school. Chapter 6 has details on testing.

If your child has already been diagnosed as dyslexic and is eligible for extra help, or an Individualized Education Program, at school, go to Chapter 8. If you know that your dyslexic child doesn't get an IEP and you want to know what options are left, skip ahead to Chapter 9. To get straight into doing your own reading activities, open up at Chapter 13.

Not in that much of a rush? Great! You'll enjoy the traditional journey through this book, starting at Chapter 1 and working through. Take your time, and especially mull over points that apply exactly to you. This is your map for guiding your dyslexic child surely forward.

Part I
Figuring Out What Dyslexia Is All About

The 5th Wave   By Rich Tennant

© RICHTENNANT

"Our daughter is definitely dyslexic. I knew I shouldn't have played all those 'Jumble' word games while I was pregnant!"

In this part . . .

This book contains a tremendous amount of information, so in this part I help you get off on the right foot with some basic but essential facts. First, you find out what *dyslexia* really means (and what it doesn't mean). I cover its possible causes and the different forms that it takes. Then, when you're revving, I show you how dyslexia may be indicated in your child's behavior, no matter how old he is. Got your water and sensible footwear? Off you go!

Chapter 1

Understanding the Basics of Dyslexia

*T*oday in a bookstore, I got held up in the magazines section. The problem was that I just couldn't decide what topic appealed to me the most: "Sixteen foods to make me stronger, happier, sexier, and smarter," "Ten minutes to a flatter belly," or "Eat around the clock." Wouldn't it be nice if this book offered you a similar approach to dyslexia, with topics such as "Sixteen surefire ways to outsmart dyslexia," "Ten minutes to perfect reading and spelling," and "Raising a reader without lifting a finger"?

But in real life, people like to hear the truth. So in this book I give you the plain and simple truth about dyslexia — not the shortcut answers like you might find in those magazines I saw. And it all starts in this chapter with an easy-as-pie outline of what dyslexia really is, a simple sketch of how it shapes your child's life, and a lightning tour of the programs and treatments you can find in and out of the classroom.

Defining Dyslexia in Plain Terms

Plenty of children struggle with reading. Their parents get extra help for them, and after a few months, they catch up. Sometimes the problem disappears suddenly without any intervention at all.

Dyslexia isn't like that. If you're wondering whether your child has reading problems or dyslexia, and what the difference is, here's the simple answer: A child with dyslexia has *enduring* and *unexpected* difficulty with reading and writing. She's bright, you give her loads of extra help, but she just doesn't get it. A blast of extra help won't make everything right for her because she needs a different kind of help over a longer time than just a few months. She'll probably learn to read and write at about age 10, but all through her life she'll need to read and reread written text several times before she fully comprehends what she's read. In addition, when she writes important stuff, she'll need to complete several drafts.

Watch out: Misconceptions about dyslexia abound. Here's what dyslexia isn't:

- ✔ Stupidity
- ✔ Laziness
- ✔ Retardation
- ✔ Brain damage
- ✔ Willfulness
- ✔ Distractibility

Research about dyslexia provides insight into the possible causes of dyslexia. For instance, dyslexics use a different part of the brain when they read than nondyslexics do, and they use more of it. Dyslexia also tends to run in families. And some psychologists break dyslexia down into several types, including phonological dyslexia and visual dyslexia.

In Chapter 2, I give you the full scoop about the definition, causes, and types of dyslexia. I also tell you about different conditions related to (and often mistaken for) dyslexia.

Dyslexia shouldn't prevent your child from achieving her goals or dreams. Plenty of professors are dyslexic. They have strategies and routines that help them achieve high standards. Oh, and your child may like to know that famous folks like Tom Cruise and Orlando Bloom (Hollywood actors) and Steve Jobs (CEO of Apple Computers) are just three of the many high-flyers who have dyslexia.

Zeroing In on the Symptoms of Dyslexia

Here's the thing about dyslexia. One teacher or psychologist may tell you your child lacks "automaticity of language," or perhaps "auditory perceptual skills," while another tells you she has "dyslexia." Some practitioners never use the term "dyslexia," but psychologists who *do* diagnose it look for a fairly standard bunch of symptoms. Different symptoms reveal themselves at different ages.

The kinds of behaviors that indicate dyslexia in a preschooler include the following:

- Starts to speak late (no actual speech until after age 2)
- Says muddled-up words *(aminal* for *animal* or *gabrage* for *garbage)*
- Doesn't enjoy being read to
- Can't tell you rhyming words *(cat/hat)*
- Can't tell the difference between letters and other symbols or squiggles

The kinds of behaviors that indicate dyslexia in a school-age child include the following:

- Writes words with letters in the wrong places, like *saw* instead of *was* and *vawe* instead of *wave* (called *transposing* letters)
- Reverses letters and numbers (especially *b* and *d, p* and *q,* and *3* and *5)*
- Writes so that her words are barely legible (letters are badly formed and the wrong size)
- Adds or leaves out small words when reading (which can totally change the meaning of the text)
- Has trouble retelling a story

For now, the main thing to keep in mind is that dyslexia, unless it runs in your family, can hit you like a shot out of the blue. Your child seems fine, or even advanced intellectually, so you just don't expect her to stumble with reading and writing. That stumble, from which your child seems unable to recover, is what dyslexia typically looks like.

In Chapter 3, I give you an overview of dyslexia symptoms at any age. I focus on symptoms in preschoolers and what to do about them in Chapter 4 and on symptoms in school-age kids and how to take action in Chapter 5.

Keep in mind that undiagnosed teenagers and adults also show a few common signs of dyslexia, including a diehard avoidance of reading and plenty of diversionary tactics for steering clear of handwriting. See Chapter 3 for details.

Deciding When to Have Your Child Tested

If you're worried that your child isn't getting the hang of reading, chances are your fears are well founded. It's better to get professional advice than to waste precious months wondering whether your concerns are valid. If it turns out that your child has dyslexia, or any other learning difficulty, the sooner you get a diagnosis the better.

That said, you can't whisk your child off to a psychologist for a dyslexia assessment much before she turns 5, because dyslexia is mostly about how well she reads. When she starts school and struggles with the alphabet, speech sounds, and text, it's time to quickly have her assessed so you can quickly start the intervention that can help her most.

The tests that your child can undergo (depending on her age) include the following:

- ✔ Language tests
- ✔ Vision and hearing tests
- ✔ Early screening tests
- ✔ IQ tests
- ✔ Performance tests
- ✔ A full test battery

The person who usually runs a full assessment for dyslexia is a psychologist. Your public school district employs an educational psychologist whose services you get for free (after making a written request for assessment). If you want an outside or second opinion, you can ask the district for a listing of private psychologists in your area. If your child attends a private school, she doesn't automatically get any of these services. Private schools make their own autonomous decisions about how they provide assessment and treatment for dyslexia and, unlike public schools, aren't legally obligated to provide assessment and an Individualized Education Program (IEP) for children who qualify for special education.

For full details on testing, including how to prepare your child for an assessment and what to do with the results, check out Chapter 6.

Exploring Different Schools and Programs for Your Child

You (of course) want the best education possible for your child, but finding the best school for her becomes even more important after she's diagnosed as dyslexic. In Chapter 7, I help you figure out whether your child's current school is doing a good job and what kinds of help other schools may offer you. I provide you with a list of questions to consider as you decide what kind of school you want your child to attend. I also introduce you to the services and staff members you find at a traditional public school and give you the lowdown on the following forms of alternative schooling:

- ✔ Charter schools
- ✔ Magnet schools
- ✔ Private schools
- ✔ Montessori schools
- ✔ Waldorf (Steiner) schools
- ✔ Schools for dyslexics
- ✔ Home schooling

If your child's dyslexia diagnosis qualifies her for special education in school, she receives an Individualized Education Program (IEP). In Chapter 8, I give you the full scoop on IEPs, including the actual fine print on the IEP document, what to expect at an IEP meeting, and how to prepare for it. This preparation includes speaking with your child's teacher, making lists and gathering important documents, and making sure that you have supportive folks with you. I also cover the acts that govern IEPs (the main one is the Individuals with Disabilities Education Act, or IDEA) and let you know your child's rights under these acts.

In public schools you have the legal right to an IEP if your child is found to have a learning disability. You don't get this legal cover in a private school; each individual private school makes its own autonomous decisions.

What if your child doesn't receive an IEP? Don't worry. In Chapter 9, I tell you how to secure help without one. In school, you can stay in close contact with your child's teacher and enroll your child in homework clubs, tutoring programs, and extracurricular activities that make her feel confident. Outside school, you have several options for strengthening your child's reading abilities:

- ✔ Dyslexia therapies
- ✔ Reading clinics specializing in helping dyslexic folks
- ✔ Private, individual tutors
- ✔ General learning centers

Of course, you can also offer your help at home by helping your child manage her homework and setting her up with lots of handy gizmos (including those I mention in Chapter 19).

Whether or not your child has an IEP, sometimes you may feel like you have absolutely no control over what your child does in class. The teacher assigns work, your child struggles with it, and the process moves on like an avalanche you can't avert or escape. Well, ta-da! I'm here with fancy underground sensors and a helicopter to help you! You really *can* influence what happens to your child in school; you just need to know how.

In Chapter 10, I tell you how to team up with your child's teacher with regular conferences, make all the accommodations you want seem beneficial to everyone, and keep a paper trail so your nice manner has some oomph behind it.

Sound easy? Ah ha, maybe you've been lucky. At some point in your child's schooling you may find yourself worrying that your child is learning more about frustration than anything else, and that's where this book comes in *really* handy. In these pages, you get step-by-step guidance for avoiding disputes with teachers and pressing your point reasonably, and you get places to go should you find yourself locked in combat anyway.

Helping Your Child with Activities at Home

You've probably heard advice that tells you to help your dyslexic child at home by doing the following:

- Reading a lot of books with her
- Doing a lot of hands-on activities with her
- Telling her all the time how terrific she is

That advice is good. But it's a bit, well, obvious. And besides, it's vague. What *kinds* of books should she read? Should you think up your *own* stimulating activities (in between cooking meals, doing the soccer run, and oh, yes, going to work)? And what if your child knows you're telling her she's great simply because the parenting books tell you to say so? What do you do then?

In Part IV of this book, you get specific, practical advice on the following ways that you can take part in your child's dyslexia treatment.

- You can use great memorizing, visualizing, and rhyming tricks to help your child learn words fast. I cover these methods in Chapter 11, along with a list of 220 common sight words that appear frequently in all written text.

✔ A knowledge of phonics is crucial to reading effectively. In Chapter 12, I provide you with plenty of activities that will help your child get the hang of sounding out words.

✔ Practice makes perfect, especially when it comes to reading. In Chapter 13, I give a variety of reading methods you can use with your child, including setting up a reading routine, selecting the right books, and handling your child's reading errors kindly.

✔ *Multisensory* is a big buzzword in the world of dyslexia, but what exactly does that mean? In a nutshell, *multisensory* means "hands-on." In Chapter 14, I explain the benefits of doing multisensory activities as part of your child's education.

✔ Even everyday activities such as staying organized, telling time, and following steps can be difficult for a dyslexic child. In Chapter 15, I show you how to help your child handle everyday tasks with ease and build her confidence.

Something especially great is that you get road-tested materials in these chapters. Instead of impractical suggestions and lists of books as long as your arm — books that the author may or may not have read — you get doable ideas and a manageable quota of recommendations that I have personally tested or had tested by another parent/teacher. How's that for *really* useful! Get your hands on the best books and kits around and, if your child's teacher hasn't seen them yet, give him the heads up!

Helping your dyslexic child with reading and other activities at home has multiple benefits. The following are just a few.

✔ Your dyslexic child may not start to read until about age 10. But she's smart and good at coverup, so the rest of the world may think she's doing okay. That's where your help at home really counts. You can get a firsthand, up-close view of what's going on and clue in the teacher. If you don't clue in the teacher, and especially if your child can sound out simple words and knows a few sight words, her difficulties may not show up in school until much later (when all of a sudden pretty much everyone else but your child reads fluently).

✔ When your child goes through a hear-see-say-do routine (which I explain in Chapter 14) with new concepts, they stick in her mind better than when she does any one of those things on its own. The fancy name for this is *multisensory learning,* and in dyslexia circles, boy it's hot! You can do some multisensory stuff at home simply by getting your child into useful habits such as saying out loud stuff she wants to remember and words she's copying down.

✔ Social and sporting interests may be especially important for your dyslexic child because they give her a chance to excel and be popular. You can help at home by establishing a schedule that's strict enough for homework to get done and flexible enough to cope with play-offs and the occasional dinner of PB & J sandwiches.

Watching Your Dyslexic Child Grow

When my kids were little, I thought other people's bigger kids were, well, big. To me they looked capable and self-sufficient. How wrong was that! My kids are now middle-sized, and they need just as much help from me as they ever did and, in many ways, more. Back then, the issues I faced seemed easy — how to divide a lump of modeling clay among friends and stop them from eating it. Now, however, I have trickier issues to settle. Should I force my shy child into a soccer team for her own good and what should I do, if anything, about that heinous "other" kid who trashes *my* cherub's school locker?

Your dyslexic child needs your help long after she stops eating clay. She has subject choices to make, examinations to take, and social events to attend. She needs your guidance, and later of course, she needs you to gradually hand the reins over to her. In Part V of this book, you get practical advice for almost all things. And if I have no idea about something, like where your dyslexic child should study anthropology, I direct you to people who probably will know.

Chapter 16 is all about dyslexic teenagers. I tell you how to help her foster her independence, learn to drive, handle school challenges, and develop essential work skills.

In Chapter 17, I tell you about getting your dyslexic student into college and the choices you have for paying for it. You find out about building an impressive portfolio, researching the best majors and schools, filling out college applications, and more.

Chapter 18 is where I deal with the challenges faced by adult dyslexics. I tell you about great at-home treatments for adults and the rights you have as an adult dyslexic in the working world.

It's all here, so what are you waiting for?

Chapter 2

Pinpointing What Dyslexia Is (And Isn't)

In This Chapter

▶ Describing and defining dyslexia

▶ Delving into the causes of dyslexia

▶ Looking at dyslexia by type

▶ Comparing dyslexia to other disorders

*R*esearchers have been studying dyslexia for years. They've found that dyslexia is almost certainly a brain issue, and they know how it manifests in your child's behavior. In this chapter I give you the detailed picture of what dyslexia means in practical terms, banish misconceptions about it, check out its causes, and compare it to similar conditions.

Understanding the Real Meaning of "Dyslexia"

In the following sections, I provide a straightforward definition of dyslexia, clear up misconceptions about dyslexia, and explain dyslexia's classification as a learning disability.

Looking at the straight facts

Dyslexia has an easy, literal meaning: trouble with words. Your dyslexic child has trouble with any combination of reading, writing, and spelling. He's bright, you read to him, and he has good teachers, but unexpectedly he just doesn't get it.

The word *dyslexia* has Latin and Greek roots. The "dys" part is Latin for "difficulty," and "lexis" is Greek for "word."

Your child may have other difficulties too. He may have trouble understanding directional instructions (left/right and up/down), remembering certain math facts (sequences of numbers and multiplication tables), and recalling words when he's speaking. And for you, his difficulties may all come as a bolt out of the blue!

But that's my in-a-nutshell description of dyslexia. Here are a few more key points about the nature of dyslexia.

- ✔ Dyslexia is a disorder that affects your child's ability to read and write. A dyslexic child typically has trouble recognizing words, sounding them out, and spelling them.

- ✔ A dyslexic child also often lacks other important language skills. He may have trouble recalling a sequence of spoken words or instructions and remembering words that he wants to use.

- ✔ Dyslexics lack the ability to discriminate sounds within a word (called *phonological processing*).

- ✔ Dyslexia is a lifelong condition, but with skilled teaching, your dyslexic child can learn to read (albeit later than other children) and minimize the impact that dyslexia has on his life.

- ✔ The exact cause of dyslexia is still not completely clear, but studies show definite brain differences between dyslexics and nondyslexics. See "Weighing up brain research," later in this chapter, for more details.

- ✔ Dyslexia affects your child's self-image. It's easy for him to end up feeling "dumb" and less capable than he is, so your insight and support is especially important.

You can receive plenty of additional basic information about dyslexia from the organizations that I list in Appendix B.

Moving away from common misconceptions

Children with dyslexia must learn to overcome, or at least get around, their problems, which includes not just their own limitations but the attitudes and ignorance of people around them. Of course doing so is hard — very hard — but if your child knows the devil he's dealing with, he has every chance of laying him to rest.

Make sure that your child understands that dyslexia is a brain issue (a few of his brain wires take different paths than other people's). This disability makes it hard for him to read, write, spell, and sometimes do other things too, like telling left from right and retrieving words he's had stored in his head for years. (See "Investigating the Causes of Dyslexia," later in this chapter, for more details.) But it's not plenty of other things that people who don't know any better believe it to be. It's not

- ✔ Stupidity
- ✔ Laziness
- ✔ Retardation
- ✔ Brain damage
- ✔ Willfulness
- ✔ Distractibility

And if your child's certain of what dyslexia is and isn't, he can let other people know too!

Classifying dyslexia as a "learning disability"

Dyslexia is a "specific learning disability" (SLD). The "specific" part tells you that dyslexia specifically affects certain aspects of learning (in the case of dyslexia, reading and writing). Other specific learning disabilities include speech and articulation disorders, auditory processing disorders, nonverbal learning disability, dyscalculia, and dysgraphia, all of which can coexist with dyslexia.

The International Dyslexia Association (IDA) calls dyslexia a specific learning disability, and many schools talk *only* about a "learning disability" (LD) or "specific learning disability," not dyslexia. Why? Most school districts currently use the term SLD in their documentation, so teachers in turn use it. You may find yourself in a strange situation: An independent psychologist tells you that your child has dyslexia, but all through the school system, you talk only of SLD.

If you were to insist that the school define your child as having "dyslexia" and not the "specific learning disability" written into documents (with no option for "dyslexia"), it can hamper the process of establishing his eligibility for special education services (which I cover in Chapter 8).

You probably need to use the term SLD in school, but that doesn't mean you have to always use it. Maybe you don't like the "disability" label? Maybe you feel that "dyslexia" carries less stigma? Maybe you decide that when you're in your child's school, you'll talk about his "specific learning disability" to keep people happy, but to keep yourself and your child happy, you'll use "dyslexia" everywhere else.

In this bullet list I whiz you quickly through some pros of using both terms:

- ✔ Teachers generally use the term SLD.
- ✔ Most school districts use SLD.
- ✔ Most learning therapists use SLD.
- ✔ "Dyslexia" is like a designer-label learning condition; people think it's interesting and don't equate it with "dumb."
- ✔ "Dyslexia" is specific; it delineates your child from kids who are poor readers for other reasons.

People who don't like to use either term (dyslexia or SLD) talk about things like "learning differences," "learning difficulties," or "learning style issues."

Investigating the Causes of Dyslexia

Current studies suggest that about 20 percent of the population has a reading disability, and of those, most have dyslexia. Dyslexia occurs in people of all races, backgrounds, and intellectual levels. In the next sections, I walk you, step by step, through insights that research and experience have given us on the causes.

Weighing up brain research

The International Dyslexia Association (IDA) makes no bones about the origins of dyslexia. Umpteen studies show it, and IDA says it outright: Dyslexia is neurological in origin.

So there you have it. Just about every expert now agrees that even though brain mapping is a relatively new scientific development, and even though you can't say how much of a person's brain map is a result of heredity and how much a product of his environment, brain differences definitely show up between dyslexics and nondyslexics.

Famous folks with dyslexia

Scores of talented, and of course perseverant, people have overcome dyslexia. They've achieved it all, including becoming famous writers! Here are just a few of the dyslexics who sidestepped the obstacles and became super-successful.

Inventors and scientists

✓ **Thomas Edison:** American. Invented the light bulb. Discovered the "Edison effect," which led to the invention of the radio. Also held over 1,000 patents for devices used in other inventions.

✓ **Albert Einstein:** Originally German but lived in Switzerland, Britain, and the United States. Developed special and general theories of relativity and in 1921 was awarded the Nobel Prize for Physics.

Business moguls

✓ **Steve Jobs:** Founder of Apple Computers. CEO of Apple and Pixar, the Academy Award–winning animation studio.

✓ **Charles Schwab:** U.S. stockbroker. Established one of the leading U.S. brokerages by offering discount fees and other inducements to small investors. Wrote *How to Be Your Own Stockbroker.* Established the Schwab Foundation for Learning, whose great Web site you can find at www.scwablearning.org.

Politicians

✓ **John F. Kennedy:** Youngest U.S. president ever elected. Served exactly 1,000 days before being assassinated.

✓ **Woodrow Wilson:** U.S. president during World War I even though he campaigned against it and was awarded the Nobel Peace Prize.

Artists

✓ **Leonardo da Vinci:** Italian painter who painted in the realist style. Famous also for being a gifted sculptor, inventor, mathematician, scientist, and architect. Painted the *Mona Lisa.*

✓ **Pablo Picasso:** Spanish painter famous for using different styles like expressionism and cubism. Had a blue period and a rose period. Painted *The Three Dancers.*

Movies and music

✓ **John Lennon:** What an icon! Just two of his famous songs with the band the Beatles are "Strawberry Fields Forever" and "All You Need Is Love."

✓ **Steven Spielberg:** Produced *E.T., Jaws, Jurassic Park,* and many other brilliant movies.

Sports stars

✓ **Muhammad Ali:** Olympic light heavyweight boxing champion.

✓ **Babe Ruth:** Often called the greatest of all baseball players.

Writers

✓ **Lewis Carroll:** British author of *Alice's Adventures in Wonderland* and *Through the Looking Glass.* His real name was Charles Lutwidge Dodgson, and he lectured in math at Oxford University.

✓ **Ernest Hemingway:** Often called the most influential American writer of the last century. Wrote *For Whom the Bell Tolls* and *A Farewell To Arms.* Shot himself after battling depression.

Here's what the terrain looks like on a dyslexic person's brain map:

✔ When a dyslexic person reads, parts of his right brain hemisphere get real busy, whereas when a fluent reader reads, he uses mostly his left hemisphere. The left side of a person's brain is the side all wired up for language. When a dyslexic person reads, he uses the less efficient right side of his brain, so he works harder at reading than a nondyslexic does and takes a lot longer to read.

Researchers aren't sure yet of the neurological and chemical specifics of why this happens, but they know it's not because of brain damage. A dyslexic's brain isn't missing anything; it just works in a different way than a nondyslexic's. There may even be, as some people argue, a good reason for this. Many people say that dyslexics have accentuated spatial skills and the "gift" of being able to see things in three dimensions.

✔ When a dyslexic person improves his reading skills (by being instructed in phonologic activities — see Chapter 12 for more details), his brain map starts to look more like that of a nondyslexic.

✔ Not only do dyslexics use a different part of the brain when they read than nondyslexics, but they use more of it. In the October 1999 issue of the *American Journal of Neuroradiology,* researchers reported that when dyslexics and nondyslexics performed the same oral language activities, the dyslexics used nearly five times as much brain area. In effect, their brains had to work five times harder.

Getting into genetics

A couple of things about the cause of dyslexia are clear:

✔ Dyslexia runs in families.

✔ Dyslexics have a different kind of brain map than nondyslexics (see the previous section).

What's not so clear is whether you inherit a dyslexic brain or your brain develops that way as a result of your not being able to read. It's tricky, and all the more so because the brain is such a complex organ.

That said, most experts believe there's a genetic basis to dyslexia, and the race is on to establish exactly which gene or genes are involved. The next two bullet points show you a couple of research teams who both claim to be the first to have found a single dyslexic gene! I, for one, intend to look out for more research because this is clearly a hard nut to crack.

✔ In a 1999 issue of the *British Journal of Medical Genetics,* a team of researchers said they were first to discover a single dyslexic gene. They expressed hope that when their research is more developed, it will lead to children with a family history of dyslexia being genetically tested when they start school. You can read more at `http://news.bbc.co.uk/1/hi/health/440261.stm`.

✔ A gene called "KIAA0319," which is likely to be one of the causes of dyslexia in children, was recently discovered in Wales in 2005. Researchers at Cardiff University said, "This is a major breakthrough and the first study to identify one gene which contributes to susceptibility to the common form of dyslexia." You can read more about this study at `www.cardiff.ac.uk/newsevents/11554.html`.

To really keep your finger on the pulse of current research, visit Dyslexia Teacher at `www.dyslexia-teacher.com`, and make the occasional visit to the National Institute of Neurological Disorders and Stroke (NINDS) at `www.ninds.nih.gov/disorders/dyslexia/dyslexia.htm`.

Breaking Down Dyslexia into Different Types

Getting people to classify your child as dyslexic can be hard enough, but sometimes you may face just the opposite problem. You meet a psychologist or therapist who tells you not only that your child has dyslexia (which you've only recently got a good understanding of) but that he has one of many kinds of dyslexia!

Just so that you're one step ahead, here are the subtypes of dyslexia:

✔ **Phonological dyslexia:** Also called *dysphonetic* or *auditory dyslexia* or *dysphonesia,* this kind of dyslexia is the most common. If your child has phonological dyslexia, he has trouble identifying phonemes (sounds within words) and matching letters to sounds. He makes wild guesses and struggles to read nonsense words, and his spelling is all over the place and may include impossible letter combinations like "sfr."

Most tests for dyslexia at some point ask your child to read nonsense words like *sluft* and *prenck.* That's so that your child can't guess but has to sound out. This particular exercise can single out that a child has phonological dyslexia. (See Chapter 6 for more info about testing.)

✔ **Visual dyslexia:** This kind of dyslexia is also called *dyseidetic* or *surface dyslexia* or *dyseidesia.* If your child has visual dyslexia, he can sound out words, but he has trouble with words that don't sound out regularly (such as *who* and *any*) and therefore have to be learned largely by sight. He reads very slowly and spells phonetically (throo, skayt, dorter) without registering that the appearance of his words is wrong. To check for visual dyslexia, a psychologist asks your child to read a bunch of phonetically regular words (like *think, wishing,* and *testing*) and irregular words (like *who, they,* and *enough*) to see whether there's obvious disparity in his reading of each kind.

- **Mixed dyslexia:** Also called *dysphoneidetic dyslexia*. This term refers to a combination of phonological and visual dyslexia. Mixed dyslexics tend to have severe deficits in reading as well as cognitive functions such as visual motor integration, visual perception, and working memory.

- **Dysnomia:** Also called *semantic dyslexia, anomia,* or *naming-speed deficits*. When your child is described in any of these terms, he has trouble finding his words. He can't always remember the right word, even though he's learned it before, and instead he says "the thingy" or another less appropriate or sometimes wholly inappropriate word.

  Psychologists test your child for this by giving him a rapid automatic naming test. That's a fancy way of saying that they flash pictures of common objects (and colors, numbers, and letters) at him and see how fast he names them, if at all.

- **Double deficit:** Here's a term that tells you your child has phonological dyslexia *and* dysnomia.

- **Severe and mild dyslexia or dyslexic symptoms:** One last thing to remember about dyslexia is that whatever kind of dyslexia your child has, he can have it to a greater or lesser extent. If he has mild dyslexia or dyslexic symptoms, he may not qualify for special education in school. (A psychologist can establish the extent of your child's dyslexia.) In Chapters 6 and 8, I go into detail about who does and doesn't qualify for extra — meaning over and above the usual — help in school.

Looking at Other "Dys" Conditions Related to Dyslexia

Just when you thought I must've exhausted every possible long-winded term, here I am with a few more! Don't worry, I'll be brief, but this little bunch of conditions in the following sections is worth knowing about. They're conditions that are dyslexia-like but not quite dyslexia, if that makes any sense. I guess the simplest way for me to introduce them is to say that the International Dyslexia Association calls them "related disorders," and that's good enough for me!

Dysgraphia: Difficulty with writing

Dysgraphia means difficulty with handwriting, but — guess what? — there are three different types:

- **Dyslexic dysgraphia:** Your child's writing is illegible, especially when the text is complex. Your child does badly on oral spelling, but he can draw and copy written text relatively well and performs fine motor skills at normal speed. (Psychologists measure fine motor speed by asking your child to finger-tap.)

✔ **Motor dysgraphia:** Your child's writing is illegible, and his copied text may be illegible too. His oral spelling is normal, but his drawing is usually problematic. His finger-tapping speed is abnormal.

✔ **Spatial dysgraphia:** Your child's writing is illegible and so is his copied text. His oral spelling is normal. His drawing is terrible, but his finger-tapping speed is normal.

Dysgraphia is usually classified as a condition separate from dyslexia but often accompanied by it. A child with dysgraphia has pronounced and enduring problems with writing. His writing is a real mess all the time, and without expert help over several months, it stays that way.

Dyscalculia: Difficulty with math

Many dyslexics struggle with certain kinds of math, a condition called *dyscalculia*. It's conspicuous because your child manages perfectly fine with math tasks that don't require him to remember strings of numbers. He struggles with the following kinds of things:

✔ Counting accurately

✔ Reversing numbers

✔ Memorizing math facts

✔ Copying math problems and organizing written work

✔ Jotting down the wrong numbers in calculations

✔ Retaining math vocabulary and/or concepts

Many dyslexic children also have dyscalculia, but because most children, dyslexic or not, experience math problems at some point, a psychologist's diagnosis is essential.

Dyspraxia: Difficulty with motor skills

Dyspraxia also goes by the name "clumsy child syndrome." If your child has dyspraxia, he has trouble planning and coordinating his body movements and struggles with fine motor tasks like writing, buttoning his clothes, and tying his shoelaces. He may have difficulty coordinating his facial muscles to produce sounds, so his speech is garbled. His large motor coordination may be weak too, so he's conspicuously clumsy and weak at sports.

Researchers believe that dyspraxia, like dyslexia, isn't caused by brain damage but does start in your child's brain. They think that immature neuron development may be the culprit and are pretty certain that dyscalculia can't be cured (also like dyslexia).

Comparing Dyslexia to ADD and ADHD

Many children who have dyslexia have other conditions too. If your child has Attention Deficit Disorder (ADD) or Attention Deficit Hyperactivity Disorder (ADHD), his main problem is that he struggles to focus and to attend to what he's doing or who's speaking to him. He's restless and fidgety all the time and is likely to wander off when you talk to him. He's hard to keep on track in class and, with his unsettling behavior, stirs other children up.

ADD and ADHD share some of their symptoms with dyslexia. I give you the full scoop on these two conditions in the following sections. (Chapter 3 goes into more detail on the symptoms of dyslexia.)

Names, names, names

When you talk to other parents whose children have problems in class, you're likely to hear about all kinds of disabilities, big and small, that you never knew existed. The kicker: A lot of them may be confused for dyslexia. Here then are just a few of those numerous names.

✔ **Nonverbal Learning Disability (NLD):** Here's a disability that looks like the opposite of dyslexia! Your child has early speech, learns to read early, and is excellent at spelling. He is conspicuously weak in motor and social skills and finds it hard to understand what he reads. Why do you need to know about NLD when it's nothing like dyslexia? Because *some* of the symptoms can look the same. A child with NLD may, for example, have poor reading comprehension and awful handwriting!

✔ **Asperger Syndrome:** To all intents and purposes, this syndrome is a mild form of autism. A child with Asperger Syndrome may have symptoms of dyslexia, such as not understanding what he's read.

✔ **Semantic Pragmatic Disorder (SPD):** *Semantic* means meaning, and *pragmatic* means being practical. Put them together and you have someone who doesn't understand everyday social and practical interactions. This disorder is like mild autism and is first identified as a conspicuous delay in speech and language development. So it's like dyslexia too.

✔ **Hyperlexia:** This child is fascinated, at an early age, with letters, numbers, and patterns. He learns to read, write, and compute very early and looks like a genius. But social interaction and oral language are a different ball game for this child. He's conspicuously weak in these areas, but even though his reading and writing are advanced, he can be confused with a dyslexic because some dyslexics learn to read but struggle later on with moving to higher reading levels and writing and spelling.

Psychiatrists look for more than just the following lists of symptoms. They look at your child's age, pattern of symptoms, and degree of symptomatic behavior. They look at how long symptoms have persisted. I guess what I'm saying is that this is only a rough guide for you. Contact your doctor or psychiatrist for the closer and clearer picture. You can also check out *AD/HD For Dummies* by Jeff Strong and Michael O. Flanagan (Wiley).

Even if your child is diagnosed with ADD or ADHD, get a second opinion. These conditions are notoriously hard to pin down because all children display some of them sometimes, and a bored or dyslexic child can have pretty much all the same symptoms. Many experts warn about overdiagnosis of ADD and ADHD, so before you accept a diagnosis, be sure that your child is inattentive even when he really loves what he's doing and hyper even when he's in a big space with fun activities on hand.

And remember: Some children are identified as having the combined type of ADHD; they have features of both inattention *and* hyperactivity-impulsivity.

Examining ADD

The American Psychiatric Association has a complex formula for how your child should be assessed, but its starting symptoms for Inattention ADHD or ADD are:

- Your child often misses details and makes careless mistakes in schoolwork.
- Your child has trouble staying on task.
- Your child often doesn't seem to listen to you even when you speak directly to him.
- Your child often fails to follow your instructions or finish tasks that he starts (and it's not because he's defiant or hasn't understood).
- Your child has trouble organizing himself.
- Your child doesn't want to start tasks that he knows require his concentration over time (like homework!).
- Your child often loses things (he usually can't find his school assignments, pencils, or books).
- Most sounds, like small noises and cars passing outside a window, distract your child.
- Your child is generally forgetful.

Checking out ADHD

If your child has ADHD, he has ADD symptoms with some hyperactivity thrown in too. He's always restless. He's hyper. He's very hard to manage in a confined, controlled space like, oh yes, the classroom! To diagnose ADHD, the American Psychiatric Association starts by looking for symptoms of hyperactivity and impulsivity. And here they are:

✔ **Hyperactivity:**

- Your child fidgets. He flicks his fingers, waves his feet, and squirms around in his seat.

- Your child finds plenty of reasons for leaving his seat because to stay in it feels so horribly hard.

- Your child runs when he really should be walking and climbs all over furniture when he's supposed to be "behaving."

- Your child has trouble with quiet play.

- Kind people describe your child as "a live wire."

- Your child generally talks, and talks, and talks!

✔ **Impulsivity:**

- Your child has trouble waiting for his turn to talk. He often blurts out his answer because he just can't hold it in.

- Your child has trouble waiting for his turn in pretty much all situations.

- Your child is always interrupting or pushing in.

Chapter 3

Being Alert to Symptoms of Dyslexia at Any Age

A few weeks ago I took my two daughters on a trip. "Pack just one bag," I said and went to attend to other things, secure in the knowledge that my girls know to pack a sweater even in a heat wave (for chilly nights) and have learned from experience that nothing really replaces a toothbrush. When the two bags were packed, there was a big bulging one and an impossibly small-looking one. If I'd loaded those bags into the trunk without peeking inside them, I'd have gotten quite a shock later on when we needed to change our clothes. My oldest child had jammed the big suitcase with purses and a virtual makeup booth, while my youngest had filled her bag, more of a pouch really, with sticks and bottles. All the paraphernalia for strutting your stuff and training in wizardry.

Watching your child for symptoms of dyslexia is like packing your travel bag. You need to focus on what's important and refer to a checklist so you don't forget anything. In this chapter, I show you why you should look for signs of dyslexia at the first hint of reading trouble, and I give you details on the exact signs to look for at any age.

Understanding Why It's Important to Look for Signs

Educators agree that it's a great idea for parents to be involved with developing their children's reading skills from an early age and that this involvement is especially important when a child seems to be making a slow start. If you notice the slightest hint that your child is struggling with reading, it's crucial that you continue to look for signs that may indicate a more serious problem. The following sections explain why.

From the moment you notice your child behaving in ways that you think could be symptomatic of dyslexia, jot them down. Later you may need to give a chronology of your observational information (especially to the educational psychologist who assesses your child — see Chapter 6 for assessment details), and this way you don't forget anything.

Appreciating that dyslexia is unexpected

Here's one important reason why you need to look for signs of dyslexia: Dyslexia is unexpected. Suppose that your child is bright, capable, and, unless she's gone through a lot of failure, willing to try new activities. She's had all the opportunities you could put her way. She hasn't had any particular traumas. But despite all this, when it comes to reading and writing, she just doesn't get it. And you're taken by surprise, dumbfounded, and horrified. You see other kids, plenty of whom have barely any of the advantages your child has, surge forward. You see them start to read pretty easily and quickly progress to chapter books. But *your* child stays put. That's what dyslexia looks like — just what you really didn't expect.

But that's not all. Dyslexia has been described as an "invisible" disability. Why? Your child may show dyslexic symptoms late in her schooling. She's bright and resilient and picks up basic early reading skills, but later on, the rudimentary skills she has can't keep pace with the harder work she's given. Now you get the really big surprise. Your older child has only a basic grasp of phonics and only a small repertoire of words she recognizes instantly, and when she reads lengthy text, she has barely any comprehension. She is dyslexic, and up until now, no one picked it up. When dyslexia shows up in older kids and even adults, it's unexpected — not because the symptoms weren't always there, but because your child's strengths carried her through school and made her weaknesses virtually invisible.

Dyslexia manifests itself uniquely; each child has her own set of symptoms (from all the possibilities), and each symptom can vary in severity. Even siblings with dyslexia may have very different strengths and weaknesses in academic performance, just as they will in other areas.

Being savvy about screening tests and what one teacher can do

If your child struggles with reading and writing, looking for signs of dyslexia is important because you may be the only one to spot or at least probe into them. "But that's what the school does," I hear you say. Well, yes and no. Your child does get screened for reading problems in grades K to 2; these screening tests screen a large number of children to see which ones may be at risk for school failure. Those children are given more tests and monitored closely in class. But suppose that your child

- ✔ Does okay in screening tests but starts struggling later on.
- ✔ Scrapes through the tests even though she struggles in class.
- ✔ Does fine on what the tests measure but has trouble with other skills that weren't tested.

All of these things can happen, so it's in your child's best interest if you keep a close watch. And don't forget that teachers handle struggling kids in different ways too. Your child may have a terrific teacher who's sensitive to her difficulties and confident enough to speak up about them, but what if your child's teacher

- ✔ Mistakes your child's problems as being within the acceptable range.
- ✔ Is busy keeping every child in line and can't give your child much attention.
- ✔ Believes that dyslexia is psychobunk for "lazy" (sounds far-fetched but it happens!).
- ✔ Believes (mistakenly!) that your child really will catch up in time.

You definitely need to monitor your child's progress (or lack of it) and jot down what you see. You can then go to the teacher with your observations in hand and ask for help. And if help doesn't seem to materialize, go right back and ask again. If you can't work things out with the teacher, see the guidance officer and the principal. After that, your next stop is the district office.

If your child isn't "getting it," you're probably right to be concerned. But you won't sound convincing to the teacher if you just say, "She isn't getting it." You need to identify a cluster of specific weaknesses because that's what the professionals do. Educational psychologists who assess children for dyslexia refer to a list of symptoms. If your child shows a bunch of them, she may be dyslexic and need to take a battery of tests to get the definitive answer (I talk more about tests in Chapter 6). But the starting point is when you see that she shows dyslexia-like behaviors pretty much all of the time. And *you* can spot those behaviors probably better than a psychologist can because you see a zillion times more of your child than he does.

Avoiding the "wait awhile" trap

You want me to tell you the precise signs of dyslexia, and of course I do that later in this chapter, but first I have some important advice for you in case you get cold feet about taking your list of dyslexia-like behaviors to school.

Parents of dyslexic children frequently wait awhile before getting extra help — and later regret putting it off. Your child makes the quickest gains in learning to read in grades K to 2. She's like a sponge at this time, ready and willing to learn a lot. Later, her first enthusiasm wanes, especially if she's struggling, and learning to read takes her much longer than it takes other kids. Don't wait. If you feel something's wrong, trust your judgment, even if someone tells you to wait awhile and let development take its course. A struggling child doesn't suddenly find that everything makes sense after all. She doesn't catch up. Her problems just get worse, and then you have a job that's harder and takes longer.

Noticing Your Preschooler's Late Development

Your child starts talking late. She has trouble naming shapes and colors. She's not all that interested in stories and often walks off halfway through them. Should you worry? Maybe. Should you look for other signs and go see a professional? Certainly. If you catch your child's difficulties when she's still a preschooler, you have a great chance of helping her get up to par by the time it really counts, in grades 1 and 2.

The following list gives you the kinds of behaviors that educational psychologists have in mind when they look for clusters of symptoms that indicate dyslexia in your preschooler. I cover these symptoms (and what to do if you see them) in more detail in Chapter 4.

- Starts to speak late (no actual speech until after age 2)
- Says muddled-up words (such as *aminal* for *animal* and *gabrage* for *garbage*)
- Doesn't understand what you say until you repeat it a few times
- Can't follow more than one direction at a time
- Can't remember words
- Takes awhile to get words out
- Can't consistently name the letters of the alphabet
- Doesn't enjoy being read to
- Enjoys being read to but shows no interest in words or letters

- Has weak fine motor skills (in activities such as drawing, tying laces, cutting, and threading)
- Can't tell you rhyming words *(cat/hat)*
- Can't tell the difference between letters and other symbols or squiggles
- Can't recognize her own written name

A psychologist assessing your child will also ask you whether your child has, or has had, a lot of ear infections. Ear infections aren't a sign of dyslexia but are a complicating factor that can make dyslexia worse.

Watching Your School-Age Child Fade

Can't read. Reverses and mixes up the order of letters when she writes words. Can't remember the alphabet. These are classic signs of dyslexia in your child when she's in elementary school. You may notice the following behaviors in your child's cluster of dyslexia symptoms:

- Doesn't show a dominant handedness until about age 7.
- Has immature speech, saying words like "wed" (red) and "gween" (green).
- Can't write or tell you the sounds of the alphabet.
- Is bright and verbal but unexpectedly weak at reading.
- Talks with an advanced vocabulary when she can't recall simpler words, saying things like "We're going to the food distributor."
- Frequently uses words like "umm" and "thingy."
- Writes words with letters in the wrong places, like *saw* instead of *was* and *vawe* instead of *wave* (called *transposing* letters).
- Reverses letters and numbers (especially *b* and *d, p* and *q,* and *3* and *5*).

Letter and number reversals are common in all children, including those who don't have dyslexia, up to about age 7. So what's the difference between a child making mistakes that are nothing to be concerned about and mistakes that may indicate dyslexia? A dyslexic child makes mistakes just as often as she doesn't, and she continues making them in grade 2 and beyond.

- Writing is barely legible (letters are badly formed and the wrong size).
- Confused about directionality, such as left/right, up/down, and front/back.
- Doesn't follow through with multiple-step chores.
- Is below grade in reading and/or writing and spelling (as confirmed by her teacher, school tests, or tests done by an educational consultant or psychologist).

- Adds or leaves out small words when reading (which can totally change the meaning of the text).
- Has trouble retelling a story.
- Complains of words moving or running off the paper.
- Complains of dizziness, headache, or stomachache while reading.
- Receives grades that don't match her intelligence.

To determine whether your child's grades match her potential, you need to have her assessed by a psychologist. You may be able to see this pretty clearly without a test, though, and of course the teacher can let you know what he thinks.

- Can't remember facts like multiplication tables, days of the week, dates, and names.

Your dyslexic child also may show you signs of her dyslexia that have no direct connection to reading and writing. Her attitude, behavior, and all-around manner speak volumes. For example, she just figured out what "apple" group really means, and she feels stupid, not as good as the other kids, and angry. How would *you* react? Here are some typical behaviors you may see:

- Your child looks and acts unhappy.
- Your child seems too quiet; she's practically invisible.
- Your child stirs up plenty of trouble at home and in school.
- Your child is clearly disorganized.

For more about dyslexia symptoms in school-age kids (and what to do about them), check out Chapter 5.

Beware of report card rhetoric

The other day I was with a friend looking through her photo albums. One album spanned her dyslexic daughter's elementary school years, and in it were old school reports. My friend said, "Check these out. They all say pretty much the same thing." On every report a handful of words and phrases repeated themselves — *struggles, tries hard, slow, kind, helpful, a pleasure to teach.* "You know, she really did try and try," my friend sighed.

Harsher words may proliferate on your child's report — words like *lazy, inattentive, distractible, careless, immature,* and *daydreamer.* Don't let them get to you. The same bunch of adjectives find their way onto thousands of dyslexic children's reports, but they don't mean much, and they certainly don't help. The important thing to do is to remember that your child is doing her best in the face of adversity and that the teacher's words (though unfair and worth calling her to task on) are very good reason to get an assessment.

For a personal account of a mother discovering that her son has dyslexia, read *Reading David* by Lissa Weinstein (Perigee Books). Two aspects of the book make it unusual: The author is an educational psychologist herself but still missed (or denied) the signs, and the author's dyslexic son, David, still in school now, gives his perspective.

Recognizing Signs of Dyslexia at Older Ages

Many adults wonder if their unsuccessful (and maybe unhappy) days at school were due to undiagnosed dyslexia. Teens can find themselves wondering the same thing because even though dyslexia is now a recognized disability, children who have mild dyslexic symptoms, plenty of other strengths, and good coverup strategies may still go undiagnosed. In the following sections, I talk about the specific dyslexic symptoms that crop up in teens and adults.

Seeking out signs in teenagers

If your teenager dislikes school, doesn't do her homework, and hardly ever picks up a book, dyslexia may be the reason. Teen dyslexics may go to great lengths to avoid reading and writing, find ways to cover up their reading failure, and worry to no end about it. Here is a quick rundown of things you may see your teenage dyslexic doing.

- ✔ She avoids reading and writing.
- ✔ When she does read, she guesses at words, skips small words, and has little comprehension.
- ✔ When she writes, she muddles the order of letters inside words or leaves them out completely.
- ✔ She starts to dislike school, even though she seemed to be doing fine before.
- ✔ She doesn't do homework, and her teachers are concerned or critical.
- ✔ She tells you that she's "dumb" or "couldn't care less."
- ✔ She is more anxious and self-conscious than before (though you may have thought that was hardly possible!).
- ✔ She is withdrawn and won't get involved in as many social events (like birthday parties and sleepovers) as she used to.
- ✔ She is aggressive, abusive, or antisocial (and worrisome) in other ways.

For information on helping your teen succeed in high school and apply for college, check out Chapters 16 and 17.

Acknowledging adult symptoms

Dyslexic adults have learned to live with their difficulties. Whether they're open about their dyslexia, or even know they have dyslexia, is a different matter. Some dyslexic adults tell everyone about their dyslexia, ask for accommodations at work, and joke about their goof-ups at home. Some hide their dyslexia and go to great lengths to keep it under wraps. They don't trust that other people will understand and don't want to lose their jobs or be thought of as mental cases (a term that a dyslexic friend of mine used!). Others don't know they're dyslexic.

The stereotypical dyslexic adult exhibits the following behavior:

- ✔ Avoids any reading or writing
- ✔ Types letters in the wrong order
- ✔ Flip-flops numbers and dates, especially 3s and 5s.
- ✔ Can't fill out forms
- ✔ Is adept at hiding her illiteracy by doing things like ordering what friends eat at restaurants to avoid reading the menu
- ✔ Has low self-esteem and/or a bad attitude
- ✔ Is a high school dropout
- ✔ Holds a job below her potential and/or changes jobs frequently
- ✔ Misses minor details at her job
- ✔ Can't play sports due to poor coordination
- ✔ Can't read to her kids

Here are a few ordinary, everyday bits of information that a dyslexic adult may be unable to read:

- ✔ Figures on a salary check
- ✔ Instructions on prescription medicine
- ✔ Numbers in a telephone directory
- ✔ The menu in a restaurant
- ✔ Traffic signs, street names, and maps
- ✔ Letters, books, and homework that your child brings home from school
- ✔ TV schedules
- ✔ Instructions for building and using new toys or equipment

Dyslexia: A special burden for teens

When you talk to dyslexics and read dyslexic message boards, you find truckloads of personal anecdotes and figures about high school pressures. Some folks talk about how terrifying it is to be asked questions that they feel that they can never answer; others discuss the humiliation of not feeling bright.

For some teenagers, the humiliation becomes too much. The strain and frustration of underachieving can cause dyslexic teens to be reluctant to go to school, to throw temper tantrums before school, or to play truant. Cheating, stealing, and experimenting with drugs can also result when children regard themselves as failures. Youngsters with learning disabilities constitute a disproportionately large percentage of adolescent suicides.

More than 27 percent of children with learning disabilities drop out of high school, compared to 11 percent of the general student population (24th Annual Report to Congress on the Implementation of the Individuals with Disabilities Education Act, 2002). According to the U.S. Department of Education, 85 percent of all juvenile offenders have reading problems.

Your teenager may bury her dyslexia under a heap of defiant or self-abusive behavior. Don't be brought down or diverted by these secondary behaviors, or fooled into thinking that your teen is just about adult enough to pull herself back on track.

Adult dyslexics have to recruit help and work out clever coping strategies every day of their lives or face being isolated in a reading world. Check out Chapter 18 for additional signs of dyslexia in adults and tips on succeeding in the real world.

Referring to Your Family's History

If there's a dyslexic in your family, your child is more likely than other kids to have dyslexia. Dyslexia runs in families. Whether your family is black or white, well educated or minimally educated, rich or just getting by, it makes no difference. Dyslexia skips past race, gender, and socioeconomic barriers, and money and position won't get you a cure either. There's no cure.

Here are some interesting snippets about family patterns regarding dyslexia:

✔ Many studies show the tendency for dyslexia to run in families. If one of your parents has dyslexia, you have an increased chance of having dyslexia yourself. Figures on this "increased chance" range from 25 to 75 percent. Because of various factors (like whether a child receives good instruction and is specifically called "dyslexic"), a more accurate prediction really isn't possible.

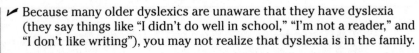

✔ Because many older dyslexics are unaware that they have dyslexia (they say things like "I didn't do well in school," "I'm not a reader," and "I don't like writing"), you may not realize that dyslexia is in the family.

✔ Researchers can make predictions about the degree of dyslexia a person will have by looking at inherited brain differences. Most experts agree that dyslexics share a certain kind of brain activity (different parts working better or worse) and that when you map this, certain topographies suggest more trouble than others!

If you struggled at school or know that you have dyslexia, or if someone else in your family fits that bill, watch your child for symptoms of dyslexia right from an early age. If she doesn't have dyslexia, you've lost nothing by watching her, but if she does have dyslexia, you've gained valuable insight and time. You may even be the only person to spot that your child needs extra help and then you spare yourself that awful "I should've known" kind of hindsight.

Part II
Determining When to Get a Diagnosis

The 5th Wave   By Rich Tennant

"I've been taking Samantha for language testing for more than three weeks now. One of these days I hope to get up the nerve to take her out of the car and inside the testing center."

In this part . . .

What's the difference between dyslexia and a simple reading delay? When do most kids start to read independently? The teacher says your child's doing fine, but should you request a dyslexia assessment anyway? This part of the book gives you answers to these and other questions you may have. In addition, it offers a clear view of what dyslexia looks like in preschool and school-age children and walks you through the complete dyslexia assessment process.

Chapter 4

Watching Your Child Carefully at a Young Age

In This Chapter

▶ Monitoring your child's early behaviors

▶ Helping your child with pre-reading activities

▶ Readying your child for school

As any parent knows, there's nothing as bleak as worrying about your child — except for worrying about him for a long time. That's why this chapter helps you move quickly from concern to action. Here you get a picture of what your preschool child's development looks like and what kinds of behavior may signify a budding problem. Then I give you games and activities to do at home that strengthen the skills a dyslexic child typically struggles with, and I cover specific abilities that your child should have before he enters kindergarten.

Keeping a Close Eye on Early Skills

Your child's preschool years are a magical time. You get to marvel when he learns to walk and speak, and just about every day he tucks some new accomplishment under his belt. Do you need to think about dyslexia now? If someone in your family has dyslexia, and/or if your child doesn't seem to be cruising past typical developmental milestones, you do.

Your child can't be definitively diagnosed with dyslexia before grade 2 or age 8 because dyslexia is primarily a problem with written words, but he can be determined to be "at risk" for dyslexia much earlier. Assessors can use tests like the Dyslexia Early Screening Test (DEST) with kids as young as 4 years old to look for weaknesses in skills like rhyming, phonemic awareness, immediate recall, hand-eye coordination, sound discrimination, and shape formation. A child has to exhibit several of these in severity to be determined at risk. (See Chapter 6 for testing info.)

What you can definitely do before school starts is be primed for potential problems, give your child plenty of play that develops his phonemic awareness (see "Listening up for phonemic awareness," later in this chapter, for details), and, if your child needs it, get him some speech therapy.

In the following sections, I give you the lowdown on language, hearing, and vision difficulties that may signal a bigger problem. I also delve into the fine motor and pre-reading skills you should monitor in your preschooler.

Talking late and unclearly

Delayed speech is a red flag for dyslexia. If your child isn't speaking by age 2 or older, you'll want to be watchful of his progress with reading when he starts school. Delayed speech doesn't mean your child will be dyslexic, but it does alert you to watch for later, more definitive signs (I talk about signs of dyslexia in older kids in Chapter 5).

Even before school starts, you should have your late talker's hearing checked (see the next section), and you may want to consult a speech therapist too just to make sure that your child's jaw and mouth muscles are as developed as they should be (if not, facial exercises can help).

If your child has muddled and unclear speech when he starts to speak, it's reason to keep an eye on him. Does he typically say things like "aminal" for "animal" and "bisghetti" for "spaghetti"? Does he stutter and fumble for his words? If so, and your child's turned 3, call your public school district. You can get free testing and speech therapy before your child starts school and for the rest of his years in school if you can establish that he needs it to receive a free and appropriate public education (FAPE). See Chapter 6 for details on testing and Chapter 8 for more about FAPE.

The following are a few more language problems that may indicate dyslexia and need the evaluation of a speech therapist:

✔ Is your child's receptive speech slightly off the mark? (*Receptive speech* is your child's ability to understand other people's speech.) Can he understand what's being said to him without it having to be repeated several times? Does he have trouble understanding the difference between "under "and "over," and "in front" or "behind"? This kind of confusion, especially over directionality, is another early indicator of dyslexia that speech therapy can help with.

✔ Is your child slow to name familiar objects? Many dyslexics struggle all their life with word retrieval. They know what they want to say but can't pluck it from their brains. They end up using sentences like "Can you pass me the thingy?" much more than other folks do. They also may use alternative words in sentences, saying strange things like "I'm going to the meal distributor" instead of "I'm going to the snack bar."

✔ Stammering is an involuntary blockage of normal speech patterns and not linked to dyslexia. That said, if your child hesitates while trying to find words and has a sort of stammer because he can't recall the words that he needs, it's a warning sign of dyslexia.

✔ Poor letter articulation is a possible warning of dyslexia. If your preschool child says "wed and gween" instead of "red and green," listen up. It's not a big deal now but becomes a red flag if he still talks that way by about second grade.

Private schools don't have to follow the special education regulations that govern public schools, but if your child attends a private school and needs speech therapy, your school district may have to pay for it. To find out more, ask your school nurse or district office. If you don't get much help there, check out the legal organizations listed in Appendix B. And if you pay for private speech therapy, check to see if your insurance plan covers all or part of your costs. The American Speech-Language-Hearing Association at `www.asha.org/public/coverage/` has useful information about insurance and other ways of having your speech therapy fees reduced.

Battling ear infections

A big dyslexia warning sign to look out for in children under age 5 is recurring ear infections. Ear infections, in themselves, don't mean your child will be dyslexic, but many dyslexic children have a history of ear infections. The infections don't cause dyslexia but almost certainly make it worse by impairing your child's ability to hear speech sounds at a time when he should be making the most progress with auditory processing.

Speaking to a speech therapist

Could your child have what speech therapists call "childhood apraxia of speech" rather than dyslexia? According to the American Speech-Language-Hearing Association, a child with speech apraxia knows what he wants to say but can't get his brain to move his lips, jaw, and tongue in readiness.

The following signs may indicate speech apraxia in your young child:

✔ He doesn't coo or babble in infancy.

✔ He may have feeding problems in infancy.

✔ When he says his first words, it takes him a long time, and some sounds are missing.

✔ He makes only a few consonant sounds.

✔ He replaces difficult sounds with easier ones or leaves out sounds altogether. (All children do this, but the child with developmental apraxia of speech does it often.)

Find out more (and guard against a possible misdiagnosis) by logging on to the American Speech-Language-Hearing Association Web site at `www.asha.org/default.htm` or by visiting `www.apraxia-kids.org/`.

The funny thing about your child's hearing is that it has what you might call everything and nothing to do with dyslexia. Experts pretty much agree that although dyslexia is all about hearing sounds, it's not a straightforward hearing impairment. A dyslexic child *hears* sounds okay, but he *processes* them all wrong.

Dyslexia is a "phonemic" rather than a hearing disorder. Your child's ears work fine, but when he identifies and makes sense of sounds (in his brain), he goes wrong. He doesn't distinguish between sounds (or *phonemes*) inside words in the same way that other children do. This kind of awareness is called *phonemic awareness,* and experts consider the lack of it the number one feature of dyslexia. A child who lacks phonemic awareness can't tell the difference between words like *tot* and *top, cot* and *cut,* and *tin* and *Tim.* For more details, see "Listening up for phonemic awareness," later in this chapter.

If you have concerns about your preschooler's hearing, consult your doctor. Get a referral to an audiologist for a hearing test (your insurance should cover at least part of the cost). If the test uncovers any problem, you can receive more private help and/or take the test results to your school district. If the district finds that your preschooler's hearing problem impacts his education, he gets free support (ongoing assessment and treatment) for as long as he needs it. "Preschool age," by the way, is age 3 to 5, but you should check cutoff dates if your child is only just 3 or nearly 6. Also check exactly what provision you get because variations can exist between school districts. And when your preschooler starts school, be sure that his file is passed to the new service provider if indeed a new body takes responsibility for him.

Seeing a range of vision problems

Your child's vision is another factor (like his hearing, covered in the previous section) that complicates but doesn't cause dyslexia. Many dyslexics complain of seeing wobbly, fuzzy, or moving letters, but experts have pretty much decided that this complaint is something of a red herring because even when letters are clearly in focus for a dyslexic, he *still* has trouble matching sounds to letters. Your dyslexic child may have vision problems (which can usually be treated with eye exercises or lenses), but his dyslexia is primarily a brain-based phonemic processing issues.

Many symptoms of vision problems are the very same symptoms that suggest dyslexia, so you need expert help in fathoming out the right diagnosis. Your child may have dyslexia, vision problems, dyslexia *and* vision problems, or perhaps something different again! Your child may have a vision problem if you notice that he does any of the following:

- ✔ Doesn't enjoy being read to
- ✔ Enjoys being read to but shows no interest in words and letters
- ✔ Loses his place along lines of print
- ✔ Gets eyestrain or red or watery eyes when he looks at books
- ✔ Complains of blurred, double, or moving print
- ✔ Squints, frowns, or rubs his eyes while looking at books
- ✔ Tilts his head or holds his book too closely when he looks at books
- ✔ Covers an eye to look at print
- ✔ Has trouble spotting items that are alike and different
- ✔ Avoids close-up tasks
- ✔ Is easily distracted
- ✔ Has a short attention span
- ✔ Needs a lot of breaks from paper-and-pen activities
- ✔ Tires quickly when he draws and traces
- ✔ Has trouble copying and tracing shapes and letters
- ✔ Reverses letters and numbers
- ✔ Has poor self-esteem
- ✔ Complains of headaches
- ✔ Has poor hand-eye coordination
- ✔ Appears awkward or clumsy

According to the American Academy of Ophthalmology, children should have a complete medical eye exam by their fourth birthday and routine eye exams about every two years thereafter. A pediatric optometrist can tell you some sobering statistics:

- ✔ About one in every five schoolchildren has an undetected vision problem.
- ✔ A school's vision screening test doesn't pick up every kind of vision problem.
- ✔ Your child can have 20/20 eyesight (meaning normal distance vision) and still have problems coordinating both his eyes as a team, tracking print across a page without losing his place, or adjusting focus when he looks from near to distant things.

Looking out for lazy and turned eyes

If your child has an undetected vision problem, he can develop symptoms that look like those of dyslexia. If he has dyslexia already, a vision problem makes things worse. Even when your child gets regular vision tests, problems can go undetected, and parents may be so accustomed to seeing a symptom, like their child having a slight head tilt when he looks at books, that they no longer notice it. Here is some information about two really common eye problems.

✔ *Amblyopia,* or lazy eye, is when one of your child's eyes doesn't work as well as the other. About 3 percent of children under age 6 have amblyopia. Treatment usually includes eye exercises and an eye patch, but if you don't treat it early, your child may have poor vision into adulthood. If your child squints or closes one eye to see, has generally poor vision, and/or complains of eyestrain or headaches, he may have amblyopia.

✔ *Strabismus,* or *deviating eyes,* is when your child's eyes don't look toward the same object together. The turn can be constant or intermittent, and if it's intermittent, it may be hard for you to detect.

Early examination is especially important if any other member of the family has had amblyopia or strabismus (deviating eyes) before.

For more information and a directory of optometrists, log on to the Optometrists Network at `www.children-special-needs.org/`.

Even though experts are pretty certain that vision problems aren't the cause of dyslexia, some dyslexia treatments (such as Davis Dyslexia Correction and the Irlen Method) pay special attention to correcting your child's visual tracking (following words along lines of a page). I talk about these dyslexia treatments in more detail in Chapter 20.

Having trouble with playing and dressing

Children with dyslexia commonly have poor hand-eye coordination and fine motor skills. A dyslexic child may have trouble throwing and catching, and tasks like tying his shoelaces, buttoning his shirts, or threading beads may throw him into a fury. He may be late to develop a dominant hand too. He may switch between his right and left hand to write, catch a ball, or do other hand tasks, and he may not become right- or left-handed until about age 7. Even then, he may use one hand for writing and the other for catching!

Plenty of children have poor hand-eye coordination and go through a time of being *ambidextrous* (able to use both hands), so (as with all the signs I mention here) these behaviors are only potential indicators of dyslexia. They don't indicate dyslexia for sure unless they persist in school and form part of a cluster of symptoms (see Chapter 5 for dyslexia signs in school-age kids).

Displaying weak pre-reading skills

Certain additional pre-reading problems can be potential symptoms of dyslexia. If your child struggles with several of the pre-reading behaviors I list here, right through grade 1, and he's otherwise bright and responsive (so you're surprised by this glitch with language skills), ask for an assessment. I walk you through the dyslexia (or "learning disabilities") assessment process in Chapter 6. You can also try some of the activities I feature in the next section to help your child strengthen his pre-reading abilities.

- **Your child can't identify sounds inside words.** By the time they go to school, most children can tell you when words sound alike or different. They can give you a string of "buh" words, like ball, balloon, bench, and bun, and enjoy alliteration ("an alligator ate Alice"). A child with dyslexia usually doesn't understand what the fuss is about. He doesn't hear the pattern in the "buh" words or appreciate the fun in alliteration.

- **Your child can't tell you rhyming words.** Most children can rhyme by the time they go to school. They can anticipate rhyming words on the ends of verses and will happily tell you a few of their favorite nursery rhymes. A child with dyslexia usually doesn't do this. Rhyme is something he just doesn't get.

- **Your child isn't interested in words or letters.** Preschool children usually enjoy writing letters and their name all over the place. A dyslexic child usually doesn't.

- **Your child can't identify letters from squiggles.** A dyslexic child takes longer to get to know letters than other children do. By the time he starts school, he usually hasn't learned to identify all the letters and may confuse letters with each other or letters and random squiggles with each other.

- **Your child can't retell a simple story.** Small children can tell you a story, albeit in an extended, roundabout way. They're not succinct or sophisticated, but they get there. A child with dyslexia usually doesn't get there. He finds it hard to recall sequences of events, so retelling a story is virtually impossible for him.

- **Your child isn't interested in hearing stories.** Some dyslexic children don't enjoy hearing stories. They don't follow plots, don't understand wordplay, and may walk right off in the middle of a story that other kids are begging for more of.

- **Your child can't write or recognize his own name.** A dyslexic child may be unable to write or recognize his own name by the time he starts school.

Engaging in Pre-Reading Activities at Home

In the previous section, I touch on a few pre-reading difficulties (like not hearing rhyme or recognizing letters) that can be forerunners of dyslexia. But what practical strategies can you put to use at home to address them?

Plenty of language activities prepare your child for reading. You can loosely classify them as activities that build the following skills:

- **Print awareness:** When your child understands that print runs left to right and top to bottom, he's primed for following sentences in pages of text. Your dyslexic child needs plenty of print awareness because directionality (left to right) is especially tricky for him.

- **Phonemic and phonics skills:** Before he can read, your child must get a few skills under his belt: phonemic awareness (hearing sounds in words) and phonics (matching letters to those sounds). In preschool and kindergarten, you want your child to do a whole bunch of singing, rhyming, and saying different letter sounds so that he develops phonemic awareness and, from that, solid phonics skills.

I delve deeper into these areas in the following sections.

Developing print awareness

When some children start school, they have no idea how to hold a book or follow along the lines and pages in a book. *Your* child knows which direction written words run in, how chapters break a book into sections, how books tell you things, and how they're written by authors, because you read to him. Print awareness is a relatively easy thing to help your child with — you simply read to him and point out the direction of the text, the parts of the book, and so on — but an important precursor of reading nevertheless.

Zeroing in on phonemic and phonics skills

Your child needs to get on top of *phonics,* that is, being able to sound out letters and words. To do that, he must develop a bunch of sequential skills that start with phonemic awareness. People get pretty technical about "phono" terms, but I of course give you the simple explanation right here!

- **Phonemic awareness:** Before you give your child any instruction in the letters of the alphabet, he must be aware that words are made of chunks of sound. This appreciation of sounds is *phonemic awareness.*

✔ **Phonological awareness:** When you hear the term "phonological awareness," it's about sounds too — only more of them! When your child has phonological awareness, he has a fairly sophisticated appreciation of sounds. He can identify many chunks of sound, like prefixes (*un-aware,* for example) and rhymes (in word families like *make, take, rake,* and *sake,* the *ake* part is called a *rhyme*).

✔ **Phonics:** After your child is aware that spoken words are made of sounds, he needs to discover that written letters and chunks of letters represent those sounds. This attaching of letters to sounds is *phonics.*

✔ **Morphological and orthographic awareness:** At the same time that your child gets comfortable with regular, easy-to-sound-out words like *stamp* and *pink,* he has to get to know a few harder words. Words like *who* (that don't sound out) are pretty hard, and so are words like *brought* and *niece* (that have unusual sound-spelling chunks). And then there are prefixes (like *un, dis,* and *pre*), suffixes (like *able, tion,* and *ly*), contractions (like *can't* and *don't*), and stuff like that to learn! The prefixes and suffixes kind of learning is called *morphological awareness* (recognizing the parts of words that convey meaning), and getting to know which letters typically come together and look right (like *ck* but never *kc*) is called *orthographic awareness.* (Chapter 11 has full details on memorizing and rhyming tricks to help with difficult words.)

Some people also talk about "phonographics" or "graphophonics," which are interchangeable terms. The *phono* part means sounds, and the *grapho* part means written appearance, so the whole thing means getting to know the chunks of sound inside words and how they look.

The following sections focus on skills you can work on with your preschooler: phonemic awareness and phonics.

Listening up for phonemic awareness

Your preschooler is initially at the phonemic awareness stage, so you need to help him hear the sounds that words are made of. What's your best approach?

The following activities are great for helping to develop your child's phonemic awareness:

✔ Help your child hear the sounds in songs and rhymes by leaving key words out when you sing them. Your child provides the words using the rhyme as his guide.

✔ Have fun with alliteration ("The dotty dinosaur danced with doves") and read rhyming stories. Visit your library to find a good selection and ask the librarian for suggestions. Even if a librarian can't answer your question off the top of her head, she has lists of award-winning books and classics that she can print for you.

✔ When your child is at the computer, encourage him to play games that make him listen carefully. For a CD-ROM that's specially designed to fine-tune your child's auditory discrimination and phonemic awareness, check out the Earobics program. The at-home version for prekindergarten and kindergarten children, called "Step 1," is PC and Mac compatible and costs $59. Find out more by logging on to www.earobics.com or calling 888-328-8199.

If you're looking for a super fun CD-ROM that helps your child with sounds and words without him even realizing it, check out "Bailey's Book House." It has seven games, is compatible for a PC or Mac, and has been loved by parents and teachers for years. Produced by The Learning Company, it's available online for $24.99 by logging on to www.learningcompany.com/ and clicking on "4-5 preschool." It's worth browsing this site because plenty more popular educational CD-ROMs are available here.

Acquiring phonics skills

Once your child gets the idea that words have sounds inside them and can come together in cute rhyming patterns, like "I saw a bear on the stair in his underwear," he's ready to match sounds to letters.

You help your child remember the shapes and sounds of letters by having him get his hands on them; a dyslexic child learns well when you help him use all of his senses, not just his vision and hearing. Have him draw letters in shaving foam, make them from modeling clay, and trace them on your back with his finger. Help him remember the sound that each single letter of the alphabet makes by associating the letter to an object or character. (I give more phonics exercises in Chapter 12 and multisensory exercises in Chapter 14.)

When your child gets to know a letter as a story character, he remembers it better. For example, the letter *a* can become Annie Apple who looks like the letter *a* with a stalk and leaf attached and takes part in stories and songs. Annie Apple is part of a program called Letterland, which originated in the United Kingdom but is used in countries all over the world. It's an extensive kit of books, tapes, CDs, CD-ROMs, and flashcards, but you can get plenty of mileage from the basic soft-cover ABC book ($9.50) and the Alphabet Songs CD ($14.50). Check out Sammy Snake, Eddie Elephant, Clever Cat, and the whole bunch of products at www.letterland.com. For a Californian program based on the same principles but using zoo characters, check out Zoo-phonics at www.zoophonics.com. The basic program for home — video, cards, CD-ROM (PC version only) and more — costs $145 (get directly to the kit at www.zoo phonics.com/products.html).

Before you use these products, you may want to check with your child's school. If teachers already use Letterland, Zoo-phonics, or any other similar program, they'll probably want you to use the same thing too.

Preparing Your Child for Kindergarten

You want your child to be as prepared as he can be for kindergarten. If you notice him doing things like wandering off when you read him stories, even really interesting ones, and having no interest in writing his own name, you especially want to make sure that his other skills are more developed (so you have less to keep a watch over). The next sections let you know what kindergarten teachers hope to see in their new charges (on top of all the pre-reading stuff I go through in the previous sections).

Stirring up good feelings about school

 In a perfect world, your child starts kindergarten by bouncing straight into the classroom and emerging hours later, radiant, and replete with newly acquired knowledge! If he doesn't quite cut that kind of figure, here's the basic feeling-good-about-school standards that his teachers hope for:

- Your child knows roughly what routine to expect in class.
- Your child understands that the teacher is there to help him.
- Your child understands that other children want to be his friends.
- Your child is mostly excited to be there.
- Your child has no real separation anxiety.

Telling little kids the honest truth

Your child may show symptoms of dyslexia, like poor fine motor coordination, before he starts school. He may understand that he's not quite as skilled as friends the same age. And if that's the case, it's likely that he's more than a little nervous about starting school. You need to prepare him by giving him accurate information. When you tell your child about school and take him to school orientation days, be honest with him. Saying things like "It'll be easy" and "You're a big boy now" may not be quite what he needs to hear.

A friend of mine who tried to prepare her son for catching the school bus by telling him things about big boys catching buses all by themselves thought she was doing okay until her son looked at her in disbelief and said, "Mom, I'm not big, I'm little. Are you *really* just going to leave me to catch a bus all on my own?" My friend managed to get her son on the school bus without incident by doing it in increments. First they followed the bus by car, then her son caught the coming-home bus only, and by the end of the week, her *little* boy was doing the whole thing with ease.

Helping your child with language skills

If you suspect that your preschool or kindergarten child has dyslexia, you'll want to look closely at his language skills. Teachers hope for the following skills, and a dyslexic child typically needs to work on at least three of them:

✔ Identifying the beginning sound of some words

✔ Recognizing rhyming sounds

✔ Identifying some alphabet letters

✔ Recognizing some common sight words, like "stop"

✔ Telling you a simple story

✔ Recognizing his written name

✔ Trying to write his name

For tips on strengthening basic language skills, see "Engaging in Pre-Reading Activities at Home," earlier in this chapter.

Nurturing other academic skills

Some children with dyslexia struggle to remember sequences of numbers and directional concepts (like under and over). From the list here you can see that these skills feature fairly prominently in kindergarten, so the more practice you give your child before he starts school, the better.

✔ **Understanding general times of day:** Is it morning or late afternoon? Most children have trouble with times of day, but a dyslexic child may be more confused than most. Unless it's actually dark or he's just got up, he can't tell you whether it's morning, afternoon, or evening, let alone what hour. See Chapter 15 for tips on helping your child figure out time.

✔ **Understanding directions such as up, down, in, out, behind, and over:** Behind or in front, left or right — which is which? That's the kind of question that can plague a dyslexic all his life. Many dyslexic adults like doing practice runs when they leave familiar territory because they know that they have little hope of following directions for getting safely back. See Chapter 15 for help with directions.

✔ **Counting up to 10:** Many toddlers can count up to ten, and by the time they start school, nearly all children manage it. A dyslexic child may not. He can't keep the sequence in his short-term memory. See Chapter 9 for tricks on introducing simple math concepts to your child.

✔ **Recognizing shapes (square, circle, triangle, and rectangle):** The fact that your preschooler can't tell a circle from a square may be one of the first things that set your alarm bells ringing. See Chapter 9 for tips on helping your child pick out shapes.

✔ **Tracing basic shapes:** Most small children can trace around shapes soon after they learn to hold a pencil. A dyslexic child typically draws as much off the shape as on it.

✔ **Naming colors:** Dyslexic children may have trouble naming colors. Psychologists testing young children for dyslexia usually include a rapid naming test in which your child is asked to quickly name colors, objects, numbers, and letters. To help your child remember these classifications, spend several days on one color, such as red, before introducing others (one at a time).

✔ **Sorting items by color, shape, and size:** If colors and shapes are hard for your child, sorting pictures by these features is extra hard. Many children later diagnosed with dyslexia had this kind of problem early on.

✔ **Identifying parts of his body:** If your preschooler always has trouble naming his body parts, it's reason to watch his progress carefully to see if other dyslexia signs appear.

Encouraging fine motor skills

Children with dyslexia often have trouble disciplining their pencils. They have a hard time writing letters, their fingers get all tangled up in scissors, and threading beads and pasta tubes onto string can be a nightmare.

For a preview of the kinds of small, fiddly hand-movements, otherwise known as fine motor skills, that teachers love to see in your child, check out this list:

✔ Your child puts simple puzzles (up to 12 pieces) together.

✔ Your child uses scissors correctly.

✔ Your child draws and traces with pencils.

✔ Your child can fasten buttons and zippers.

✔ Your child can unscrew lids from child-sized jars of craft materials.

The only way for your preschool child to get better with fine motor skills is to do more of them. He needs to squeeze clay, pick up beads, fit jigsaw pieces into place, and get his finger and hand muscles pumping. For a smorgasbord of things to do with sandpaper, modeling clay, and gloop (a soapy, ooey, gooey mix you make yourself), flip to Chapter 14.

Shop online for cool puzzles, toys, games, and creative kits designed especially for children with special needs by visiting Dragonfly Toys at www.dftoys.com/specialneeds/dragonfly/usa/.

Showing your child what's sociable

Dyslexia isn't a behavioral disorder. Your child won't behave badly or unusually because he has dyslexia but might, of course, act up or draw attention to himself in other ways if he's frustrated, infuriated, or demoralized as a result of his dyslexia. Your child's teacher naturally (and idealistically!) hopes that all the children in her class have the following basic social skills:

- ✔ Your child uses words, not fists.
- ✔ Your child speaks clearly.
- ✔ Your child plays with other children.
- ✔ Your child follows simple directions.
- ✔ Your child can tell you what he needs and wants.
- ✔ Your child waits his turn.
- ✔ Your child goes to the bathroom by himself.
- ✔ Your child is inquisitive and asks questions.
- ✔ Your child enjoys hearing stories.
- ✔ Your child says "please" and "thank you."

Putting your child in charge of his personal information

A dyslexic child might struggle with remembering sequences of numbers, like telephone numbers. Here are the essential things, telephone number included, that teachers hope your child knows:

- ✔ His full name
- ✔ His age
- ✔ His address and telephone number
- ✔ His family members' names

Chapter 5

Acting Quickly with Your School-Age Child

When your child goes to school, you can't help wondering how she compares to classmates. Is she keeping up? Does she have the same strengths and weaknesses as her friends? Is she really a little slower to read than her sister was, or is your memory hazy? In this chapter, I tell you what does and doesn't constitute reason for having your school-age child assessed for dyslexia.

Understanding Why a Quick Response to Reading Problems Is Critical

If a teacher tells you that your 5-year-old child isn't developmentally ready to read, he may be right. But if he says the same thing when your child is 7, and you can see that your child has a deep and enduring confusion with words, he's wrong. A few children do learn to read later than others (at age 8 or 9), but they're children who need motivating and Band-Aid type help, not the ones whose difficulties go deeper and farther.

Dyslexic children don't suddenly just "get it" but continue to struggle while the majority of children overtake them. Their acute difficulty with written text is obvious at ages 5 to 7, when nearly all the other kids are easily "getting it." Without intervention, the learning gap between your dyslexic child and her classmates just grows and grows.

Dyslexia doesn't just get better on its own. The quicker you treat your child's dyslexia, the quicker and easier it is for her to make headway. On the other side of that coin, the longer you wait to treat your child's reading problems, the more they compound. She misses out on the language extension that reading gives her, she misses out on all the knowledge that classmates are gaining through their reading, her grades drop, and she dislikes school because every classroom subject requires at least some reading.

All of this makes sense, and a lot of research supports it. Two major studies include the Roper Poll Study in 1999 and the "Teaching Children to Read" report in 2002. From these and other studies on how kids read and what happens when they struggle, here's what we know for sure:

- ✔ Parents typically don't have enough confidence in their own judgment to act quickly on their child's reading problems. They often wait over a year before getting extra help.

- ✔ With intensive reading instruction, 95 percent of struggling children age 9 or below can achieve average reading levels.

- ✔ A quick response to your child's reading problems is critical because older children don't learn to read as quickly or easily as the under-10 age group. Only 25 percent of children age 10 and over ever catch up.

- ✔ Kindergarten and grade 1 are the best grades of all for reading intervention. With intensive instruction, a kindergartner catches up to her peers four times more quickly than a fourth grader does.

In some alternative schools, like Waldorf schools (see Chapter 7 for details), children aren't formally taught to read until after age 7. This isn't a problem for nondyslexics because in earlier grades they learn a lot of pre-reading skills, so they're well primed for a quick start. Your dyslexic child won't make this quick start and needs extra help.

So what's the moral of this story? As soon as you see clusters of dyslexia symptoms (which I cover in the rest of this chapter), have your child assessed. I talk at length about tests in Chapter 6.

When you give children extra help with reading, the young ones do best. Children under 7 make the best progress, and children ages 7 to 10 do well too. After age 10, however, only 25 percent of children ever catch up to grade level. Argh, what if your child is 10, 11, 12, or older? Don't panic. The statistics sound alarming, but you're reading this book, so you're obviously a person who gets things done. It's never too late for someone to learn to read, but the key, as with all things that are worth doing, is to practice consistently and frequently. Your older child needs to work harder and longer than she would have if she were starting her remediation at age 5, but she can still achieve the same end. Chapter 2 has the scoop on symptoms you see in older kids and teens; when you've determined that your older child or teen indeed has dyslexia, check out Chapter 16 for ways to help her succeed.

Noticing Dyslexic-like Behaviors at Home

If you're not sure whether your child struggles enough with reading and writing for it to be something to worry about, she'll probably provide you with the answer. Children who struggle in class soon realize that they are low performers and find ways to internalize or externalize their hurt.

In the next sections I talk about ways in which you can deal with three fairly typical behaviors your dyslexic child may display at home: unhappiness, disorganization, and, of course, the constant struggle with words.

 Your own observations of your child's behavior are just as important as observations that the teacher makes and test results. Many dyslexic-like behaviors are things you see at home, and of course, you're in the best position to see whether your child is beginning to dislike school. Your child usually puts on her best face for the teacher, so if you jot down the fact that your child tells you she's sick every morning before school, but makes a quick recovery on weekends, you can confidently let her teacher know. If the teacher says something like "But she's so happy in class," you won't start doubting your own memory. Jot down specific incidents and dates so you have a full-color picture of how your child is doing. Jot down the good things too so you can see whether certain times in school are better for your child than others.

Struggling with written words

Dyslexic children always struggle with written words. Your dyslexic child probably dislikes reading, making mistakes like reading *was* for *saw* and *horse* for *house* and skipping right past small words like *it*. When she writes, she likely puts letters in the wrong order inside words (called *transposing*), leaves out letters all together (called *omissions*), and faces letters like *b* and *d* the wrong way (called *reversals*). These actions are all typical signs that your child may have dyslexia. I go into more detail about these and other word-based signs in the sections "Laboring with reading" and "Writing with difficulty," later in this chapter.

The information that you probably want most from this book is how to help your child develop her reading and writing skills. I devote whole chapters to those answers too (see Part IV), but so that you have an outline of the important points, in simple terms, here's what the research says:

- ✔ Your child needs to do plenty of phonemic and phonics activities because she lacks matching-letters-to-sounds skills. (*Phonemic activities* teach your child that words are made of sounds. *Phonics instruction* shows your child how to match letters and letter combinations to those sounds.) I give you a wide variety of phonological activities to try in Chapter 12.

- ✔ The best instruction for dyslexic children is structured, systematic, and explicit instruction in phonics, delivered through multisensory activities (check out Chapter 14 for more about these activities).

Feeling unhappy

Your child knows she's at the bottom of the class in reading, doesn't like going to school, and dreads getting homework. What can you do about it?

You can tackle her unhappiness by talking it over with her. Let her know that you realize she feels humiliated because she can't read like the other kids (even ones that don't seem as bright as her), that you know she tries hard, and that you want to help. Together you can pinpoint her specific difficulties, do reading and writing exercises to help reduce her problems, and get an assessment for dyslexia. (I give you more details about building your child's self-esteem with positive talk in Chapter 15.)

And, perhaps most immediately helpful to your child, you can tell her about dyslexia and the many gifted and famous people who have it. Children with dyslexia nearly always say that when they realized that clever and talented people have dyslexia, they felt empowered, inspired, and happier! (See Chapter 2 for a list of famous folks with dyslexia.)

Being disorganized

At school your child has a messy notebook, desk, and locker. At home her whole daily schedule is slightly off course. She has trouble getting ready on time, turning up where she's supposed to be, and doing whatever it was you asked her to do.

The best advice that parents of dyslexics say they have for helping a child with her disorganization is to forget about fighting it. Your child is unlikely to one day wake up with a perfectly organized mind and military-like habits to match, but she *can* harness every helping device known to civilized man. In Chapter 15 I talk at length about understanding clocks and calendars, establishing and keeping a morning routine, and other organizational issues. For now, however, you just need to know that, while your child may never be a virtual Mary Poppins, she can at least be a girl whose pocket organizer and cell phone pretty much organize her life for her!

Asking Your Child's Teacher to Look for Dyslexic-like Behaviors in Class

You need to be able to talk about dyslexic-like behaviors with your child's teacher so that your child's difficulties don't get brushed off as her not being "developmentally ready." It's easy to mistake dyslexia for more superficial reading problems, so if you're at all uncertain, tell the teacher what you're thinking (and the dyslexic symptoms you see), so you're both on the same page.

You want your child's teacher to help you monitor your child's behavior and pinpoint where she needs help. Start by telling him what behaviors you've noticed in your child and how persistent they've been. Phrase what you say in terms of your child ("Jane has trouble reading long worksheets"). Ask the teacher what he's observed and what test results and examples of your child's work he can show you. Jot down what he tells you, what you tell him, and what you ask for. The paper trail that you start now will be handy later on, as a baseline, so date it and make it as much of an at-a-glance document (with headings and bullet points) as you can.

In the next sections, I take a close look at your child's reading, writing, and spelling and then list other symptoms her teacher can look out for in class. If the teacher is receptive to your comments, you may want to give him a copy of these symptoms so he can simply check off any that he sees. (I provide more information on working effectively with your child's teachers in Chapter 10.)

An indicator of dyslexia that the teacher doesn't see, but that you can tell him about, is family history. If someone in your family has dyslexia, your child's chances of having it are greatly increased. See Chapter 2 for more details on the link between dyslexia and family history.

Laboring with reading

When you take a close look at the way your child reads, you see that what at first looks like a big muddle in fact has patterns. A dyslexic child makes particular kinds of reading errors:

- ✔ She reads a word on one page but doesn't recognize it on the next page or the next day.

- ✔ She reads single words (without story line or other clues) slowly and inaccurately.

- ✔ She misreads words as other words with the same first and last letters or shape, saying things like "form" instead of "from" or "trial" instead of "trail."

- ✔ She adds or leaves out letters, saying things like "could" instead of "cold" or "star" instead of "stair."

- ✔ She reads a word that has the same letters, but in a different sequence, like "who" instead of "how," "lots" instead of "lost," "saw" instead of "was," or "girl" instead of "grill." And when she makes these kinds of mistakes without pausing or trying to figure out whether what she's reading makes sense, it clues you in that she's not comprehending what she's reading.

- ✔ She confuses look-alike letters like *b* and *d, b* and *p, n* and *u,* or *m* and *w.*

- ✔ She substitutes similar-looking words, like "house" for "horse," even though they change the meaning of the sentence.

- ✔ She substitutes a word that means the same thing but doesn't look at all similar, like "trip" for "journey" or "cry" for "weep."

- ✔ She misreads, leaves out, or adds small words like "an," "a," "from," "the," "to," "were," "are," and "of."

- ✔ She leaves out or changes suffixes, saying, for example, "need" for "needed," "talks" for "talking," or "soft" for "softly."

- ✔ She reads out loud with a slow, choppy cadence. Her phrases aren't smooth, and she often ignores punctuation.

- ✔ She may be visibly tired after reading for only a short time.

- ✔ Her reading comprehension is poor because she spends so much energy trying to figure out words. Her listening comprehension is usually heaps better.

- ✔ She may have trouble tracking (following words and lines across pages). She skips words or whole lines of text.

- ✔ She tries to avoid reading or other close-up tasks and has plenty of excuses on hand for why she can't read right now.

✔ She needs a lot of snacking, bathroom, or resting time between very short bouts of actual reading.

✔ She complains of physical problems, like eyestrain, red or watery eyes, headaches, dizziness, or a stomachache, when she reads.

✔ She squints, frowns, rubs her eyes, tilts her head, or covers one eye to read and holds books too closely to her eyes.

✔ She complains of words moving or running off the paper.

Writing with difficulty

A child with dyslexia usually shows a huge difference between her ability to tell you something and her ability to write it down. She tends to do the following:

✔ Avoid writing.

✔ Write everything as one continuous sentence.

✔ Not understand punctuation. She doesn't use capitals or periods or uses them randomly.

✔ Not understand the difference between a complete sentence and a fragment of a sentence.

✔ Misspell many words even when she uses only very simple ones and is "sure" she knows how to spell them.

✔ Mixes up *b* and *d, m* and *n,* and other look-alike letters.

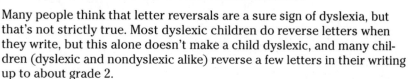

Many people think that letter reversals are a sure sign of dyslexia, but that's not strictly true. Most dyslexic children do reverse letters when they write, but this alone doesn't make a child dyslexic, and many children (dyslexic and nondyslexic alike) reverse a few letters in their writing up to about grade 2.

✔ Take ages to write.

✔ Write illegibly.

✔ Use odd spacing between her words. She may ignore margins completely and pack sentences tightly on the page instead of spreading them out.

✔ Use a mix of print and cursive and/or upper- and lowercase.

✔ Not notice her spelling errors. She reads back what she wanted to say, not what she actually wrote.

✔ Use both hands for writing up to about age 7. Most children choose a dominant hand at about age 5.

If your child does many of the things I list here and writing is her conspicuous Achilles' heel, she may have *dysgraphia* (also called a visual-motor integration problem), a kind of dyslexia characterized by poor, often illegible handwriting. Chapter 2 had the full scoop on dysgraphia.

Making predictable spelling errors

Typically, a dyslexic child spells far worse than she reads. Her spelling looks like the "inventive" kind that teachers expect to see in emergent readers in grades K to 2 even when she's well past those grades. She has particular difficulty with vowel sounds and often leaves them out. With much effort, she may be able to memorize Monday's spelling list long enough to pass the spelling test on Friday, but she can't spell the same words two hours later when she wants to write them in sentences.

A child with dyslexia also does the following:

✔ Misspells frequently used words, like "they," "what," "where," "does," and "because," despite practicing and practicing

✔ Misspells words even when she's copying them from the board or a sheet

✔ Has erasures, cross outs and undetected errors all through her writing

---

Having the gift of dyslexia

Many talented people have dyslexia, which has led some folks to regard dyslexia as a gift. They say that the incidence of dyslexia among gifted people is higher than it is among nondyslexic people and that dyslexics tend to have engineering and creative types of talent. I just need to alert you to the fact that your child can be both gifted and dyslexic at the same time. Whether your child's dyslexia enhances or stymies her talents is a whole different matter. The dyslexia-is-a-gift contingency maintains that dyslexic people do excel in certain areas:

✔ They are good at hands-on learning and seem, almost intuitively, to figure out how to do things.

✔ They have strong graphical skills and can visualize objects in a moved or altered state.

✔ Dyslexic children tend to excel in constructing models, coloring, and drawing.

✔ At an early age they are extra curious about how things work and love to tear things apart and rebuild or fix them.

✔ They love to invent things and have mechanical talent.

✔ They have vivid imaginations. They are creative and known for their musical ability.

✔ They can view the world from different points of view. They can process so much information that if it's not filtered, what begins as a talent ends up being a tangled mass of confusion.

Coping with other classroom tasks and issues

If your child has dyslexia, her teacher should spot many of the reading, writing and spelling errors I list in the previous sections. Other things may be conspicuously out of line with your child's intellect and bright personality:

- Noticeable and unexpected low achievement
- Conspicuous disorganization
- Distractibility or a short attention span
- Hardly any sense of direction
- Persistent left/right confusion
- Difficulty making sense of instructions
- Difficulty remembering words and learning new words
- Immature speech (such as "gween" for "green")
- Inability to always understand what is said to her
- Difficulty finding appropriate words in telling stories
- Trouble with time, counting, and calculating
- Difficulty sequencing days of the week and months of the year
- Failure to finish work on time
- Appearance of being lazy, unmotivated, or frustrated
- Awkwardness/clumsiness

Behaving unusually

The following sections cover problematic behaviors that a dyslexic child may display at school.

Acting invisible

Dyslexic children develop all sorts of strategies to cover up their weakness in reading and writing. Being an obliging, sweet-natured, no-trouble child who blends into the background in school is one of them. When teachers describe your child in too-good-to-be-true terms, beware! Many dyslexic children manage to go through whole grades in school without being noticed. They become masters of cover-up, and no one realizes what's going on. This is all fine and dandy in the short term but has disastrous long-term consequences, such as when your child fails school tests and you've wasted precious time when you could've been giving her extra help.

So if you see that your child is learning the art of invisibility in class, help her learn new things. She needs to develop phonemic awareness (the awareness that words are made from a limited number of chunks of sound — see Chapter 12 for more details) and asking-for-help strategies.

Making trouble

A bunch of children are sitting outside the principal's office, and your child is one of them. She's in trouble for misbehaving, acting silly, or giving the impression that even if the president himself is asking her to tow the line, she's not going to.

Children commonly react to academic failure by failing in behavior. Why? Because then all eyes are on your child's bad behavior and not on her failure in reading and writing. She's labeled as unruly, but that's much easier for her to bear than being thought of as "dumb." Watch out for bad behavior. Remember that bad behavior is a symptom of something deeper. And whatever you do, don't take it personally!

It's really important to pinpoint bad behavior and nip it in the bud before it gets out of hand or becomes a habit for your child. Does the behavior happen at certain times, only during some lessons (like reading time), or in reaction to a certain set of conditions? Don't focus on the "behavior problem," but instead, work as a team with the school to determine the real root of the behavior.

When your child drives you and everyone else crazy and you feel like she's dragging your whole family down, remember that bad behavior masks other things. Your child is stressed, and her misbehavior is a way of showing it. She doesn't really mean to hurt you; it's just that she's hurt, angry, and frightened herself. Try to break the problem down into small bits and tackle one bit at a time. Look for practical solutions. Don't blame her — or yourself.

Chapter 6

Testing Your Child for Dyslexia

*Y*ou've watched your child struggle with homework, seen other kids outstrip him in class, and at times wondered whether his teacher is too busy to see what's really going on. Now you want answers:

✔ What exactly is my child struggling with?

✔ Does he have dyslexia?

✔ How do I have him tested?

✔ If he takes a test, will he get extra help?

In this chapter I give you the answers to these questions and more.

Before you even get started with having your child tested for dyslexia, you need to be comfortable with the term "dyslexia" and help your child get comfortable with it, too. But wait, you've heard your school talking about a "learning disability (LD)" or a "specific learning disability (SLD)," so which term — dyslexia, LD, or SLD — should you be psyching up for? Probably all of them! Don't worry too much about this, but know that different school districts use different terminology to mean the same thing. LD and SLD are accepted terms wherever you are, but in many school districts that's where the classification ends. Dyslexia is one type of SLD, but to avoid excessive terminology and paperwork, and hence get applications for special education moving quickly, districts may document dyslexia as SLD and teachers may talk about dyslexia as simply LD.

If your child attends a private school, a whole different set of rules applies. Or there may be no rules to govern how a learning disability is assessed and provided for. In public schools you have the legal right to an assessment and special education if your child is found to have a learning disability. You don't get this legal cover in a private school, and each individual school makes its own autonomous decisions.

Deciding When to Get a Diagnosis

A great reason for having your child diagnosed is to find out exactly what's going wrong for him, especially if other people tell you he's doing okay and you suspect he's really not! But that's just a part of it. Here are a whole bunch of reasons to head purposefully toward someone with letters after her name and assessment tools in front her:

✔ You find out whether your child has dyslexia.

✔ You find out whether he has other problems, like attention-deficit hyper-activity disorder (ADHD) or dysgraphia (difficulty with writing).

✔ You get a baseline from which to gauge your child's progress.

✔ If your child qualifies as having an LD, he gets special education. Special education is the extra help a child gets when he's diagnosed with an LD. It usually means he sees the resource teacher a few times each week. The *resource teacher* is trained to deliver special education to the children who are eligible for it. She usually has her own room in school in which she teaches special programs to small groups of children. (See Chapter 8 for more about this education.)

✔ Test results help your child's teacher understand his difficulties and make accommodations for him.

✔ You get insight into the best help you can give your child at home.

When your child struggles with reading, you hear a lot of "wait awhile" advice. You're told things like your child isn't "developmentally ready" to read yet or "he'll grow out of it" or "plenty of children start reading late."

Most children start to read between the ages of 5 and 7 and make their quickest progress at this time. This time period is a window of opportunity in your child's reading development, so if you see that this window isn't opening up for him, act quickly. He needs extra help right now. Trust your instincts. If you think your child is falling behind, he most likely is, even if teachers tell you he's doing fine. Don't get delayed or sidetracked by bad (albeit well-intentioned) advice. Research shows clearly and unequivocally that for struggling kids the "wait awhile" notion is just plain wrong.

Up to age 10, your dyslexic child can still make great progress if he's given good help. After age 10, things get harder. He needs more help more often, and you must be sure that whoever helps him (that person can be you) is homing in on his weak skills. I talk about the essential skills that dyslexics lack in Chapters 3, 4, and 5.

It's never too late to find out whether you or your child has dyslexia. In fact, the older you get, the easier the testing process becomes. Older children and adults are experienced and articulate. They can demonstrate their dyslexia by giving a complete verbal account of their difficulties. A psychologist may need to give them only one or two formal tests. See Chapter 18 for specific info on testing adults for dyslexia.

Examining Different Kinds of Tests

Names, names, names. When your child is assessed for dyslexia, you may hear so many fancy test names that pretty soon you'll be screaming for mercy. And figuring out exactly what each test measures can be an uphill slog too.

In this section I make things easy for you. I classify tests according to what they measure and give you a smattering of those scary, long-winded titles.

Adults are better able to describe their difficulties to a psychologist than children are, so adult testing for dyslexia usually entails a bit of talking. An adult may take a test, such as the Wechsler Adult Intelligence Scale (WAIS)-Revised, as a measure of his general ability. In addition, he takes reading and writing tests similar to the ones that I list here (only they're adjusted for adults) and gives a full personal account of his school life and literacy skills.

Looking at language tests for preschoolers

Did you know that your school district can test your child for speech and language development even before he starts school? Well, it's true and worth looking into if you're the least bit concerned about your 3- or 4-year-old (see Chapter 4 to find out more about signs to watch for in your preschooler).

Call your district and keep the number handy. The district is responsible for any testing you may need in future. Additional options for testing include colleges (ones that have child health and development courses) and independent speech and language centers (log onto www.speechville.com for a database of services in your state). You can also get great advice from the American Speech-Language-Hearing Association (ASHA) at www.asha.org, phone 800-638-TALK (8255).

When your child is in school, the school district is responsible for testing her for learning disabilities. If you want a second opinion or can make a case that the district isn't sufficiently staffed or resourced to give you proper testing, then the district must pay for you to get proper assessment elsewhere.

Speech difficulties are not the same thing as dyslexia and can't result in your child getting dyslexia (because dyslexia is there from birth). But untreated speech difficulties can make dyslexia worse, and even if your child doesn't have dyslexia, can lead to reading difficulties further down the line.

Preschooler language tests give your child the opportunity to listen and talk, look and talk, and chat generally about things. You can be fairly sure that at some point the speech therapist will show your child pictures and ask questions such as "What is this?" What is happening?" and "How is this different?"

Making sense of vision and hearing tests

If you're worried that your child rubs his eyes all the time or seems to respond to you only when you ask him something for the third or fourth time, head straight to your doctor. Don't be afraid to get a second opinion either.

Early testing is best. Your child gets routine vision and hearing tests in the first two years of school, but if you suspect a problem earlier (or later), see your doctor.

The symptoms in the following list are all possible signs of a vision problem:

- ✔ Head tilting
- ✔ Squinting
- ✔ Rubbing eyes frequently
- ✔ Holding books at an unusual angle or distance
- ✔ Headaches
- ✔ Dizziness
- ✔ Tiredness

Here are some possible signs of a hearing problem:

- ✔ A lot of ear infections
- ✔ Excessive shouting and talking loudly
- ✔ Not answering you
- ✔ Mishearing words
- ✔ Frequently asking you to repeat yourself

According to the American Academy of Allergy, Asthma & Immunology (`www.aaaai.org/patients/publicedmat/tips/recurrentinfections.stm`), your child is having too many infections if he gets more than four per year.

There are two types of ear infection: outer and middle ear. Outer ear infections are most often caused by swimming, but middle ear infections are linked to all sorts of factors, such as having had a respiratory tract infection or having been exposed to secondary smoking. For plenty of good information on ear infections and speech delays, check out `www.keepkidshealthy.com/welcome/infectionsguide/earinfections.html`.

Routine eye tests at school detect obvious visible defects in your child's eyes (such as cataracts, squints, or crossed eyes) and whether your child can follow movement in his field of vision (up, down, and side to side) and is not short- or long-sighted. Secondary-school-age children may also be tested for color-blindness. Routine hearing tests detect whether your child's hearing is within the normal range of volume (loudness) and pitch (high and low sounds).

You need to know that vision and hearing tests may not tell you about visual and auditory "discrimination" (or "perception" or "awareness"). You may hear these terms in a dyslexia assessment, and they have nothing to do with whether your child *receives* visual and sound information. The terms refer to how your child *processes* (or doesn't process) information.

If vision and hearing tests don't tell you anything about dyslexia, why have them done? To rule out vision and hearing problems that look like dyslexia or to fix up these problems so they don't make your child's dyslexia worse. (If you treat vision and hearing issues and your child *still* struggles with reading and writing, it could be dyslexia.)

In dyslexia assessment, *visual discrimination* is your child's ability to tell the difference between different letters and different orientations of a letter. *Auditory discrimination* is the ability to identify different sounds in words; it's often used synonymously with *phonological* (or *phonemic*) *awareness*.

Surveying early screening tests

Schools typically test, or screen, children for reading problems halfway through kindergarten or in first grade. A 5-year-old child can be tested for dyslexia (remember that schools usually call it "learning disability") even though he can't yet read because he should still have pre-reading skills. He should be able to do the following:

- ✔ Name the letters, such as *ay, bee, see.*

- ✔ Tell you the letter sounds — "a" (like in *apple*), "buh," and "cuh."

- ✔ Play with letter sounds, such as words with similar letters *(bat, ball, bench)* or rhyming words *(cat, hat, mat).*

If your child can't do these things (whether or not a test picks it up), he needs extra practice, and you may want more testing. To find out exactly how to give your child extra practice, flip to Chapter 12.

Understanding IQ tests

An IQ (Intelligence Quotient) test measures your child's aptitude or what he's capable of. (Psychologists don't always say that IQ tests measure "aptitude." They may use the words "potential" or "ability.") Two tests pretty much dominate the field:

 ✔ Wechsler Intelligence Score for Children III (WISC III)
 ✔ Stanford Binet IV (SBIV)

Your child must be at least 6 years old to take the WISC III, but children as young as 2 years old can take the SBIV! Both tests measure a whole bunch of stuff, like long-term memory (what day comes after Thursday?), practical knowledge (what should you do when you cut yourself?), and visual discrimination (which pictures look the same?).

Comprehensive IQ tests like the WISC III and SBIV are typically part of the battery of tests used by psychologists to determine whether your child has dyslexia or any other learning disability. They can be administered only by psychologists, and from them you get measures of many subskills.

IQ tests have been around for a long time because psychologists have considered them to be among the most reliable tests of ability that we have. Theoretically, your child's IQ score should stay pretty much the same regardless of what kind of a day he's having. Even if he's nervous, hot, hungry, sick, or upset, his good old IQ score shouldn't change all that much.

Some parents find that their child's test results are *very* different, depending on factors like who gives the test. When their child feels uncomfortable, he scores lower than when he likes the test administrator and feels relaxed.

One huge flaw in IQ testing has been brought before the courts in California. The IQ test (as part of the testing for LD) was ruled biased against African Americans because as a group, their scores were unreasonably low and led to their overrepresentation in special education. As a result, it looks like the IQ test and the IQ discrepancy way of determining whether a child has a learning disability will be ditched nationwide. What's IQ discrepancy all about? If your child's IQ is average or above but his performance on language and other performance tests is below average, he has an *IQ discrepancy.* As a rule of thumb, if a psychologist finds that your child is performing at a level about two years below his actual age and has a normal IQ, it shows he needs special education, and the psychologist must look closer at his tests and identify his disability.

Because of increasing criticism of the IQ discrepancy way of testing for LD, a lot of people (who know what they're talking about!) want a response-to-instruction way to test for LD. This means that a child is monitored after being given extra instruction, and if he doesn't improve (in response to that instruction), a diagnosis of LD may be made. Using this process, test findings are more directly tied in to subsequent instruction.

For the time being, in most places, the IQ test is still key in the test battery used to identify an LD (I talk about the battery later in this chapter). If your child scores much lower in tests of skills (like reading, writing, and spelling) than he does on a test of his IQ, it shows that his performance is lower than you'd expect from his aptitude (his IQ). He officially has an LD.

A psychologist also may find discrepancy *within* the IQ test because the IQ test has several parts that measure things like verbal IQ and performance IQ.

Picking out performance tests

An IQ test (covered in the previous section) measures your child's aptitude — what he's capable of regardless of how he performs. Other tests are designed to measure your child's performance. You may want to grab yourself a coffee and a snack because a lot of performance tests are out there! I divide the tests into four simple groups:

- ✔ General skills
- ✔ Auditory and visual motor skills
- ✔ Phonologic skills
- ✔ Oral reading

These tests are part of the battery for assessing dyslexia. Because dyslexia is mostly about reading problems, your child can't really get tested before about age 6, but once he is in grade 1 (or above) and reading just isn't happening for him, you can have him tested.

Testing for general skills

Many performance tests give you a big picture of how your child is doing. They measure things like reading, math, writing, and general knowledge. The test administrator especially looks for a gap between your child's written and oral skills because dyslexics are typically bright and knowledgeable in most oral tasks but weak at reading and writing tasks (that seem simple to other people). That's why parents get mystified. They know that their child is bright and clever; therefore, they can't understand why his reading and writing, and some aspects of his spoken language, make it look the opposite.

Here are some of the popular tests of general skills:

- California Achievement Test (CAT)
- Detroit Test of Learning Aptitude (DTLA-3)
- Peabody Individual Achievement Test-Revised (PIAT-R)
- Wide-Range Achievement Test (WRAT-3)
- Woodcock Johnson Psycho Educational Battery

Testing for auditory and visual motor skills

A test battery for dyslexia typically includes at least one test of auditory skills and one test of visual motor skills. Here are some you may hear about:

- **Test of Auditory Perceptual Skills (TAPS):** Does your child mishear directions, say the wrong word ("steps" instead of "ladder") or leave words out of his speech altogether? If so, a psychologist may use this test to measure his *auditory perceptual skills*, or how he processes the information he hears (*auditory* means hearing).

- **Lindamood Auditory Conceptualization Test (LAC):** Here's another test of auditory skills. This one measures how well your child identifies letter sounds on their own and inside words.

  The word "Lindamood" crops up a lot in reading tests and programs because Ms. Pat Lindamood has written, alone and with colleagues (Ms. Nanci Bell), reading tests and programs (Lindamood-Bell Program) that are popular in schools all over the United States.

- **Bender-Gestalt Test for Young Children:** This is a test of *visual-motor integration,* or how well your child draws what he sees. If your child has a lot of trouble with this kind of task, it means he may have, or be at risk of having, LD.

- **Beery Developmental Test of Visual-Motor Integration:** This test measures visual-motor integration too. Your psychologist will probably choose either the Bender-Gestalt or the Beery depending on his familiarity with either one and what your school district requires.

Testing for phonologic skills

Whether the teacher gives your child a five-minute test or the psychologist puts him through five hours of testing, someone will look at your child's phonologic skills. That's because dyslexia is a phonologically based condition. A dyslexic's problem isn't that he can't see or hear letters and words; it's that he can't easily *process,* in his brain, the letter/sound/word information (the phonologic stuff) that he hears and sees. A child may be bright and be able to tell you about complex things but has trouble identifying letters (and some numbers), reading, spelling words, and sometimes recalling (from his head) the word he wants to use when he's talking.

You really need to understand what these tests do rather than what names they go by. In plain terms, they ask your child the following kinds of things:

- Can you tell me the name of this picture?
- Can you point to the word that names this picture?
- If you take *p* off *pat* and put *c* there instead, what do you get?
- Can you write *stamp*? Can you read these funny sounds: *isk, eemp, thalep*?

Many tests of phonologic skills don't have "phon" in their names so you have to figure out for yourself that they're testing phonologic skills! The tests here *do* have "phon" in their names, so it's easy to see what they're all about.

- Comprehensive Test of Phonological Processing in Reading (CTOPP)
- Phonological Awareness Test (PAT)
- Togesen-Bryant Test of Phonological Awareness (TOPA)
- Yopp-Singer Test of Phoneme Segmentation

Testing oral reading

A dyslexia assessment can test every kind of language and problem-solving skill you can think of, and math and reasoning, too. Here's one last test that you're really likely to hear about. The Gray Oral Reading Test has been around a long time. Psychologists like to listen to your child read because when he hates doing it, is slow, and makes a lot of mistakes, it's a good sign he's dyslexic. The Gray Test measures the number and types of mistake your child makes with oral reading and is a real favorite.

Charging up for a test battery

When you look into the possibility of having your child tested for dyslexia, you find people talking about a *battery* of tests or a *test battery*. What they mean is a whole bunch of tests, both IQ and performance, that measure a whole bunch of skills.

The school or, more specifically, the school district, puts your child through a battery of tests to decide whether he has a learning disability (LD). To have this testing done, you must give a written request to your school district or to the school district via your school principal. The district is legally obliged to reply to your request (within a set time, usually 60 days) and test your child, as long as your child is clearly struggling in class. If testing reveals that your child qualifies as having an LD, he gets special education and an IEP (Individualized Education Program). You can read more about special education and the IEP in Chapter 8.

When you decide to file your request for testing, it's often because a teacher recommends that you do.

Choosing Your Test Administrator Wisely

You can have your child tested for dyslexia by the school educational psychologist (who works for your school district) or by an outside, independent educational psychologist (whom you pay). Or you can do both. In the next sections, I walk you through your options.

Selecting a specialist within your child's school district

The first person you need to go to when you want your child to be assessed in school is the classroom teacher. The courteous thing to do is to see your child's teacher before you see anyone else. Besides, if you skip her in the chain of command, it can come back to haunt you. You may ask the school psychologist for help only to find that he sends you right back to the teacher to start your quest at the right place. But even if that doesn't happen, you want your child's teacher on board from the outset so she knows you're concerned and ready to push your child's case. Hopefully, she agrees that your child should be tested and alerts the right people, and testing happens within a few weeks. Better still, she preempts you and asks you for your consent to have your child tested.

Taking the do-it-yourself testing route

I've been told that I can find anything I want on the Web, but I haven't wanted all that much until now. But now I want online testing that isn't just a pile of junk, and guess what, it's out there! If you want to test your child yourself (or test yourself!), you can create a relaxed atmosphere, behave like a detached but kindly administrator, and see what you turn up.

Here are some places to start your search for online tests:

- ✔ Worldwide tests that purport to measure dyslexia: www.dyslexia-test.com.

- ✔ British Schonell Reading Test: http://members.tripod.com/~gleigh/

readtst.htm. This test is alive and well even though I remember it being popular with resource teachers, then called "remedial" teachers, 20 years ago.

- ✔ British Burt Reading Test and the Schonell Spelling Test: Reading Reform Foundation at www.rrf.org.uk.

- ✔ Australian read-aloud tests and spelling tests: www.literacytesting.com.

Anyone can use these tests (no matter where you live), but they're obviously not the same as personal face-to-face tests, so you may want to use them just as a starting point.

In either case, you give your written request, it goes to the district, and the district psychologist has your child take a battery of tests. Other people (like the resource teacher) can help the psychologist with some of the tests in the battery, but only he is qualified to administer the IQ test. (If your psychologist doesn't use an IQ test, he'll use another test, like the Woodcock Johnson Psycho Educational Battery.) The psychologist's interpretation of test results is key to the decision your school district makes. Then you're asked to come to a meeting at school where you're told the results and the actions that the district proposes in response to them.

What are the pros of this option? If your child is tested in school, it's free. You have fewer bureaucratic steps to take. You know that the district accepts the assessment results, the teacher is already in the loop, and your child gets special education, no questions asked, if test results show he's dyslexic.

On the con side, you get no choice of who carries out the tests, you can't choose the venue, and you get no voice about the testing day. Also, the psychologist is sure to be very busy, so you may wonder later (if you're skeptical about the test results) whether he did a thorough job.

Investigating independent testers outside your child's school district

Plenty of people can test your child, but typically only a psychologist can give you test results that are accepted by school districts. In addition, insurance companies may contribute toward the cost of testing only when it's given by a psychologist. Other practitioners, who usually call themselves consultants, therapists, or tutors, can give you an assessment that helps you (or them) design a practical program for your child, but they typically don't give a dyslexia assessment. (They refer you to a psychologist because they know about the school district/insurance company thing.)

The title "consultant" or "therapist" implies that the practitioner has more qualifications than a tutor. It may even mean that the person is qualified (usually with a psychologist's certification) to provide you with a diagnosis that your school district will recognize. You'll want to check this out by asking the therapist what her qualifications are and then running this past your school district.

Only some practitioners use the term "dyslexia," so if you want to hear about dyslexia in a diagnosis, make sure you find out whether a practitioner is looking for it *before* you hire him. If he doesn't specifically look for dyslexia, find someone who does.

What are the pros of using an independent tester? Why do people pay for independent testing (which can run into thousands of dollars)? Here are five good reasons to opt for independency:

- ✔ The district won't test your child. It's not heartless but feels that your child definitely won't qualify for extra help and the money it would cost to test him should go to needier kids.

  It's unusual for the district to refuse your request for assessment because if you get your child tested independently and results show that he *is* eligible for extra help, the district could (legally) be in a tricky spot.

- ✔ The district says it will test your child, but you don't want to wait (usually for up to 60 days — the time most districts typically specify).

- ✔ The district already tested your child, but you're not in full agreement with the results. You want a second opinion.

- ✔ Your child is embarrassed by his problems. He doesn't want any kind of special education and will accept only the most low-key help. You want to protect his self-esteem (he has a hard enough time as it is) and don't see this as a battle you can really win. You can afford to pay for private services, so you decide to get private practitioners to assess and tutor your child.

- ✔ You place importance on having control over who gives the test (you want someone who's nice to your child) and when and where it's given. You want confidentiality, too (you may not want the school to know the test results).

What's the down side of independent testing? You pay for it. If you want your child's school to know the results (which is advisable but still your choice), you must make a time to see the teacher and then explain the situation. In that case, you'll have a lot of photocopying and distributing of information to do.

For a list of independent educational psychologists, ask your school district. To find parents, therapists, and dyslexia groups who can advise you, check out Appendix B. Another resource to call is a nearby university. Education, psychology, or special education departments often offer courses and summer classes for children as part of their research into learning disabilities.

Adults use an independent psychologist for assessment unless they're assessed through a government-funded vocational rehabilitation (VR) office. Chapter 18 has the details of getting an assessment when you're an adult.

Preparing Your Child (And Yourself) for Testing

Before the school tests your child, give your child's teacher any paperwork you've saved, like pediatric reports, vision and hearing test results, and a list of things you've observed your child struggling with. She can give the paperwork to the district psychologist, or alternatively, you can deliver the information to your district office yourself. If you're having tests done by someone outside of the school system, give him all the same information and your child's school reports, too.

Giving the test administrator the information you have well before the test makes good sense. He needs time to look it over so he can use it as another piece in his complete diagnosis.

This checklist gives you the material to gather together to make a portfolio for your child:

✔ A brief account of when your child started to walk and talk

✔ A brief account of warning signs you've seen (see Chapters 3, 4, and 5 for more about general and specific symptoms)

✔ A brief account of things your child's teachers have said about him and the kinds of reading instruction they've given him

✔ Medical information (especially about eyes and ears)

✔ Formal tests and reports from school

✔ Samples of his writing and spelling

✔ Samples of books (or lists of books) he reads

✔ Lists of words that are hard for him to read and write

Tests are scary for most people, but for a dyslexic, who's used to low scores and embarrassment, they can be much worse. Remember to tell your child that he's being tested so he can do better and not feel so bad in class. Tell him there are no wrong answers or grades. Walk him through some practice questions too (ask the teacher for some) so that he knows how to mark his answers (if he has to pencil in boxes or circle the right answer) and pace himself, and what to do if he doesn't know the answer to a question.

One aspect of testing that you may want to mentally prepare yourself for is the parent questionnaire. A teacher or psychologist may ask you to fill out a questionnaire, which you probably won't like, before your child is tested. The questions include things like these:

- ✔ Was your child delivered normally?
- ✔ Is your child often sick?
- ✔ Does your child have friends?
- ✔ Has anyone in your family had reading problems?
- ✔ Do you read to your child at home?

You may feel like you're on trial, so remind yourself that these tests aren't designed purely to make you squirm — even if it feels like it. The psychologist actually uses this information to get a clear picture of factors (like frequent school absences) that may have contributed to your child's reading failure. Fill out the answers, relax, and roll with the punches. You're getting a reminder of how your child feels about being tested and how you need to tell him he's not on trial, not dumb, and not being graded.

Receiving Test Results and Putting Them to Work

By now you have a good idea of the tests and test administrators that are out there and which, if any, you need. But are you reminding yourself that, most of all, test results have to work for your child? Knowing that your child is dyslexic or trusting that the school will take things from there isn't enough; you must steer or dictate what happens next. If your child gets extra help in school, you need to check that it's working. If your child isn't making progress, you need to pinpoint why and try something else.

You also need to follow up to see whether your child still gets the same amount of help in a few months. Your child may let slip that he doesn't see Mrs. Brown (the school resource teacher) three times a week anymore, but only once, so you need to keep regular tabs on the help your child is supposed to be getting. If your child goes to a tutor instead of receiving in-school help, you still need to be watchful because you can't assume that professionals have everything all sewn up.

Dyslexia is an ongoing condition. Your role as supporter and advocate is ongoing too. Your job is to constantly match tasks to your child rather than have people force tasks on him. Not everything works for your child, so you both need to get good at mixing and matching. Your child has individual needs, and you know them better than anyone else. But you also need to help your child do more for himself. The older he gets, the more he needs to speak up for himself and let teachers know exactly what kinds of activities and learning aids help him perform on an equal footing with other students.

In the following sections, I tell you the terms you often hear in test results and how to proceed with your child's education, whether or not he qualifies for special education.

Breaking down terminology in test results

When the test administrator explains your child's test results to you, you're bound to hear some terminology you may not be familiar with. Here's a heads-up about the meaning of some of the common phrases:

- ✔ **Age:** A test age of 7.2 means your child performed like an average child aged 7 years and 2 months.

- ✔ **Auditory access:** Can your child pull sound-information (like names of things and parts of words) from his mind? This is auditory access, which is often measured by asking a child to quickly name pictures. If your child can't quickly name common objects, like a toothbrush, vase, and curtain, his auditory access is weak.

- ✔ **Auditory memory:** Can your child keep bits of sound-information in his mind for a short time? This is auditory memory, which is often measured by asking a child to remember a few words over a few minutes. If your child can't recall a sequence of numbers, like 5 3 6 1, right after being told (and asked to remember) them, he has weak auditory memory.

- ✔ **Percentile ranking:** If your child gets a percentile ranking of 14, it means that of 100 average children, he's 14th from the bottom.

- ✔ **Phonemic skills:** This has to do with *phonemes,* or the smallest chunks of sound inside words (like c-a-t and sh-ou-t). Your child's grasp of phonemes is tested when he's asked what sounds he hears inside words.

- ✔ **Phonologic skills:** This refers to general sound, letter, and word skills, such as being able to rhyme and name letters. If your child can distinguish different sounds inside words and words that sound alike, he has good phonologic skills.

- ✔ **Standardized:** A standardized test has been given to hundreds of children, so the test administrator has a normal bell curve of scores on which to plot your child's score. He knows how kids in general perform on this test and how your child scores relative to the general population that the test is for.

Finding out that your child has an LD

If your child's tests show that he's performing far below the level you'd expect of him, he will be diagnosed as having an LD (learning disability) and will get special education.

You may be told that your child has a "learning disability," a "specific learning disability," or a "specific language disability." The terms "specific learning disability" and "specific language disability" are really just ways of saying your child has dyslexia. There are other learning disabilities, but dyslexia is the most common.

Other learning disabilities include *dysgraphia* (difficulty with writing), *dyscalculia* (difficulty with math), and *dyspraxia* (difficulty with motor skills) but not (yet) ADHD, which your dyslexic child can have along with dyslexia.

The following sections give you the details on working with an officially recognized LD child in school and at home.

Seeing LD at work in class

You're probably wondering what happens when the paperwork is filed away and your child gets into class as a newly assessed child with an LD. Specifically, your child's teachers must accommodate his needs in class and document exactly how they do it in his Individualized Education Program (IEP), which is a written and working document specifically about him. You attend IEP meetings to review how well things are working, but you need to keep in touch with the teacher and resource teacher because the meetings typically happen only once a year (ridiculous isn't it!).

The resource teacher is usually the one who's ultimately responsible for setting up your child's IEP and seeing that everyone follows through. She gives your child what you might think of as remedial instruction, usually in her room with just a few other students.

Watch your child's reading and writing. If he's not making progress, meet his resource teacher and request some practical changes, like having enlarged print for your child or allowing him extra time to finish assignments. Bring up your concerns at your IEP meeting — and keep doing that! Flip to Chapter 8 for complete details on the IEP.

The resource teacher is hopefully a nice, approachable person who has many strategies at her fingertips to help your child. If you're lucky, she may also be trained in one of the reading programs that have evolved in recent years to regulate what resource teachers do. Here are some popular programs designed especially to move struggling readers forward (see Chapter 7 for details):

- **Lindamood-Bell:** Of the several Lindamood-Bell programs, the Lindamood Intensive Phonological Sequencing, called LIPS for short, is the most common. In a LIPS program, children become aware of the actions their mouths make when they say different sounds.

- **Orton-Gillingham (O-G):** This program is probably the most common of all. It's been around a long time, and most other programs describe themselves as being influenced by O-G.

- **Slingerland:** In a Slingerland program your child learns the sounds inside words and does a lot of writing.

- **Spalding:** Spalding programs are offshoots of O-G with an emphasis on writing.

Now when a teacher asks you, "Has your child done Orton-Gillingham?" you know what she's talking about. These programs are often named after the people who wrote them (that's why they have unusual names), and they're structured, phonological, and sequential — just right for a struggling child.

Responding to an LD at home

After you know that your child has an LD, don't think that you're not qualified to help him. No matter what terminology you use, the same basic truth holds your child struggles in class and needs as much love, support, and assurance as you can give him because he's having a tough time. Imagine how it must feel for him to be constantly lagging behind classmates and trying to hold his own. Imagine the kind of teasing he puts up with. You're his greatest ally when it comes to feeling good about himself, so gear up for the ride! You can help him out with schoolwork too of course, and be every bit as good at helping him as the professionals (once you know how).

To look deeper into helping your child out emotionally, flip to Chapter 15 and for help with at-home activities, check out Chapters 11 to 14.

Discovering that your child won't be recognized as having an LD

School districts have a limited amount of money to go around, so not everyone can get special education. Even when your teachers see that your child struggles and you're certain he needs more help, chances are your child won't qualify as having LD. About five children in each class (or about 20 percent) struggle with reading, but only about half of them, at best, qualify as having a learning disability (and are therefore entitled to special education).

Test results separate children eligible for special education from those who aren't eligible, but in reality benchmarks can be different in different places. Your child can be eligible in one school district and not in another. Also, a school or private psychologist may tell you that your child has only mild dyslexia and therefore isn't eligible for special education.

What can you do when the school tells you that your child's test results (whether they're from the school or an independent tester) don't qualify him for special education? You can take the following steps:

- ✔ Dispute the test scores and get private testing done
- ✔ Consider Section 504
- ✔ Get help from school by being friendly
- ✔ Get independent tutoring
- ✔ Tutor your child yourself
- ✔ Home-school your child

The following sections discuss the details of these options.

Disputing the school's test results

If you disagree with the school's evaluation and ask for an independent opinion, called an independent educational evaluation (IEE), the school district must help you get one and may have to pay your costs. To fight your case, find someone (who talks in down-to-earth terms) to tell you about your rights. Luckily, I've tracked down great help for you so you can save a bundle of time and energy. Interested? Check out Appendix B for more information.

When you contact someone for help, be selective about what you say and stay focused. Off-load and grumble to other parents who have been through the same things as you, but with a professional, be professional. Jot down a list of things you want answers to and stick to your point. After someone tells you your rights and how to proceed, you can then find an independent tester (I talk about independent testers earlier in this chapter). If the independent tester confirms the school's results, you'll probably want to end your search. If the independent tester disagrees with the school's results, you can take your new information back to the school. Hopefully you reach a resolution, but if not, you may be looking at legal proceedings or at least gathering more evidence. In either case, you can find people to help you by checking out Appendix B at the back of this book. The legal people and organizations like the International Dyslexia Association (IDA) know about this kind of thing.

Considering Section 504

When your child is assessed as having an LD, he receives special education, and his rights are spelled out in the Individuals with Disabilities Education Act (IDEA). If your child doesn't qualify as having an LD, another legal safety net may apply. It's called Section 504 (of the Rehabilitation Act of 1973), which is for children who have conditions like ADHD, which don't count as learning disabilities.

Section 504 says that schools must make "reasonable accommodations" for children who have a "functional impairment" that "substantially limits a major life activity." Also, Section 504 says that schools must have a Section 504 official. If you want to look into Section 504, ask your school to give you its parents' rights manual and set up a time to see the Section 504 official. "Accommodations" doesn't mean that your child gets the same help that a child with a diagnosed LD gets (unless your school is *really* nice to you!), but he *can* get assistance like having test questions read aloud to him rather than having to read them for himself. I talk about accommodations in Chapters 9 and 10.

Securing help from school by being friendly

When you worry about your child, your whole world seems darker. You can find yourself being angry all day, sleepless half the night, and not in the best state to say productive things to teachers. Try to have an "I'm reasonable and caring" image upfront even when you have dark thoughts whirling around out back. Try to believe that teachers really *do* want to help your child, and if it doesn't seem that way, it's probably because your teacher is overworked or really *does* think your child will catch up. Whatever the reasons, the important thing for you to do is to focus on your child's practical needs.

The best way to make things easier for your child in class is to make it easy for the teacher to help him. Suggest (politely and reasonably) practical things that will help your child. Thank the teacher for any effort he makes for you and offer to help in any way you can.

Be calm, helpful, and friendly to your child's teacher. Let him know that you aren't criticizing him and you respect his competency, but you need help in making things easier for your child. Convey the belief that if you both work as a team on your child's behalf, he can succeed in class. I talk about building a good relationship with the teacher and asking him to make classroom accommodations in Chapter 10.

When teachers often see your face in school and know you help out at fairs, in the cafeteria, during Library Week, and at other school events, your child registers higher in their consciousness. They're more likely to talk about him and think of him when new things are available.

You may find after-hours school clubs to help your child too. Ask about homework clubs, volunteer tutoring, and social or athletic groups that can boost your child's self-esteem. Also try to befriend people who always know what's going on in school. Networking and keeping in the loop can make a big difference to your child. See Chapter 9 for more details on these options.

Finding independent tutoring

If your child is struggling in class, you may decide to have him privately tutored whether or not he gets extra help in school. When you look for a tutor or learning center, consider the following:

- ✔ The cost of the lessons
- ✔ The distance you must travel
- ✔ The tutor's qualifications and experience
- ✔ Whether the tutor gives structured, phonological, and sequential instruction (remember those buzz words?)
- ✔ Whether you can sell the idea to your child

Check out Chapter 9 for more about finding and using a tutor.

Tutoring your child yourself

No matter what happens in school or with an outside tutor, you can help your child at home. Don't think that because you're not a dyslexia-trained teacher you can't be effective. Of course the term "dyslexia" brings up scary-sounding things like "multisensory" teaching and "phonological" skills, but these terms are really just fancy words for stuff that doesn't need to be difficult. You can help your child (just as much as a teacher or tutor can) and save yourself a lot of money and commuting time.

To get the naked, practical strategies that successful teachers (of dyslexics) use, flip to Chapters 11 to 14.

Home schooling

Home schooling is getting more and more popular and may be an option you want to know about. If you home-school, you get to monitor your child's performance closely and adapt lessons to suit his strengths, and you don't get the usual homework strife. The drawback is that your child's social life takes a massive cut. In Chapter 7, I tell you why parents choose to home-school, what they teach, and how successful they are. (You can also check out *Homeschooling For Dummies*, by Jennifer Kaufeld, published by Wiley.)

Looking at Your Options When You Decide Not to Test

Should you ever do without testing altogether? Most people get tests done because they want to know exactly what's wrong and how to move forward. They want a starting point as a way to gauge progress. Sometimes, though, you may consider all the factors (the LD label, the likelihood that you won't get special education, and your child's anxiety) and decide to do without testing (and move straight to tutoring, asking for small accommodations in class, and helping more at home).

You should skip testing only when your child's problems seem mild (see Chapter 3 for a list of general symptoms) and after you've had a discussion with your child's teacher. Overall, the solution for diagnosing dyslexia is indeed testing, so if you have any doubts about what to do, have your child tested.

This list gives you reasons why no testing at all may be an option for you:

✔ You can't afford it. If this is the case, don't think that your child will be disadvantaged. Big, comprehensive tests are good, but so are small, quick tests. Sure, you get all the bells and whistles with a test battery, but the bottom line is that you need to know what practical instruction your child needs. A good teacher can tell this from quick, inexpensive commercial tests she has in class or from tests she devises herself. This kind of test, which measures only your child's skills without comparing them against other children's scores, is called a *criterion-referenced test.* If you'd like to try one out, flip to Appendix A at the back of this book.

✔ You have a great relationship with your child's teacher and know that she goes the extra mile for your child even though he's not formally identified as having an LD. You pretty much know that your child won't qualify for special education anyway because you see other kids in class struggling just as much as your child and have talked it over with teachers and parents who have been in the same boat.

If your child is struggling in school, the teacher sees it and will most likely do his best to help your child in class, regardless of whether test results boost your case.

✔ You know a good tutor and believe that your child will make progress with her. She'll give your child a quick, useful assessment so you save the stress of two to five hours of testing (which will say the same things but in fancier words!), save money, and sidestep the LD label in school.

✔ You read this book, checked out the Web sites listed in the back, and joined your local branch of IDA. You know your child has weak phonologic skills, you know he needs a lot of practice with sounding out, and you're helping him yourself or getting a tutor. You don't feel you need to fork out a few hundred dollars for someone else to tell you what you already figured out for yourself. Great, what are you waiting for?

In case you think that doing without testing sounds overconfident, I should tell you that I talk to plenty of parents who manage to identify and treat their child's problems by themselves. They network, work with their child each night, monitor his progress, and see him move into higher reading groups in class and score better grades! Two parents I know who took the do-it-yourself approach are now training to be special education teachers.

Part III
Exploring Your Options for Schools and Programs

The 5th Wave   By Rich Tennant

"I realize that your son's dyslexia diagnosis raises many questions, but let's try to address them in order. We'll discuss the IEP, meet with your son's teachers, and then determine what color ribbon you should wear."

In this part . . .

Of course you want the best school, the best teacher, and, naturally, the best reading program for your child. But in the real world, how much choice do you really get? Does every alternative school cost a fortune? Is the best reading program (for dyslexics) already being used in your child's school? Can an Individualized Education Program (IEP) really make that much difference to your child's chances in school? This part is crammed with the answers to all these practical questions — and a lot more besides.

Chapter 7

Choosing the Best School for Your Child

*Y*our child needs extra help in class, and naturally you want her educated in a place where she gets a lot of it. You have a few important decisions to make when it comes to selecting her school.

If your local public school has a great resource teacher who uses a good program with your child and sees her every morning for an hour, you're on to a great thing! Assuming that you see your child making steady progress and know that she's happy, this is the ideal scenario. And it happens for a lot of children.

But sometimes your child gets hardly any time with the resource teacher, and neither of you likes her anyway. Then you have to take a look at the big picture. Maybe your child is generally happy in school, so a good choice for you is to send her to a private consultant for the special instruction she misses out on in school. On the other hand, if you've heard of a great school especially for dyslexics, you may want to put up with the initial stress of changing schools for the long-term benefits.

In this chapter, I give you a list of traits to consider as you decide on a school for your child. I also describe the features and staff members of traditional public schools and explain the alternative schooling options that your child has.

Questioning the Kind of School Your Child Needs

Your child needs a lot of support to overcome her dyslexia. She needs to mix with people who understand her and don't bring her down. Maybe she has special talents to be nurtured, too. Here are the questions you need to ask when you make the crucially important decision about which school to send your child to:

- ✔ How many children are in a class?
- ✔ What kind of support will my child get with reading?
- ✔ Do the teachers seem happy and sensitive to all the children's needs?
- ✔ Does the school use a reading program like Orton-Gillingham (see "Homing in on school programs," later in this chapter)
- ✔ How much group work do students do?
- ✔ How much homework will my child get?
- ✔ Can my child use a computer for most of her assignments?
- ✔ Does my child's prospective teacher use a classroom buddy system?
- ✔ Does the school have a homework club?
- ✔ What extracurricular activities does the school provide?
- ✔ Does my child have friends in the local public school?
- ✔ How much are parents involved in the school?
- ✔ Does the school have a tutoring program?
- ✔ Does the school encourage you to help in class and feel free to drop in anytime?
- ✔ Does my local public school have a good resource teacher?
- ✔ Does my local public school look well equipped with things such as new books and computers?
- ✔ Do the teachers at the local public school seem happy and friendly to the children?
- ✔ Is the principal at my local public school approachable?
- ✔ Does the local public school welcome my visits?
- ✔ Is there a local charter school? (A charter school is an alternative public school. It must follow the same rules as regular schools in some ways, but in other ways, it follows its own charter, which is drawn up by staff and parents.)

✔ Are other schools within easy traveling distance for me?

✔ Do I have special requirements, like wanting a Catholic education for my child or advanced instruction in violin?

✔ Can I afford private school?

✔ Can I afford to send my child to a private tutor or consultant (to augment her public education)?

After you prioritize your questions, you and your child need to visit the local public school in the hope that at least many of the things you want are offered there. Phone the school to arrange a time for your visit. Keep your child in the loop so she can be mentally prepared (and have her coolest outfit ready!). When you get there, go through your questions, try to see classes in session and visit the places that will be important to your child socially, like the lockers and cafeteria. Through this mix of academic and social information, you should get a feel of what the school is like and can do for your dyslexic child.

The question of whether your child gets special education and an Individualized Education Program (IEP), which I discuss in Chapter 8, applies only to public schools. Private schools aren't bound by the same laws as public schools and make their own decisions about providing for dyslexic children. Most parents stick with a public school, so that's what I focus largely on in this chapter.

Decisions, decisions: Do you have a choice of public schools?

Your house sits within a designated school district. Within that district, one elementary school is closer to you than the rest, so it's your "home" school. If your house is equidistant between two schools, your school district decides which school is your home school. Your child must go there unless

✔ The school doesn't have room for her (in which case she is wait-listed).

✔ You can show, or the school acknowledges right off the bat, that your child's special needs can't be met at that school.

If you show that your child needs to go to a school with special facilities for her (that your local home school can't give), your school district must cover the costs. You must persuade the district superintendent though, so you need a clear case and any supportive documents (like test results) you can get. The district prefers that your child attend her home school of course, so it will aim to accommodate her needs there. You have to be on the ball when the teachers tell you (informally if your child doesn't have an IEP, or formally during an IEP meeting if she does) what kind of help your child will get so you can ask for changes or additions and monitor how the talk pans out in practice. (In Chapter 10 I talk more about the kinds of help or accommodations your child can get in class.) And from the outset you should be prepared to go to school often, if need be, to push your child's case.

Looking at What a Traditional Public School Offers

Your local public school has to account for the way it spends its money and show that it makes appropriate provisions for children with disabilities. In real terms, this means that as long as you can show that your child needs it, she gets a few kinds of extra help. In the following sections, I lead you through the assessments, special instruction, and other services to watch out for and, if they're missing, inquire about.

Supplying assessment services

One good thing about your local public school is that it gives your child free dyslexia assessment. You file a written request with the school district and get an answer within a set time (usually 30 days). An educational psychologist runs your child through a battery of tests, and if she's found to have dyslexia (or a learning disability), she gets special education. See Chapter 6 for full details on testing.

You'll probably hear about your child's "learning disability" or "specific learning disability" rather than her "dyslexia." Dyslexia is one specific kind of learning disability, but teachers don't often use the word (because they don't feel qualified to do so). Your school psychologist may not use it either, simply because his mandate is to deal with "learning disabilities."

Your child may have dyslexia but still not qualify for special education. She may be struggling, but not enough (about 2 years behind) to qualify for special education. If you just depend on the public school for special education in this instance, you don't get it until your child's problems worsen to the required low level of performance.

Homing in on school programs

If you're brand-new to special education and reading programs, boy have I got some alphabet soup for you! At some point during your child's education, you're going to hear weird terms like "Orton-Gillingham" and "Lindamood-Bell." These are names of popular reading programs. I run through them here so that when a teacher tells you your child gets Lindamood-Bell, you can nod sagely and ask, "Do you prefer it to Orton-Gillingham?"

Ready? In this section I describe 17 programs, any one of which your child is likely to come into contact with in a public school. A couple of them are straightforward and inexpensive enough that you might like to try them out at home. (I feature a few of these reading programs, along with other dyslexia treatments, in even more detail in Chapter 20.)

Most of the following programs are used predominantly in public schools, but they may also be featured in private schools and learning centers. For more about sending your child to a tutor or a learning center, check out Chapter 9.

- ✔ **Orton-Gillingham (O-G):** Developed by Samuel Orton and Anna Gillingham in the 1930s, this is the granddaddy of multisensory, phonics and research-based programs. In real English that means that it engages a few of your child's senses while she learns phonics rules and patterns, and it's backed by plenty of research. Everyone knows about it, it's the most popular program of the bunch, and several other programs are offshoots of it. Plenty of teachers and tutors are trained in O-G techniques, so you can find programs in schools and centers, and you can train in it yourself too if you want. For info, visit www.ortonacademy.org or call 845-373-8919.

- ✔ **Lindamood-Bell:** This is a bunch of programs designed by Ms. Lindamood and Ms. Bell. The most widely used is Lindamood Intensive Phonological Sequencing — LIPS for short —for the clever reason that the program makes children become aware of the actions their mouths make when they say different sounds. Programs are short and intense. Your child gets one-on-one help through four to six weeks, four hours a day (yep, you heard right!). You usually go to a Lindamood-Bell center or a trained tutor and pay, or your school resource teacher may give your child a milder variation of the same thing. For info, visit www.lblp.com or call 800-233-1819.

- ✔ **Project Read:** Project Read is most often used in schools, not centers. There are five curriculum strands (phonology, linguistics, written expression, and two kinds of reading comprehension), so it can be used in regular and special classes and with all ages. For info, visit www.projectread.com or call 800-450-0343.

- ✔ **Slingerland:** This program is designed for classrooms and there are summer programs too. Children learn the phonetic sounds and do a lot of writing. For info, visit www.slingerland.org or call 425-453-1190.

- ✔ **Spalding:** This is an adaptation of Orton-Gillingham with an emphasis on writing. This program is used in schools and learning centers in several countries, and an online parent course will soon be available. For info, visit www.spalding.org or call 602-866-7801.

- ✔ **Corrective Reading:** SRA (now joined with McGraw-Hill) has been producing learning kits or programs for decades. The one you hear most about in schools and learning centers is Corrective Reading. In a Corrective Reading program, the teacher reads out instructions from a manual (word for word) to a small group of students, and all the students read and fills in their workbooks as instructed, all at the same time. This program is also called SRA, Distar, and Direct Instruction (DI). For info, visit www.sraonline.com or call 888-772-4543.

✔ **Reading Recovery:** This program, which originated in New Zealand but has spread to schools and learning centers across the globe, is for children in grade 1 and is an intensive blast of daily instruction for 12 to 20 weeks. It's not a program that's up there with the favorites for teaching dyslexics because it doesn't tag itself as phonics-based or multisensory, but it gives children individual instruction and a lot of reading at their level and gets good results with most participants. For info, visit www.reading recovery.com or call 614-310-7323.

✔ **LANGUAGE!:** This is a popular program for middle and high school students in part because it incorporates all 18 reading and language arts curriculum strands. It's also used in some learning centers. For info and materials, visit www.language-usa.net or call 800-547-6747, ext. 266.

✔ **Wilson:** The hallmark of this program is that teachers show students how to tap out sounds in words to help them remember them. Originally it was for older students, grade 5 and above, but now it has materials for younger kids too. You find the Wilson program in schools and sometimes being used by therapists and learning centers. For info, visit www.wilsonlanguage.com or call 800-782-3766.

✔ **Lexia Herman Method (**also called **Herman Method):** In this program, students complete 21 levels of instruction, each with a spelling and handwriting component. Instruction is multisensory and phonics based (as pretty much all reading programs for dyslexics are) with an emphasis on comprehension. The Herman Method is used in schools by teachers who take workshops to learn it but may be used by those teachers outside of school too. For more information, go to www.hermanmethod.com.

✔ **Read Naturally:** This program is specifically for improving your child's reading fluency and is used by schools and by some therapists and learning centers. Your child does repeat readings of short pieces of text. She reads the text out loud while listening to it on a tape recording and times her reading speed for each separate reading. She reads progressively faster at each reading and gets more confident. For the bigger picture on Read Naturally, go to www.readnaturally.com.

✔ **Success for All (SFA):** This is a school-based reading program for disadvantaged or at-risk children in grades pre-K to 6. Schools that use the program get support (like on-site coaching) from the Success forAll Foundation, which is funded by donations. The foundation also produces other programs, like Curiosity Corner and Kinder Corner for little children and the Reading Edge for adolescents. Check it out at www.successforall.net.

✔ **Early Intervention in Reading:** This is a program with a difference. It's for use in schools only and is an easy and relatively inexpensive way to give regular classroom teachers training in providing struggling readers with the explicit phonics instruction and guided reading that they need. Teachers get Internet training and learn how to give struggling children

20 minutes of daily instruction, in a small group (up to 7 students) within the class. For more information, visit www.earlyinterventionin reading.com.

✔ **Davis Learning Strategies:** Ron Davis, dyslexic and author of *The Gift of Dyslexia,* has built a small dyslexia-busting empire! You can take your child to a Davis center for assessment and tutoring (which I go into in Chapter 20), and now teachers can attend Davis workshops and buy Davis boxes (full of materials for small group instruction) to use in class with struggling readers. Check it out at www.davislearn.com.

The programs that I list next are smaller, less popular programs than the ones I just described, but they're still great and used by plenty of resource and special education teachers. You don't get the training courses and substantive research that come hand-in-hand with the bigger names, but you can buy what you need quickly and easily, whoever you are. The publisher for all the next programs is Educators Publishing Service (EPS books; www.epsbooks. com), whose Web site you may enjoy browsing because it has masses of great stuff on offer. Since the programs I list next are readily available to parents, I give you prices and a quick summary of what you get for your money.

✔ **Alphabetic Phonics:** An offshoot of the O-G program, this multisensory curriculum teaches elementary and high school children to mark sounds with symbols. You get a teaching manual ($11), workbooks ($12.55 each), and a lot of other materials if you want them. For info and materials visit www.epsbooks.com (click on Dyslexia Materials) or call 800-225-5750.

✔ **Recipe for Reading:** This program, for children in grades K to 6, is comprised of a teacher's manual, workbooks, storybooks, and other bits and pieces too. The whole package is straightforward and attractive. The manual currently sells for $20.75, and the workbooks are around $10 each. For info, visit www.epsbooks.com (click on "dyslexia materials") or call 800-225-5750.

✔ **Explode The Code:** Here's a program that consists mostly of simple sequential workbooks. Each workbook costs about $7, which makes this program one of the least expensive around.

Just because a program has a good track record doesn't mean that your child will succeed in it. Different children like different methods, so don't think you've come to a dead end if your child hates a program everyone else raves about. Try another one. Look for a teacher or tutor who has experience with struggling kids. Even if she doesn't talk about Orton-Gillingham or Lindamood-Bell, she may still do great phonetic and multisensory activities with your child (see Chapters 12 and 14 for more about these types of activities). Watch how your child fares. You don't need a PhD in reading programs to see whether she's getting the hang of sounding out, enjoying the tutoring, and becoming a better reader.

Giving help above and beyond the classroom

Public schools can do great things for your dyslexic child outside of class. When enthusiastic teachers and parents come up with ideas and give their time, all kinds of things, like homework clubs and tutoring clubs, can happen.

Here are some of the clubs and activities you may want to ask about in a school:

- **Buddy system:** Your child can be a younger child's buddy or get taken under an older child's wing herself. Either way, this is great stuff! Schools that put kids to work being friends and helpers for other kids are great places to be.

- **Homework club:** If your school runs a homework club, it could be worth your while to check it out. Older kids often help out in homework clubs, and if that's the case in your school, you may be able to commandeer a kind, interested one to take special care of your child!

- **Special responsibilities:** Good teachers know that giving a child special responsibilities, like being lunch monitor or litter patroller, works wonders for her self-confidence. If your child isn't already doing a special job, put in a good word for her.

- **Specialty one-off programs:** Sometimes a school offers a short, one-time program to help kids with things like assertiveness. Keep your ear to the ground so your child doesn't miss out. If you can't volunteer in school, get friendly with another parent who's always there so you get to hear what's going on.

- **Sports and arts:** I know that these things are pretty obvious, but I feel that I have to give it a quick mention anyway. Encourage your child in any nonacademic activities she enjoys. She needs many ways to feel happy and successful because happy children are better equipped to weather the knocks that dyslexia can bring.

- **Tutoring for your child:** Most schools ask parents to volunteer to listen to kids read. Often they set up programs in which a parent regularly works with a child once or twice a week. Listen up for this kind of program because after a volunteer parent knows how to help your child, great reading progress can come from this special one-on-one coaching.

- **Your child tutoring other children:** On the surface, asking a dyslexic child to tutor another child may seem ridiculous, but it works. As long as the teacher finds something your child can cope with, like marking spellings from an answer sheet, your child can feel useful and important (and who doesn't need that!) and brush up on her own skills in the process.

Providing sensitivity to your child's needs

A couple of years ago I asked my child's teacher if my child could do a slightly different weekly spelling list than the other kids. I gave my (really great) reasons and offered to provide the list and come to class each week to help mark it if that would help. The teacher said, "If I let one child do it differently, they'd all want to." She also spent a lot of time yelling at the kids and telling them they were the worst she'd ever taught, but that's a whole other story!

This teacher was inflexible, which is exactly what you don't want. It shouldn't happen of course, especially if your child has been officially deemed dyslexic (or learning disabled), but it does. I could start a lengthy tirade about the awful things I've seen happen to dyslexic kids, but instead — because it's more productive — I tell you about the great things I've seen teachers (who take the trouble to put themselves in your child's shoes) do. In schools and classrooms that are sensitive to a child's extra needs, you see these kinds of things:

✔ **Small group activities:** Your dyslexic child probably enjoys small group activities because she can talk tasks through with her group and contribute to it in ways that emphasize her strengths and sidestep her weaknesses (for example, drawing posters or taking photos instead of writing). In a small group, your child also feels more secure. Fewer eyes are upon her than when she has to ask or answer questions in the whole class.

✔ **Partners working together:** As long as both partners get along, partnerships are a perfect fit inside your dyslexic child's comfort zone. An understanding partner may allow your child to dictate words for her to write, assume responsibility for tasks that take the least writing, and develop a friendship in the process.

✔ **Creative projects:** Here's where your dyslexic child gets to shine. She shows her artistic, dramatic, and technological skills and gets better at thinking of ways to apply these skills to other classroom projects, too.

✔ **A designated classmate that each student can call on when she needs help:** At one time or another, all children forget what they're supposed to be doing for homework and need to call a friend. You can pretty much expect your dyslexic child to stress about homework often, so a friend on the end of the line (phone or Internet) is a must. Help your child keep and use a reliable contact list.

✔ **Use of computers and tape recorders:** Older dyslexic children can save themselves a lot of trouble by becoming computer savvy and knowing how to use a tape recorder. It's worth trying to keep abreast of technology or even just keep pace with your child's technological know-how if you can manage it. If not, maybe a friend can help you out.

✔ **Word lists posted on walls:** After you show your child how to sound out the parts of words that sound out easily, and highlight other parts, tape those words to a bathroom or other much-viewed wall. If you have a whole list of spellings, try to put them into word families too (like *round, sound,* and *pound*).

✔ **Classroom help from parents:** When parents help in class, the teacher gets more time with students. Your dyslexic child benefits, along with everyone else.

✔ **Scheduled time with the teacher for every child:** One-on-one teaching is the most effective teaching your dyslexic child can get. Scheduled, personal time with the teacher is a definite plus.

✔ **Respectful tone of voice in use by everyone, including the teacher:** Your dyslexic child has enough to deal with without having to listen to a teacher yell at students or other students yelling at each other (or being rude in other ways). A respectful classroom in which the teacher has kind but firm control is the ideal.

✔ **Full recess time for everyone (detentions aren't common):** Your dyslexic child needs her school recess time. In a great classroom, the teacher deals with issues like noncompletion of assignments in ways that don't deprive children of their wind-down (and eating) time.

A responsible position

Recently my child's teacher told me he planned to give my child special responsibilities. "She'll rise to the occasion," he said, "It sounds terrific," I said. A few days later, my child came home from school with this to say:

"Guess what, mom? I'm now officially a very important person. Mr. Peterson gave me a truly responsible job. I'm shoe tidier, and if one single shoe is out of line, I have full permission to go right in there and fix it. If I do a great job, maybe I'll be promoted to hats?"

My daughter, evidently being tongue-in-cheek, was really telling me she'd seen right through our plot, but even so, I could tell she was a teensy bit proud to be shoe tidier. She held her elevated position for several weeks, and those shoes hardly knew what had hit them.

A few weeks later I went through much the same thing with my older daughter. She was invited to join the after-school art club but pronounced that it was really the after-school dork club (and she's dorky enough as it is without drawing attention to it!). I listened to her complain, and poke fun, but sure enough, she joined the art club and had new experiences to grumble (in a typical teen way) about. Any reasonable responsibilities that you give your dyslexic child can make her feel more confident. Even if she grumbles about a job, it still gives her a feeling of independence and being relied upon. And your dyslexic child, more than other children, needs to strengthen her people skills and work ethics so they can outshine the weak spots in her literacy skills.

Meeting the Staff in a Traditional Public School

When I walk into my kids' school, it hits me right away — this really is a nice place (and I think I'm a pretty good judge by now because I've worked in several schools and sent my kids to several more)! The secretary is nice to me, kids walk past and say "Hi," and I don't see a line of miscreants waiting outside the principal's office. When the principal herself appears, lo, she smiles at me and sometimes stops to chat!

In the following sections, I introduce you to the main folks at any given public school. If you get a good feeling after meeting with all of them, you can feel more comfortable about putting your dyslexic child's education in their hands.

Familiarizing yourself with the classroom teacher

Please, oh Lord, let me have a good teacher. If your child has ever had a really bad school year, you know (and yards of research substantiates it) that the teacher is the single most important factor in your child's success in class. In the following sections, I explain the qualities of a good teacher for a dyslexic child and show you how to improve your chances of getting your child happily paired with one. (For complete details on working productively with teachers, see Chapter 10.)

Sizing up qualities in a good teacher

A good teacher for your dyslexic child sets up her classroom in the ways I talk about earlier in the chapter: She fits small group activities into her programs, matches up buddies, encourages creativity, and maintains a warm but disciplined atmosphere in her classroom. She has some special skills too because your child has a few special needs. She is

- ✔ **Approachable:** Your child can always go to her after class and ask for extra guidance.

- ✔ **Flexible:** If one strategy doesn't work for your child, she's happy to try another.

- ✔ **Aware:** She understands that when your child can't do things in the same way as other kids, it doesn't mean she can't do them at all. Your child shouldn't be allowed to skip tasks; instead, she needs to try out different strategies until she finds her fit.

Requesting a specific teacher for your child

Teachers get together at the start (or end) of the school year to decide which child goes with which teacher. The principal oversees the process, but the teacher your child just left probably wields most power. It sounds mercenary to cultivate a friendship with your child's teacher so you can get preferential treatment, but of course, that's exactly how the real world works. Dyslexia can be taxing enough (for your entire family) without finding out that your child gets the super-uninspiring, yell-rather-than-talk, teacher from hell.

It hardly seems fair that you don't get to choose your child's teacher does it? Since that's the case, however, let me outline some things you can do to raise the odds of your getting a good teacher.

✔ Fill out the optional information sheet that you get at the end of the school year, the one that helps teachers place your child next year. You're not allowed to say honest things like "I don't want bad-tempered, boring Mrs. Kent," but you can say things like "My child responds best to quiet, gentle discipline" and hope for the best. If you fill the form out, at least you have a chance that your voice will be heard.

✔ Be friendly with your child's current teacher so you can brazenly ask her (if you dare) to allocate your child to a specific teacher the following year. I was once at a school where parents were quietly and dutifully filling out their information forms when a parent marched straight into the classroom and said, "Judy, Connor hates Mrs. Raynor, so you have to put him with Mr. Clark." And yes, the next year Connor was in Mr. Clark's class!

✔ If your child gets special education, talk to her resource teacher. Tell her which classroom teacher you'd like for your child so she can add her comments to the selection process. (See the following section for more about resource teachers.)

✔ Talk to the teacher you'd like your child to have. Maybe she will remember you and ask if she can add your child to her list (as long as no one else has other plans).

✔ When the new school year begins, if you don't like your child's teacher, go to the principal right away. If you present a good case, the principal may put your child into another class, but if you wait longer than about three weeks, she's likely to tell you it's too late.

Both parents should see the principal, but make sure that you present a united front. Be calm, clear, and tactful. Specify what's going wrong in concrete terms, but avoid personally criticizing the teacher ("Shelby is unhappy" rather than "Mrs. Smith is awful"). Be firm and persistent.

✔ If your child hates going to school and you don't know whether to complain or sit a bad year out, remember that your child can fall seriously behind in the early years. Write down all the incidents and comments your child tells you about, and date each one. Take this record with you to the principal and ask, on the basis of your child's stress or academic failure, for a change of class. Take someone (preferably someone who's good at negotiating) with you if you need to.

No luck? Ask to see the counselor and/or the district superintendent. Again, keep documenting what you're concerned about (for example, low grades, punishments, or snide comments). If you feel that the school, not just the class, is causing your child to fail or be miserable, and your record of events shows it, you may even (after a lot of fighting) get your district to agree to move her to another school within the district. If all else fails and you're prepared to take extreme measures, move to another house so you can send your child to a school you've researched and love the look of.

If it sounds like I'm scaremongering by telling you to march boldly into school with your issues, it's because I hear from a lot of parents whose children are struggling in class. They're not sure whether their problems are big enough to warrant serious complaint. They're not sure whether they should keep quiet because the school on the whole is nice, their child has friends, and so on. Here's what I think is the deciding factor. Your child's reading problems don't get better by themselves; without intervention, they get worse. If your child doesn't get good intervention or she gets great help with the resource teacher but she's so unhappy in her classroom that she can't learn, speak up. Now. Trust your own judgment and don't wait for someone to give you the okay. And if your child is seriously unhappy (she cries most days, has bad dreams, or has started wetting the bed), you're not overreacting by wanting to change a class or even school. In fact, you should be making it a priority.

Acquainting yourself with the resource teacher

A typical public school has a resource teacher who's responsible for keeping your child's Individualized Education Program (IEP) running smoothly and productively. Typically, your child goes to the resource room a few times each week to get small group instruction with the resource teacher. It's up to your school, though, to decide exactly what your child gets, and that's influenced by budget and staffing. (See Chapter 8 for complete IEP details.)

Resource teachers do great work, but just like in any other job, you get good and not-so-good ones (and even with a great resource teacher, she and your child may not click). If your resource teacher runs a special dyslexia treatment program, like the Orton-Gillingham program, you're likely to be pleased with what you see. (I cover Orton-Gillingham and other dyslexia treatment programs in the section "Homing in on school programs," earlier in this chapter.) Does a good program always equal good results, though? No. The teacher factor is still crucial. Your child learns much more from a teacher she likes than from one she doesn't like, so ideally you want a good teacher (see the section "Sizing up qualities in a good teacher," earlier in this chapter) who uses a good program.

Ah, but maybe even that isn't strictly true. Plenty of great resource teachers use their own eclectic mix of strategies rather than a commercial program. They (as well as the program users) understand how important phonetic understanding is for your child, and they're great at livening up the work, too. Teachers are under a lot of pressure to train in new programs, but you still can't beat experience, empathy, and an open, lively mind. You should be able to spot these qualities simply by talking to a resource teacher and checking out her classroom. (See the section "Providing sensitivity to your child's needs," earlier in this chapter.)

Resource teachers and special education teachers deliver special education to children who are entitled to it. If your school has both kinds of teachers, the resource teacher usually works with more moderately disabled children, and she may teach gifted children too. She is often trained in reading programs, like Orton-Gillingham, while the special education teacher has training in things like how to include wheelchair-bound children into normal school life.

Checking out school specialists

Your child is assessed for dyslexia, or a learning disability (LD), by a district-employed psychologist and may meet a few other specialists too. The psychologist works full time for the school district or is contracted to do assessments. He is qualified to diagnose your child and is the only person who can administer some of the tests that your child takes as part of the whole battery of tests for LD. You can get the specifics on assessment in Chapter 6. If your child needs other services that aren't provided by regular school staff, like speech or physical therapy, and these needs are part of her IEP, the school district provides them, too. Your child will visit a specialist, or the specialist will come to school to visit her. Treatment continues for as long as the IEP team says it should. I tell you all the ins and outs of IEPs in Chapter 8.

Paying special attention to the support staff

Here's a thought: You probably have almost as much contact with the school secretary as you do with your child's teacher. You speak to the secretary any time you make an appointment to see the school psychologist, speech therapist, or other specialist or when your child forgets her lunch, stays home sick, or has an outside appointment. If you're nice to the secretary, your life runs smoother.

Sounds easy, doesn't it? I'm a (fairly) honest person, however, so I feel compelled to warn you that you may encounter an officious school secretary or two. Of course, I speak only from my own encounters, but well, some of them haven't been pretty. I've groveled shamelessly to many a secretary for things as trivial as use of the school phone (and only for the briefest of local calls too). All I can say is that when you deal with the school secretary, you're in the midst of real power, so tread warily!

Oh, don't forget to grovel to the janitor, too. He can let your child in the classroom after hours when no one else can, and you can bet your life you're going to need that some time when your child swears someone took her homework (due tomorrow) from her bag and put it right back in her desk.

Taking note of the principal

In a small elementary school, you may have a lot of contact with the principal. Especially if he has an interest in children with special needs, he may talk to you about your initial concerns and attend subsequent IEP meeting that you go to, but he doesn't have to, though. Often you deal almost exclusively with teachers, and in fact you may hope for that because meetings with the principal may mean you have a problem that you haven't been able to resolve at the lower ranks.

Meeting the principal and getting on friendly terms with him is easy when your child is in a small elementary school. When your child goes to a big middle or high school, however, it's much harder. The principal is harder to track down and has all the responsibility of being at the helm of a big organization. Even if you schedule a meeting with him, he may not remember you a few weeks later.

Realistically, you can count on not having much to do with the principal of a big school unless you have serious complaints. Even then, the principal is near the end of the line of people you need to contact (the classroom teacher, resource teacher, and guidance officer come earlier in the line). Jot down some contact details about him (and also about the district superintendent) and file them away safely, just in case.

Getting the Scoop on Alternative Schooling

If you think that your child won't get all the help she needs in your local public school or you have other reasons for wanting to keep your child out of the public system, you have a few options. You can choose from schools that operate by their own unique set of beliefs, schools that meet your religious needs, and schools that cater specifically to dyslexics. In the following sections, I give you a quick tour of the whole caboodle.

You can claim tax deductions for your child's specialized tutoring and schooling as long as you can show that a doctor recommended it. Your expenses are treated as medical, and the basic rule is that you can deduct only amounts that exceed 7.5 percent of your adjusted gross income. For the fine details, read IRS Publication 502 (Medical and Dental Expenses), downloadable from www.irs.gov/publications/p502/ (click on Forms and Publications and then on Download Forms and Publications by: Publication Number).

Finding out about charter schools

A charter school is a free public school with more self-regulation than a regular public school. It is state funded but writes its own charter that must comply with some district guidelines but leaves teachers and parents free to choose methods and curriculums. Forty-one states have charter schools, and if you have one in your school district, you're eligible to enroll your child.

What are charter schools like? Unique. Because each one develops its own charter, I can't give you shared key features. Here though are a few things you may find:

✔ A child-centered, less formal curriculum

✔ A cooperative setup in which parents must volunteer in class or in other ways that help the school, for a set number of hours each semester

✔ Innovative new teaching methods

✔ Community involvement

To find out whether a charter school is located near you, visit the US Charter Schools Web site at www.uscharterschools.org. To get the scoop on what kind of special help your child can expect, contact your particular school. If you like the idea of online education, you'll be interested to know that there are currently more than 60 cybercharters serving more than 16,000 students in 15 states. You can check that out on the same US Charter Schools Web site.

Feeling the pull of magnet schools

Another type of public school you may want to consider is a magnet school. Magnet schools originally started out as a way to help schools desegregate. They offered attractive options to black students (so they'd be drawn as if by a magnet), and that, without the racial part, is still what they aim to do today.

What kind of options do you have with magnet schools? Each magnet school has a special focus, like preparing students for musical, scientific, or military careers. If your dyslexic child has her heart set on a particular career path, you can see what every magnet school in the country offers and requires from prospective students by logging on to the Magnet Schools of America Web site at www.magnet.edu.

If you choose a magnet school, you'll probably want to include private tutoring in your plans because magnet schools don't usually offer specialized treatment for dyslexia. See Chapter 9 for more details about tutoring.

Choosing a private school

If you choose to send your child to a private school, check out the same kinds of things that you'd look for in a public school (see the section "Questioning the Kind of School Your Child Needs," earlier in this chapter, for a list of considerations).

Technically, Montessori schools, Waldorf schools, and schools for dyslexics (which I cover in the following sections) are considered private, but when I talk about "private schools" in general, I'm discussing a wider range of schools that fit special requirements you may have. Private schools, in this context, include religious schools and single-gender schools (all boys or all girls).

Just like in any school, you find good and not-so-good teachers, so take extra care to sit in on a class and talk at length to your child's prospective teacher. Is she easy to talk to, and does she seem flexible and accommodating?

Private schools aren't governed by the same laws as public schools and don't have to provide special education to your dyslexic child. You have to ask a private school what kind of help it will give your child. You also need to understand that whatever help your child does or doesn't get, you can't rave about your rights under the Individuals with Disabilities Education Act (IDEA), which I cover in Chapter 8. (Actually, you can rant and rave if you like, but it won't get you very far.)

If you don't want your child to attend a private school full time or you can't afford it, ask about summer school. Many schools offer summer classes, and they're usually popular (so enroll early!).

Examining Montessori schools

Montessori schools began in the early 1900s with Maria Montessori, an Italian physician and educator. Now you can find Montessori schools all over the world — and not just for little kids. Key features of Montessori include the following:

- Classes have 20 to 30 students and two or three teachers.
- Students in the classes are mixed ages and start at age 2.
- The alphabet and sounds are introduced at age 2 with materials like letter blocks and sandpaper cutouts.
- All children get to do a lot of hands-on activities. Children help themselves to specially designed materials from low shelves.
- Teachers watch your child and give her new materials when she looks ready.
- Teachers introduce your child to specific stimuli (like dance and music) when she's thought to be at the most receptive age for them.
- Your child learns as an individual and starts doing group work only in high school.
- Classes are quiet, clean, and orderly, with an emphasis on self-care and responsibility.

Will your dyslexic child thrive in a Montessori school? Maybe. Montessori schools introduce your child to phonetics at an early age (before difficulties set in) and use multisensory and noncompetitive strategies, and that's all great. The downside is that your child may not master reading early on, and then she may need specialized tutoring (even though you're already paying big dollars for Montessori!).

If you like the look of a Montessori school near you, do your homework. What exactly can the school do for your child to help her with her special needs? For the fine details on Montessori, check out these three Web sites: www.montessori.com, www.montessori.org, and www.montessori.edu.

Walking the Waldorf (or Steiner) path

Back in 1919, Dr. Rudolph Steiner, an Austrian, started a school that was funded by a Mr. Waldorf. Now there are more than 600 independent, private Waldorf (sometimes called Steiner) schools in over 32 countries. Waldorf schools aim to educate the whole child, "head, heart, and hands," without competitive grading and with protection from the harmful influences of broader society. Waldorf schools have these key features:

- ✔ Letters are only introduced in grade 2, and children learn to read from their own writing.

- ✔ In grades 1 to 8, your child keeps the same "main lesson" teacher.

- ✔ In the younger grades, all subjects are introduced through artistic mediums.

- ✔ All children learn to play the recorder and to knit.

- ✔ All children learn a stringed instrument from grade 3 on.

- ✔ Children don't use textbooks until the fifth grade. All children have main lesson books, which are workbooks that they fill in during the course of the year.

- ✔ At the elementary level, teachers don't grade children but write a detailed evaluation at the end of each school year.

- ✔ The use of electronic media, particularly television, by young children is discouraged.

So is Waldorf right for your dyslexic child? Hmm, maybe not. Your child gets plenty of loving care at a Waldorf school but is taught to read late in her school career. Also, while teachers can give her extra help, they may not have the time or expertise to give as much of it (or the right kind) as she needs.

If you like the sound of Waldorf, you need to carefully check what happens if your child struggles with reading and writing. For all the ins and outs of Waldorf, check out the Association of Waldorf Schools of North America at www.awsna.org and also www.waldorfanswers.org.

Deciding on a school for dyslexics

Many private schools cater specifically to children with dyslexia. Some of them are boarding schools. They all have Web sites and brochures that you can browse through after you recover from the shock of how much you pay! The big advantage of these schools is that your child is surrounded by students just like her and all the teachers are focused on teaching her in a dyslexic-friendly way. The factors that may put you off are financial and geographic. You have to pay for these schools, and you may have to travel a long way to take your child there each day (unless your child boards, which has its own drawbacks). In addition, even before you get into those issues, you have research to do. Every school is different, so you have to get a feel for each one individually. For a list of K to 12 schools and links to their Web sites, go to www.ldresources.org.

Thinking about home schooling

Home schooling may be an option you don't want to dismiss out of hand. These days, you can find many places to turn for help with planning curriculums. In addition, home schooling may be cheaper for you than private schooling or tutoring. Here are a few things to ponder:

- Home schooling your dyslexic child can work out cheaper than sending her to private school and you don't have to travel long distances.

- Plenty of home-schooling curriculums, online courses, and support groups are available all over the place. Parents of dyslexic children often say that being able to pick and choose from curriculums is the biggest benefit of home schooling. They can find materials that suit their child instead of trying to push their child through the one-size-fits-all public system.

- Children who are home-schooled generally do well in tests against publicly schooled children.

- Home schooling allows you to respond to your dyslexic child's academic needs but also to protect her emotional health (if she was teased or felt depressed at school).

- You can always send your dyslexic child back into the public system.

Must a home-schooling parent have vast reserves of patience and calm? Not necessarily. Home-schooling parents say that as long as you're reasonably level headed and can get along with your child without too many showdowns, you may be pleasantly surprised by how stress-free home schooling becomes once you know the ropes. And of course you can make your own discoveries about flexible, fun lessons and teaching your child phonics through multisensory techniques.

If you're considering home-schooling your dyslexic child, plenty of Web sites and books are available to check out. In fact, all that research can get overwhelming, so here are just three Web sites that, for my money, get the "informative but simple" award:

- At www.geocities.com/Athens/8259/special.html, you get a list of links. It sounds boring, but it's not, because the list is easy to read and each site is briefly described.

- At www.homeschool.com, you get straightforward general information that includes a page about phonics home-teaching packages.

- Ever thought about part-time home schooling? The Illinois Department of Education has a Web site that explains how it works. The rules are different in each state, but at this site, www.illinoisloop.org/homeschool.html, you at least get the drift.

Almost every state has home schooling networks. Just type "homeschool net-work" and the name of your state into your Internet search engine. In addition, check out a home-schooling magazine at www.homeedmag.com.

After you decide to take the home-schooling plunge, you need materials. In the next sections, I give you suggestions for sets of readers (reading and writing), workbooks, and other bits and pieces that are super-handy things to have alongside your abacus and cane. *Homeschooling For Dummies* by Jennifer Kaufeld (Wiley) is also a great resource.

If your child goes to regular school (and you're home-schooling only part time), check that she doesn't already use these books in class so you don't double up.

Reading textbooks

With so many kids' reading books to choose from, what kinds of texts should your dyslexic child be using? For all-by-herself reading, your child needs attractive books with well-spaced text spread comfortably throughout the pages. Most words should sound-out regularly, and it's helpful if new and tricky words, like *enough* and *who,* are given in a separate list your child can look at before she launches off. And so that your child can read several books before having to search anew, you may want to focus most of your book search on series. In the next list, I describe book series that you can be sure satisfy all or most of the good-reading-books-for-dyslexics characteristics I just outlined.

- ✔ **The Alphabet Series:** This is two volumes (1 and 2) of storybooks. You get color short stories and, at the back of each book, questions to ask your child and sight words she should learn (so flip to these first). Published by Educators Publishing Service, the books are available at www.epsbooks.com (click on Decodable & Leveled Readers). The cost per set of 13 books is $59.95.

- ✔ **Bob Books:** These are small books in a box with 12 books per box. Boxes come in Levels A, B, and C with more than one box per level. Bob Books are great for all kids because they are phonetically leveled and the illustrations are cartoon characters of indiscriminate age. They're published by Scholastic and available at all good bookstores at a cost per box of $16.95.

- ✔ **Dr. Seuss:** The easiest books in this classic series are *Hop on Pop, Cat in the Hat,* and *Green Eggs and Ham.* Check out the word families in the back of *Hop on Pop.* Published by Random House, the books are available at most good bookstores for $8.99 each.

- ✔ **Primary Phonics:** In this series, you get five sets of readers with ten books per set. The text is phonetically controlled, and the illustrations appeal to a broad readership. You can buy separate workbooks too. They're published by Educators Publishing Service and available at www.epsbooks.com (click on Phonics/Decoding). The cost per set of ten books is $20.95.

✔ **Reading Rainbow Readers:** Each book in this series is comprised of short stories with a theme (like "Silly Stories" and "Pet Stories"). The brief, phonetically controlled text has story lines. The books are published by SeaStar Books and available at all good bookstores for $3.99 apiece.

✔ **Real Kids Readers:** This series has three levels (1, 2, and 3). The text is phonetically controlled, and because of the real-life photos, the books appeal to a wide age range. They're published by Millbrook Press and available at all good bookstores for $4.99 each.

Workbooks

Having a few workbooks that your child can write in is a handy starting point for home schooling. But a lot of workbooks that look nice on the outside and purport to be straight forward turn out to be confusing for your child to follow. You need books with simple instructions and a sequential progression of phonics activities. Here are the ones I like:

✔ **Building Spelling Skills:** This series includes a set of six workbooks, available for grades 1 to 6. Simple, repetitive lessons each focus on a different bunch of words. You can obtain these books, published by Evan-Moor, at www.evan-moor.com (click on Language Arts). Each book costs $16.99.

✔ **Explode the Code:** This series includes 17 books so far. The first three (preschool) books are *Get Ready for the Code* (Book A), *Get Set for the Code* (Book B), and *Go for the Code* (Book C). Next are books 1 to 8 with some half numbers (such as 1½) in case Johnny needs more practice. Published by Educators Publishing Service and written by Nancy Hall and Rena Price, the books are available at www.epsbooks.com (click on Phonics/Decoding) or by calling 800-225-5750. The teachers guide books cost $7.95, and the workbooks each cost between $6.25 and $7.

✔ **Reading Freedom (Activity Books 1 and 2):** Published in Australia, these books are easy to order online. Use them after Johnny knows the letter sounds and some sight words. They have a grown-up appearance that older kids like. Published by Pascal Press of Australia and authored by Hunter Calder, the books are available at www.pascalpress.com.au. Activity books cost $16.95 (AU) each, and the teacher resource book is $39.95 (AU).

✔ **Reading Reflex:** This book tells you how to teach your child phonographix, or, in other words, that letters are sound-pictures. You get instructions for making letter cards and having your child slide them together to make words, word games, and short stories to read. Published by Free Press and written by Carmen and Geoffrey McGuinness, the book is available in all good bookstores and online bookstores for $16.

✔ **Recipe for Reading:** This program, for children in grades K to 6, is comprised of a teacher's manual, workbooks, storybooks and other bits and pieces. The publisher is Educators Publishing Service, and the authors are Nina Traub, Frances Bloom, et al. You can obtain the books by visiting www.epsbooks.com (click on Dyslexia Materials) or calling 800-225-5750. The manual currently sells for $20.75, and the workbooks are around $10 each.

✔ **See Johnny Read!:** Here's a book I have a certain fondness for! It's for parents of boys who struggle with reading. You get real-life stories and a SPRint program to use (sight words, phonics, and reading). You're asked to give your child 20 to 40 minutes of daily reading and to do a one-hour lesson with her once or twice each week. Published by McGraw-Hill and written by yours truly, Tracey Wood, the book is available in all good bookstores and online bookstores for $12.95.

✔ **Teach Your Child to Read in 100 Easy Lessons:** This long-standing, well-regarded book takes you step by easy step through teaching your child the basics. It's good for very beginners. Published by Fireside and written by Siegfried Engelmann, et al., this workbook is available in all good bookstores and online bookstores for $20.

✔ **Toe by Toe:** This is a workbook/manual in one. You get one book of exercises and progress charts and are told to tutor your child for 20 minutes a day. Your child progresses to the next lesson only after passing a mastery test. Published by Keda Publications (United Kingdom) and written by Keda and Harry Cowling, the books are available at www.toe-by-toe.co.uk. The cost is $45.27.

Extra materials

Some teaching tools and extra bits and pieces are especially handy for teaching letter sounds and spellings to dyslexic children. In the following list I give you the inexpensive, portable items that I always like to have among my own teaching paraphernalia.

✔ **Lowercase letter cards:** For a set of inexpensive letter cards or letter blocks, check out the resources at Creative Teaching Press. You may want to browse because there's a smorgasbord of attractive products here. Buy these products at a school supplies store or online at www.creativeteaching.com (click on Parents, then Products, and then Letters). Each set costs about $5.

✔ **Book-sized whiteboards:** Kids like writing on a whiteboard. Buy two, and you can write words and play word games together. You can find them at any school supplies store for about $7.

✔ **Flashcards:** Flashcards can help your child practice phonics rules and patterns she already learned. These three packs, by Frank Schaffer, each have 100 clearly printed word cards that you can group into families. *And* the cards come in sturdy little boxes that you can pack in your car or bag. You can buy them from school supply stores or online at `http://elementary-educators.schoolspecialtypublishing.com` (type in the ISBN number to find them) for $6.99 each.

  • **Easy Blends and Digraphs:** ISBN: 0-86734-412-1

  • **Easy Vowels:** ISBN: 0-86734-410-5

  • **Easy Sight Words:** ISBN: 0-86734-403-2

Here are some other places to start looking for books, toys, guidelines, and more:

✔ **Charts and graphs:** Help your dyslexic child represent her ideas pictorially rather than in writing by downloading, for free, pie charts, bar graphs, and other diagrams at `www.edhelper.com/teachers/graphic_organizers.htm`.

✔ **Images:** For inspiration about turning words into images, check out `www.picturemereading.com` or call 800-235-6822 or 619-462-3938.

✔ **Mark Twain:** If you want to tell your child that Mark Twain is said by some people to have been dyslexic, you can read up about him and other interesting stuff, at this cute school Web page: `www.waunakee.k12.wi.us/midlschl/commarts8.htm`.

✔ **Note taking:** Check out `www.sas.calpoly.edu/asc/ssl/notetaking.systems.html`.

✔ **Puzzles and toys:** At Dragonfly Toys, `www.dftoys.com/specialneeds/dragonfly/usa`, you get goodies targeted at children with special needs.

✔ **Reviews:** For recommendations on new products, surf `www.parenting.com` (under Software of the Year). For software and book reviews, go to `www.familyfun.com`.

✔ **Speed reading:** For a manufacturer's blurb on speed-reading, visit `www.accelerated-achievement.com/speedreadingFAQ.html`.

✔ **Spelling rules:** At `www.usingenglish.com/weblog/archives/000021.html` and `www.alt-usage-english.org/I_before_E.html`, you can find a discussion about the efficacy of the "*i* before *e*" rule.

Chapter 8

Investigating the Individualized Education Program

Oh my gosh, the Individualized Education Program (IEP) can be intimidating. An IEP is a detailed written plan of exactly how special education is to be delivered to your dyslexic child. In this chapter, I walk you through all the important points: the basics of an IEP meeting and document, how to guarantee a successful IEP meeting, the services your child receives with an IEP, and the legal issues pertaining to IEPs.

All public schools are legally obliged to provide disabled children — including dyslexics, because dyslexia is a learning disability — with special education and an IEP. Private schools do *not* have to provide special education or an IEP. Each private school makes its own decisions about providing (or not providing) for students with disabilities.

Probing into the Basics of an IEP

An IEP keeps everyone honest and on their toes! It's a binding, written account of who does what, when, and how in the delivery of your child's special education. It specifies names, times, and dates so individuals are accountable for carrying out specific actions by specific times. The following sections give you basics of an IEP meeting and the actual IEP document.

The nuts and bolts of an IEP meeting

The IEP is written in school, in an IEP meeting, by a team you're on! The IEP meeting must take place within 30 days after your child is found, from the time of assessment (see Chapter 6), to be eligible for special education (and therefore an IEP). The school must give you ample notice of the meeting time and place and do its best to schedule it when you can be there. It's best, of course, if both parents can attend the meeting, but if that isn't possible for you, send in your place a friend or a family member who's well versed in your child's history and education, or an advocate.

If you can possibly avoid it, don't skip an IEP meeting. You don't get that many meetings, so each one is important. At each meeting you have a chance to talk to all involved parties together in one place and make sure that your voice is heard and documented.

The school must tell you who will be on the IEP team and give you any documents you ask for (like your child's school records, the school's blank IEP form, or notes the team members are presenting). People typically on the team are you, the classroom teacher, the resource teacher, a school district person who can allocate money, and a district person who translates things into plain talk for you (such as how Section 504 affects you — see the section "Recognizing how Section 504 and ADA fit in," later in this chapter).

You're allowed to take someone with you to the IEP meeting to morally support you and help you keep on track. You can also take a professional or other knowledgeable person with you. Good professionals to take to meetings are people who call themselves advocates. See the section "Knowing your rights — and your child's," later in this chapter, for details.

Your child also is allowed to be at the IEP meeting. He benefits by this because he gets practice in speaking up for himself and being clear about his own goals. Do some role-playing ahead of time to prepare him. Have him practice explaining which school activities in particular cause him strife and what kinds of ideas he has, if any, for making things easier.

Children younger than about 7 years old may not benefit that much from attending an IEP meeting because it's hard for them to define their problems and ideas. Besides, a grown-up meeting can be boring even for grown-ups! You may simply want to talk to your younger child at home and take his ideas to the meeting. If your child is older than 7, you may still want to represent him rather than have him attend the meeting. This decision is based on how much benefit you think there is to be had from having your child attend.

If your child comes to the IEP meeting, let the school know in advance. If he's there, the conversation will change because teachers may not want to say things like "Tim bullies other kids" or "Tim talks aggressively." Team members need to phrase their concerns in sensitive, constructive ways, and your child needs to be assertive but open to suggestion. You may want to include your child in just the second part of the meeting so you get adult-only time (and the chance to talk about Tim's heavy handedness). Usually the coordinator of the meeting sets the stage for your child's inclusion.

You will spend a few hours at your child's first IEP meeting, but after that, you get IEP meetings only annually (unless you ask for more frequent reviews). Your child gets reassessed for eligibility every three years, and if he's made great progress, he may no longer qualify for special education. If he still qualifies for special education, his IEP and IEP meetings continue.

For more details about IEP meetings, see the section "Ensuring a Successful IEP Meeting," later in this chapter.

The fine print of an IEP document

The IEP is essentially a document of who does what, when, and how. It holds individuals responsible for actions within a time frame. The IEP must describe your child's present performance, unique needs, and the specific and practical ways in which the school will meet those needs. An IEP document includes the following information:

- **Baseline:** The IEP starts with an appraisal of your child's current education level so that you have a baseline from which to chart his progress. Members of the IEP team share test and observational information about your child so that everyone's clear about his here-and-now strengths and limitations.

- **Goals:** The IEP team then outlines short- and long-terms goals for your child and benchmarks to watch for. Goals are stated in specific, measurable terms so you don't end up with vague goals like "Johnny will improve his reading speed." Instead you see "Johnny will work on Fast ForWord with Mrs. Jones every morning for 20 minutes. He will take the weekly test every Friday morning and the ABC test on November 30."

- **Ongoing evaluation:** The IEP tells you how the school will keep you informed of your child's progress. You can expect regular updates (by e-mail, mail, phone, or whatever you agree upon) and can ask for a meeting at any time if your child doesn't seem to be moving forward.

✔ **Accommodations:** The IEP explains the special education services and accommodations provided to address each of your child's goals/needs. It also explains the date that the services will begin, their frequency, and their location. At any time you can ask for changes to the type and amount of special education your child receives (like time with the resource teacher), the type and amount of other services he receives (like speech therapy), and the type and number of goals that are set for him (like recognizing 100 sight words).

✔ **Transitioning:** Transitioning is when your child moves from elementary to middle school or from middle to high school, and his IEP must prepare him for it. About halfway through the year preceding transition (sometimes even earlier), your child is shown what to expect in his new school and gets plenty of dry runs. When he approaches the end of high school, he gets help with choosing a job or college and grooming himself in preparation. (Chapter 17 has additional info on applying to college.)

Considering the cons of an IEP

The pros of an IEP are self-evident to a lot of people, especially those who would love to get special education for their own child but don't qualify, but some folks believe that there are disadvantages. These parents worry about the IEP for the following reasons:

✔ A stigma is sometimes attached to being a special education kid.

✔ The IEP meetings can be harrowing.

✔ Books and other materials that mainstream students receive may not be allocated to special education students, so they miss out on updated and challenging materials.

✔ The resource teacher may have a general special education degree but may not be trained in specific reading techniques.

I'm not going to whitewash over these concerns because they're entirely valid, and the stigma issue can be particularly worrying for older students. Kids who get special education *do* get called "dumb" by other kids and must prepare for that and learn to deal with it. Hopefully your child gets used to "wearing" his learning disability in elementary school and can deal with it in later years. If he can't bear to be a special education kid, try to find a compromise (like reducing, but not eliminating, his hours away from regular class) before you think of withdrawing him from special education. Few parents want to give away this help.

You'll at times feel worn out by pushing your child's case or having to listen to hours of edubabble as part of the IEP meeting. You'll tire of justifying your every request and having to listen like a hawk to every detail so you're sure you're ending up with the best deal. But, and this is a considerable but, having extra help in school and learning to overcome the drawbacks is better than going without extra help at all.

Ensuring a Successful IEP Meeting

Many parents take whole courses about effectively representing their child in IEP meetings. They read up on advocacy (at the Web sites of organizations listed in Appendix B) and contact the Council of Parent Attorneys and Advocates (www.copaa.org) to sign up for workshops.

That being the case, *you* certainly want to be prepared for an IEP meeting. In the following sections, I give you the info you need at that foundational level.

Preparing yourself

Before I tell you about preparing for the IEP meeting, I have an analogy for you to visualize. Ready? I'm not the kind of cook you can rely on. At times I cook great things, but often something's missing, like onion in the curry, butter in the mashed potato, or meringue on top of the meringue pie. Do you have that picture?

Now here's my point. When it comes to something as serious as your child's IEP meeting, don't rush the preparation. Preparation is everything; preparation is key; preparation is crucial. Why? Because if you don't have the essential ingredients of a successful IEP meeting — knowing what you're entitled to and the right spiel to use — you may end up getting a poor deal for your child. The following sections explain the preparatory steps that can help ensure a successful IEP meeting.

Speaking with the teacher

Before the IEP meeting, you'll want to have a conversation with your child's teacher and ask the following questions:

- ✔ Who will attend the meeting and what will be discussed?
- ✔ How is my child coping in each of his subjects?
- ✔ How good is my child at concentrating, completing tasks, following instructions, and organizing his work?

You'll also want to tell the teacher the kinds of things you want to bring up at the IEP meeting so you (hopefully) form a little alliance with her.

Don't bypass your child's teacher unless you really can't work things out with her. She can be your best resource. If you get her on your side, you may get the same kind of help, just by asking, as you would get after weeks of cutting through red tape. See Chapter 10 for additional info on working with teachers.

Making lists and organizing documents

Making lists and gathering relevant paperwork before the IEP meeting are important; everyone needs to be prepared to talk about the same issues. You shouldn't lose or forget important topics amid the talk and general activity.

As soon as you know you're going to an IEP meeting, start making a list of things you want to discuss, including the following:

- ✔ **A list of specific things you want to tell and ask the IEP team:** You can include such things as how well your child is doing on a new reading program or that he doesn't seem to be benefiting from a program at all.

- ✔ **Your child's strengths and weaknesses:** You may want to mention your child's out-of-school behavior or strengths if they impact what he does in class and his own view of his strengths and weaknesses. This information is especially useful if your child is the type who's always obliging and seemingly happy in school but complains about schoolwork the minute he steps through the door at home.

- ✔ **What you expect your child to learn this year, especially in reading and writing:** Be as specific as you can. For example, you can pinpoint his reading speed, comprehension, or instant recognition of sight words.

- ✔ **What you envision your child doing when he leaves school:** If you envision your child going to college, his teachers need to know before he makes high school subject choices. Colleges prefer some subjects over others; for example, they may ask that all students study a foreign language (and pass the exam on it).

- ✔ **Strategies that you know have helped your child:** These can include things such as phonics and strategies for remembering sight words.

In addition to making a list of questions, call the school before the IEP meeting and ask whether a draft of the school's proposed IEP is available. If it is, ask for a copy and find out whether you can give, in advance, your reactions and a list of the issues you want to raise.

If this IEP meeting determines your child's eligibility or reassessment, tell the school that you want assessment results in hand before the meeting. You'll be better prepared for the meeting and get no surprises. Ask a professional or knowledgeable friend to help you interpret the assessments if needed.

Finally, photocopy documents (like test results from a private tutor) that you want everyone to see. Put them in a folder and take it with you to the meeting.

No matter what you ask for or discuss at any point during the IEP process, take notes from your conversations and date them. Keep a notebook for phone calls, save all e-mails, and put every document into your folder.

Surrounding yourself with supportive folks

Plan for both parents or guardians to be at the IEP meeting. Ask a supportive, knowledgeable friend to go with you, and let the school know in advance whom you're bringing.

Have an experienced advocate go with you (see the section "Knowing your rights — and your child's," later in this chapter for details) and any professional, such as your child's previous teacher, whose input can lend support to your requests. Again, let the school know whom you're bringing. If a professional can't make the meeting, she can give you a written report to take with you instead.

Many parents develop good relationships with the people on their IEP team, go to meetings on their own, and encounter no confrontation, surprises, or disappointment. But if you're concerned about what the outcomes might be, or feel the school professionals aren't meeting your child's needs or your requests are being ignored, don't go on your own to an IEP meeting. You'll feel better with someone you know and trust at your side. If that someone listens carefully and makes notes, it may make quite an impression on the rest of the team. You have a witness and notes to refer to if you need to contest an issue later on, and with those notes in hand, you can later mull things over more slowly. Another way to keep a careful note of what happens in the IEP meeting is to tape-record it. Ask in advance whether you can do this.

Making the meeting work for you

If you think people aren't listening to you, if you feel crowded in by the professionals, or if you find it hard to follow what's being said, the IEP meeting can be stressful. To help you go in there with a can-do attitude and come out with the feeling of having achieved something, I provide some pointers in the following sections.

Asking for straightforward language

The team identifies your child's current level of performance (or how he did on his last IEP) by examining his test results and samples of his work. Be sure you understand the measures. Don't be too shy to ask teachers to put their technical jargon into down-to-earth terms. And tell the team about relevant observations you've made ("Part of the reason for Tim's low score on Rollicking Reading is that the text is boring").

Teachers and specialists who know each other and talk the same jargon can be intimidating. Keep in mind, though, that your knowledge of your child's needs is greater than theirs, and you have every right to make sure that your child's needs are met. If team members use terms that you don't understand, ask them to explain. Be firm and persuasive but not confrontational.

Stating a preference for specific goals and clarifying your concerns

The team sets short- and long-terms goals that must be measurable. A teacher can't just say something like "I will make Tim a better reader." She must specify and quantify: "Tim will read at level A on the Z test by December 1 and at level C at the end of the year."

If you don't like the goals that team members propose, say so. Say what you'd prefer. You can ask that behavioral goals (like helping him sit still for longer) be included if you think they'll have an impact on his learning.

You are an *equal* member of the team, so go to the meeting and chip in. Make sure that practical, measurable annual goals, and subgoals toward them, are written down. You must propose or agree with the goals.

If you don't agree on something, ask other team members to give explicit, concrete reasons for their statements and state your concerns clearly and reasonably. Phrase your comments in terms of your child (such as "Tim fails on this program") and avoid personal criticism of teachers (such as "You always make him . . ." or "You never listen to . . ."). If the meeting is making you feel frustrated or angry and you need time to cool down, ask for a recess. If you think you need more time to review what's been said, request that the meeting be continued at another time.

Don't be put off by answers like "We don't have the resources" or "He'll grow out of it in time." Be persistent, because your child is one of many, and that's the only way to push his case to the fore. Keep your goals in mind and remember that your child needs your support. He can't get help without you, and every extra day he waits is a day when he falls farther behind.

 Don't sign the IEP if you don't agree with it. You must be 100 percent happy with everything written in the IEP, and if you're not, don't sign it. If the team says you must sign just to verify that you were there, write something like "I do not agree with. . . ." The school has to address your objections because it can't implement the parts of the IEP you disagree with.

Because the IEP is a legally binding document, it's your safety net. Later, if you think your child isn't progressing, you can say that X goal isn't being achieved so you'd like a review meeting. You can ask for review meetings throughout the year.

Surveying the Services That Your Child Receives with an IEP

The resource teacher at school will probably have the most to do with implementing what's written in the IEP, and she most likely is specially trained. Your child sees her to get the special education he is entitled to.

With the resource teacher, your child gets tailor-made extra help. Examples of this help include working with a special reading program like Orton-Gillingham (see Chapter 7 for more about this program and others) and reading books with limited vocabulary. It may not seem like enough, but it's way more than non-IEP kids get!

Your child usually goes to the resource room — a quiet, supportive place — to work with the resource teacher. The resource room is often equipped with computers and materials that your child gets easy access to. Your child can read lower-level books in the resource room, and other kids won't tease him.

Because the resource teacher sees fewer kids than mainstream classroom teachers do, you can contact her more easily, and she has a good knowledge of your child. She can ask other teachers to make allowances for your child, such as giving him a buddy who reads especially hard text out loud to him, and allowing him extra time to finish assignments.

Teachers who are experienced with working with children with special needs have special ways of presenting new information to the class, too. They talk in short, clear terms and change from one topic to another by saying transitional sentences like "Now I'm going to talk about *ch* words. After that, you'll write some of your own *ch* words." They write key words on the board alongside lengthier text. They establish helpful routines, like having sheets that summarize topics, and make diagrams available for kids to take home.

Looking at the Legal Nitty-Gritty of IEPs

If the title of this section has your eyelids drooping and your mind lazily floating off to sweeter places, wake up! I promise not to overwhelm you or bore you to distraction here, so hang around. In the next sections, I give you the bottom line about your rights and what you should do if you find yourself in a rift with your child's school. And face it, that's handy stuff to know.

Examining the acts governing IEPs

When your child qualifies for special education (because he was assessed and found to have dyslexia or a learning disability — see Chapter 6 for details on the assessment process), he must have an IEP. This requirement is laid down in the law, so there are no ifs, buts, or maybes about it. The following sections cover the all-important acts pertaining to IEPs.

You probably won't delve deeply into laws affecting children with disabilities unless you get into a confrontation at school. Then you can skim through this chapter and call one of the organizations listed in Appendix B (especially your local Parent Training and Information Center and Disability Law Center) that can tell you everything you need to know and put you in touch with someone called an advocate. *Advocates* are wonderfully helpful people who guide you through the grievance process and support you at meetings. I talk more about them in the section "Knowing your rights — and your child's," later in this chapter.

Getting the IDEA

The main law that governs the whole special education process and how assessments and IEPs must run is the Individuals with Disabilities Education Act, which everyone simply calls the IDEA. The original IDEA was passed in the 1990s, but it was updated in December 2004 in the Individuals with Disabilities Education Improvement Act. Its current form regulates pretty much everything having to do with special education, including how states receive federal funding for providing for disabled children in school and precisely what an IEP should include.

The way that each school district enacts the IDEA is different. That's because each state has its own laws, and each district interprets federal and state law its own way, usually in response to how local courts have dealt with individual cases. Keep in touch with the big organizations (like the International Dyslexia Association) because its employees take a daily look at court cases and amendments to the law.

At Wrightslaw (www.wrightslaw.com), you can find a rundown of IDEA 2004 and, if you need more detailed info, a whole book about it (for $14.95).

Recognizing how Section 504 and ADA fit in

If your child qualifies for special education, he also is automatically eligible for protection under Section 504 of the Rehabilitation Act of 1973 and the Americans with Disabilities Act (ADA) of 1990.

- ✔ **Section 504 of the Rehabilitation Act:** This civil rights law protects people with disabilities who are in federally funded programs or services (which, of course, includes public schools). It requires schools to provide a "free and appropriate education" (known as FAPE) to your child and specifies the due process you can go through if you have a serious complaint about your child's IEP.

- ✔ **ADA:** This civil rights law protects people who have a "physical or mental impairment that substantially limits one or more life activities." It applies to workplaces more than schools but can be useful in adding force to your case. ADA can be handy for parents of children in private school; it applies to nonsectarian (but not religious) private schools.

Advocates and attorneys can explain how these laws relate to your specific case. To get free advice, contact your Parent Training and Information Center or any of the big organizations like the International Dyslexia Association (IDA) and the Learning Disabilities Association (LDA) listed in Appendix B.

If you're told in an official assessment that your child doesn't have dyslexia that's serious enough to qualify him for special education services but has mild dyslexia or dyslexic tendencies, he may still be eligible for support (like having test questions read to him or getting extra time on tests) under Section 504 and under the ADA. A paper trail strengthens your case. After you gather evidence of your child's needs and your requests for help, you may get it under Section 504 and ADA. Start the ball rolling by requesting a meeting with your teacher and principal.

Knowing your rights — and your child's

Things that sound great on paper don't always come out that way in practice. In real life, your child's teacher has a lot of things on her plate and a lot of other children to take care of. Your school's budget is stretched. The staff at your child's school may not be specially trained to help your child. Even if all parties are doing their best, you can feel shortchanged by what the IEP translates into in practice. When that happens, you should get the help of a trained advocate or consider getting training yourself. If you do, you can talk the legal talk, and you have a much better chance of getting what you want.

Advocates have had guidance from special education attorneys and may have been through the IEP process themselves with their own children. They have attended many IEP meetings and workshops (though currently there is no special certification) and know the kinds of things you should ask for, what kinds of issues can become sticking points, and the terminology and approach that you should use to receive the best results. Their fees can run up to $100 an hour (some work for free). You can get all the details at the Council of Parent Attorneys and Advocates Web Site (www.copaa.org).

So you know the kinds of things that an advocate can help you with, the following sections cover some of the legal hoopla to steel yourself for.

To find out more about IEPs, visit the National Dissemination Center for Children with Disabilities at www.nichcy.org and click on A-Z Topics and then on IEPs. For loads of legal advice (in ordinary language!) and to get details about advocacy, consultations, and training, visit Wrightslaw at www.wrightslaw.com. For a list of advocates and attorneys in your state, visit the Council of Parent Attorneys and Advocates at www.copaa.org and click on "Find an Attorney/Advocate."

Receiving a free, appropriate, and inclusive education

Your child is entitled to a "free and appropriate public education," often shortened to FAPE. You're not legally entitled to ask for the "best" education for your child. If you complain that your child isn't getting the "best," your school can use the language you use against you. In court, the school can simply say, "This parent is wholly unreasonable. She wants the best!"

If you ask for X, Y, or Z reading program for your child, the school isn't legally obliged to give it to you; it only has to give you an "appropriate" program. If you're incensed that you can't specifically ask for, say, Orton-Gillingham for your child, weigh your options. You can call the school to task for not providing your child with instruction backed by research if you think that's really the case. Or you can save time and energy and focus on getting other goals instead, like more one-on-one time with the resource teacher.

Your school district won't pay for private services unless it acknowledges that it can't provide them itself. If you decide to pay for private services yourself, inform the school in writing. Date your letter and explain that you think your child isn't getting a FAPE at school. Later, if you get good results from the private services and poor results from the school, you may have a great case for claiming reimbursement.

Your child also has the right to be educated in the "least restrictive environment" for him. Least restrictive is really another way of saying inclusive; your child must be included in regular classes as much as possible (but he still wants some time with the resource teacher).

Obtaining records and requesting reviews

You're entitled to see and get copies of all school records. You also have the right to get an IEP meeting every year, and you can ask for review meetings in between. You must get progress reports at least as often as you would get regular school reports.

The specific act that lays down your access to records rights is the Family Educational Rights and Privacy Act, or FERPA. You can find out all about it at www.ed.gov/policy/gen/guid/fpco/ferpa/index.html.

Deserving due process

You have the right to a due process hearing, meaning that if you want to contest something or ask for extra, you get to have your case heard by an independent hearing officer. This is like going to trial. You make your case against the school, which in turn makes its own case.

Before you get to the due process hearing, you may also be offered mediation, a lower level of the dispute process in which a mediator listens to the case and tries to resolve it before it escalates into a due process hearing.

Chapter 9

Securing Help without an Individualized Education Program

··

In This Chapter

▶ Tapping into school resources

▶ Choosing private tutors, learning centers, and more

▶ Helping your child at home

··

An Individualized Education Program (IEP) is a written working plan of exactly how special education is delivered to an eligible child. The hard truth about IEPs is that not every child gets one. More importantly, not every child who seems to be in need of one gets one. In this chapter, I tell you which direction to go when it's *your* child who goes without. I cover resources in and out of school and methods that you can use to support your child at home.

If your child doesn't qualify for an IEP, she may still be eligible for extra help under Section 504. In this chapter I talk about getting help without an IEP or Section 504, but if you flip to Chapter 8, you can revisit the main points about both.

Making the Most of Choices in School

If your child struggles in school and you think or know she has dyslexia, even though she doesn't qualify for special education (and an IEP), you have options. You can ease her progress through school in a few ways, including the in-school choices I list here:

> ✔ Be nice to your child's teacher and keep in contact with him. Without badgering him, thank him for any extra help he gives your child, and when your child could use a bit more, tell him. The teacher can do small things that make a big difference to your child's happiness and success.

✔ When your child can't do her homework or classroom assignments, pinpoint where the problem lies. Think of practical ways to help and propose them (respectfully) to the teacher. He will be more amenable to your practical suggestions than to your vague complaints.

✔ Regular parent-teacher conferences come around only two or three times a year. Don't be afraid to ask for more. As long as you have useful information to share with the teacher or legitimate concerns, you can both benefit by touching base a few times each semester.

✔ Keep your eyes and ears open for special extracurricular programs in school. Let the teacher know that you want your child to be considered for homework clubs, tutoring programs (often manned by parent volunteers), and social or sporting clubs that can help her feel confident.

You can read more about extracurricular school programs in Chapter 7. In Chapter 10 I give you the nitty-gritty on working with your child's teacher.

Looking for Help Outside School

You've likely used private services for your dyslexic child or at least considered using them. You may have had your child's hearing and vision tested, you may have paid for an assessment (see Chapter 6 for assessment details), and maybe you've tried a tutor — or two dozen. Getting outside help can take a weight off your shoulders, put the spark back in your child's eye and give your child's teacher something to smile about. It can also make a sizeable hole in your wallet and leave you feeling despondent.

In the next sections, I outline the kinds of private help you can get so you have an idea of what's what before you shop around.

By the way, be prepared to shop around because dyslexia isn't a condition for which one size fits all. You need to match your child to a specialist that she clicks with, a program that makes sense to her, and a schedule she can follow without getting overwhelmed. And you need a Plan B in case, even after all your careful planning, your choices don't work out.

Scoping out specialized dyslexia therapies

Some dyslexia programs address what they see as the underlying cause of dyslexia rather than the symptomatic reading and writing problems. Such programs include the following:

- ✔ **All Kinds of Minds:** Your child is shown how to use her best learning style (because being pushed into using her weakest learning modalities is the real problem).

- ✔ **Fast ForWord:** Your child learns better listening and quick response skills (because these attention and response difficulties are the real concern).

- ✔ **Processing and Cognitive Enhancement (PACE):** This program runs your child through brain exercises (because her problem is underdeveloped specific brain skills).

You can flip to Chapter 20 to read more about these and other specialized dyslexia therapies, but upfront you may want to know the price range you can expect and the broad pros and cons:

- ✔ Prices for assessment and treatment in a specialized therapy center typically run in the hundreds or thousands of dollars.

- ✔ The good thing about these programs is that they're usually short (lasting a few weeks) and intensive (a few hours each week), so you get to see your child improve relatively soon.

- ✔ The weakness of these programs is that you can expect your child to need, in addition to them, at least some specialized reading and writing instruction.

Considering dyslexia clinics

A local dyslexia clinic can be an attractive option for augmenting your child's education in school. So you can get a general idea of how they operate, this section summarizes what happens at the Dyslexia Institutes of America, whose ten branches are spread across Colorado, Connecticut, Florida, Georgia, Illinois, and Indiana.

Dyslexia Institutes of America clinics provide a multisensory phonics-based reading program. The program also treats related problems, like poor working memory, phonemic awareness, visual perception, and visual motor integration.

Your child begins the program by having a screening test to establish whether she has dyslexia (for $85) followed by a battery of diagnostic tests (lasting two hours at a cost of $400) to pinpoint her areas of weakness. Results of the evaluation determine what goes into your child's personalized treatment plan.

Your child receives two-hour weekly sessions with certified teachers, costing $100 per session (this fee may be reduced if you pay by the month in advance). The reading component is taught one on one. Sessions are followed up with home exercises that parents are trained to do. Parents receive weekly reports on their child's progress and another assessment every six months.

The clinic director attends one parent/teacher meeting at your child's school so that teachers are kept in the loop.

You can find out more at www.dyslexiainstitutes.com or by calling the home office at 217-235-0045.

Dyslexia Institutes of America also provides treatment to adults with dyslexia.

Another option is 32º Masonic Learning Center. I really should put a Wow! icon here because here's something way cool (if that's still the term for really, really good)! Your child can get tutoring in Orton-Gillingham, one on one, twice a week, for free (see Chapter 7 for more about this method), and you can train in it for free too, if you have a 32º Masonic Learning Center near you. If you live in Massachusetts, you lucked out because that's the hub of these centers. If you don't live there, visit www.childrenslearningcenters.org and click on About the Children's Learning Centers and then on Locations (or phone toll free 877-861-0528 or 781-862-8518) to see whether these centers have come to your state.

You can use a search engine like Google or Yahoo! to find a local clinic too. Just type "dyslexia clinic" or "dyslexia institute" along with the name of your state, and see what pops up!

Paying an individual tutor

In an ideal world, your child's much-adored teacher recommends a tutor who's sensitive, fun, and qualified to the hilt to teach her the latest dyslexia-busting methods. Your child visits the tutor for a few idyllic sessions and emerges a fluent and error-free reader and writer. That's the ideal world.

In the real world, you may have a hard time finding a tutor, let alone someone who's experienced with dyslexia. And even if you do find a tutor who looks good on paper, you can't be sure your child will click with her.

So is it worth searching for a tutor? To help you answer that question, here are the potential benefits that tutoring can have for your child:

✔ Tutoring gives your child more personal attention than she can possibly receive in class (as one of 20 or 30 kids).

✔ Tutoring can provide your child with challenges to keep her excited about learning and extra support to strengthen her weak areas.

✔ Tutoring takes the pressure off parents. Even if you have a perfect relationship with your child, you probably (like most parents) have trouble helping her (especially in her teen years) with homework.

✔ Tutoring can help your child feel privileged.

Are there disadvantages? The term "disadvantages" is probably a bit harsh, but here are a few things to at least watch out for:

✔ Your child may describe her tutoring as "good," which is adequate enough explanation to her but not much help to you. You may want to schedule meetings with her classroom teacher so you can see whether the tutoring is in fact making any difference in class. See Chapter 10 for more details about having a conference with your child's teacher.

✔ Naturally you want good value from tutoring, but you need to be clear about what counts as good value. Improved grades in class are obvious indications of success, but your child's improved confidence and better attitude in school count, too.

✔ Tutoring that isn't enjoyable may do more harm than good, especially to little children. You want your elementary school child to develop a positive attitude toward school (after all, she's going to be there a long time), so if you have to drag her to tutoring, look for another tutor. The same thing applies to older children, of course, but they're a bit better at letting you know how they're feeling (and putting up a fight!).

✔ Paying for tutoring and getting your child there each week can be hard enough as it is. You don't want to end up paying cancellation fees, too. Check out a tutor's cancellation policy before you start marking your child's tutoring sessions on the calendar.

I can't take you to a bunch of tutors and point out the ones who might be right for your child, but I can tell you what to look for and where to start your search. You need a tutor who

✔ Is nice! You may think that it's not important that your child's tutor is nice, but if you've ever had to drag your child to tutoring or had to listen to her whine and grumble every time she goes to tutoring, you'll appreciate why nice is relevant. Especially if you want your child to go the distance (months or years) with a tutor, nice is something you should look out for.

✔ Strikes a chord with your child. Your child should relate to the tutor and want to please him. As a result of this relationship, she tries hard and gets better marks for her work.

✔ Is a trained and experienced reading teacher or special education teacher with experience in teaching reading. A tutor with a teaching degree and at least three years' teaching experience is a great start.

✔ Can tell you about her phonics-based and multisensory teaching methods. Phonics is the teaching method in which students are shown how to match letters (and clusters of letters) to speech sounds (see Chapter 12). In multisensory activities, your child uses a few of her senses at the same (or roughly the same) time (see Chapter 14).

✔ Can measure (in tests), and show you, your child's progress after a few weeks of tutoring. But remember: Even with experienced and effective tutors, your child may take months, rather than weeks, to make progress. You should, however, be able to see your child gaining confidence within weeks, provided that she starts to have success with tasks she previously failed.

✔ Is within your price range. Tutoring can range in cost from about $15 per hour for a college student (not the best option for your dyslexic child unless perhaps the student is training in a reading program like Orton-Gillingham and/or is dyslexic and full of handy strategies) to about $150 per hour for an experienced therapist trained in Orton-Gillingham.

Recommendations from trusted friends are great if you can get them. But if teachers and friends can't give you any leads, where can you find a tutor? Check out Appendix B. The Web sites and phone numbers I list there take you to tutors across the country. Check them out and, if they're fully booked or not really for you, ask if they can redirect you.

Tutoring is a great option for adults, too. Tutors trained in reading programs like Orton-Gillingham are usually happy to work with adults. Your local library and community college are good places to search for free or low-cost adult literacy programs.

Opting for a general learning center

A general learning center may offer you more flexibility than an individual tutor. For example, you may be able to take your child to a center at different times, including weekends. In addition, your child may enjoy seeing different tutors, and especially if your child gets small group tutoring rather than one-on-one, you may end up paying less. That's the good news.

The bad news is that tutors in centers aren't usually qualified in special needs. They don't have training in remedial reading techniques, like Orton-Gillingham, and they may not know much about dyslexia.

If your child's dyslexia symptoms are mild, if she hates the idea of visiting a dorky tutor but thinks a center is cool, or if you have a friend whose dyslexic child did well at your local center, a center may still suit your needs. In Appendix B, I give you contact details for the big learning centers that operate in most towns, and in the following sections, you get a quick summary of how they operate. There are individual differences among centers, though, so you'll probably want to use the details I give here as a guide for asking the right questions (including info on updated prices).

When someone tells you that your child gets individual instruction, check what this means. Centers that give small group instruction may still call it "individualized" because, as they explain, each child follows her individualized program even though she's part of a small group. Another piece of terminology that may catch you out is "certified." Instructors can be certified teachers and/or certified in the methods of the center (which means they're not necessarily qualified to be classroom teachers).

Huntington Learning Centers

Dr. Raymond and Eileen Huntington opened the first Huntington Learning Center in 1977, and now there are Huntington centers all across the United States. Instruction is available for children aged 5 to 17 in reading, writing, math, and phonics as well as in high school subjects and exam preparation.

All instructors at Huntington Learning Centers are certified teachers. Your K-to-3 child gets one-on-one instruction. Grade 4 children and older get small group instruction except in subject tutoring (like algebra) in which tutoring is one on one.

Your child gets a diagnostic evaluation that takes three to three and a half hours and costs $195. Tutoring costs $49 an hour for K-to-3 children, $39 an hour for standard tutoring for grade 4 and older, $65 for subject tutoring, and $75 an hour for tutoring in exam preparation (for tests like the ACT, SAT, GED, and PSAT). For more information, go to www.huntingtonlearning.com or call 800-226-5327.

Kumon Math and Reading Centers

Toru Kumon, a parent and teacher, started Kumon Math and Reading Centers 50 years ago in Japan. Today there are well over a thousand centers in North America and centers in 43 other countries. Kumon is for any child preschool to high school age who needs tutoring in reading and math. Test preparation isn't offered, but because Kumon has your child take regular tests and do self-guided homework, it maintains that its students are well prepared for taking tests like the SAT.

At Kumon Math and Reading Centers, your child learns by working through sequential worksheets that are administered and marked by instructors. She must complete her worksheets, have them marked by the teacher, and complete any corrections before she leaves (in 45 minutes) so that she gets immediate feedback and the teacher is sure she gets it.

Students typically attend Kumon twice a week year-round and do brief daily assignments (about 15 minutes) the other five days. Preschool students attend at fixed times, but other students can show up anytime during open hours.

Kumon offers two incentives programs to your child. In the Kumon Cosmic Club, your child earns points redeemable for prizes. The Advanced Student Honor Roll recognizes older children performing above their grade level.

Tuition at a Kumon center costs from $80 to $110 per month per subject, with an initial registration fee of $30 to $50. You get a small discount on the cost of having your child tutored in a second subject (either reading or math), and everyone gets an initial assessment at no extra cost. Find more information and a center near you by visiting www.kumon.com or calling 877-586-6673 (in the United States) or 800-222-6284 (in Canada).

Oxford Learning Centers

A team of educators opened the first Oxford Learning Centers in the 1980s. Now there are over 100 centers spread across the United States and Canada. Preschool to high school students can attend sessions at these centers.

Your child can take programs in reading, general skills, test preparation (for tests like the SAT), and French at Oxford Learning Centers. Oxford teachers aim to help your child with *metacognitive awareness,* which roughly means the awareness of how she learns best. For example, when your child appreciates that she has trouble with auditory processing, she moves from thinking "I don't get this" to "I need to sit at the front" and "I do better with visual information, so I may need to ask the teacher to write what she said on the board."

For 3- to 6-year-olds, the centers offers a Little Readers program in which your child gets two hours of tutoring three, four, or five times a week so she learns the "84 synthetic phonics sounds."

Parents get ongoing progress reports. Summer programs are available.

Your child gets an initial two-hour dynamic diagnostic assessment for $195. Tutoring costs $40 to $50 per hour. Oxford offers scholarship programs for eligible children. Find out more at www.oxfordlearning.com.

SCORE! Educational Centers

The first SCORE! Center was established in 1992, and now there are more than 160 centers across the United States.

Your child can drop into a SCORE! Educational Center anytime during open hours (yes, it's that flexible), twice a week, for an hour each time. Your child can get intensive membership, which means she drops in three or four times a week (prices increase proportionately). Basic subjects your child can be tutored in are math, reading, spelling, and writing. Supplemental subjects are science, problem solving, and keyboarding.

Your child works on a computer, but an instructor monitors and guides what she does. The computer programs are designed to be fun and high energy. Academic coaches are college graduates, so they tend to be young (which to your child may mean "cool"). One-on-one paper-and-pen instruction is sometimes available.

Your 4- to 7-year-old child can take an online interactive reading course (which is run in partnership with Headsprouts, an organization that offers online interactive reading lessons for children in grades K-2).

Your child sets goals and keeps a scorecard that she uses to earn prizes such as art cases, CD holders, baseballs, calculators, shirts, and hats. At the end of each session, your child gets to take basketball shots too, which sort of ties in with the name "SCORE!" The centers liken themselves to athletic training in that they are goal- and coaching-oriented, with an emphasis on helping kids reach their potential and continue to learn and grow.

Tutoring costs $164 to $189 a month. Find out more at www.escore.com or by calling 866-65-SCORE.

Sylvan Learning Centers

If you've thought about having your child tutored, you've probably come across Sylvan Learning Centers, which were started in 1979. Now more than 1,000 Sylvan centers are located across the United States and Canada, and Sylvan makes the claim that more parents choose Sylvan than any other tutor.

At a Sylvan Learning Center, your child is taught by certified teachers. Instruction is in small groups for children in grades K–12, and your child usually goes once or twice a week at a designated time. In addition to reading and writing, subjects that your child can be tutored in are math, study skills, and preparation for tests like the ACT and SAT. Live, online tutoring in reading is available for children in grades 3 to 9. Live, online tutoring in math is available for children in grades 3 to 8.

Your child earns tokens (for performance and effort) to spend at the on-site Sylvan shop, which features typical toys and games that kids love.

Your child gets a two- to four-hour initial assessment that costs $175. Tutoring costs from $47 to $52 per hour. Sylvan offers a student loan program to help you make payments.

Giving Academic Support at Home

Your child may act as if she hears about half of what you say and goes along with about a tenth of that, but without realizing it, she absorbs your habits and beliefs. If she's having a hard time in school, you can help her. In the next sections, I focus on home-based ways you can help your dyslexic child.

You may want to go all out with your support at home and decide to home-school your child. For full details on this education option, see Chapter 7.

Letting your child take the lead with homework

When your dyslexic child struggles with homework, it's easy to get into the habit of doing things for her. You see her working hard to keep up with classmates, and you want to help. Do what's best for your child by giving her practical help that leads gradually to her helping herself, such as the following:

- ✔ Type her projects for her, but also see that she starts training on a typing program so she's able to type more and more work for herself.
- ✔ Dictate spellings to her, but ask her to proofread her answers before you check them.
- ✔ Discuss books with her, but encourage her to ask relevant questions for herself.

Anytime you help your child, think about how you can take a supporting rather than a leading role. Your child must develop independence from you, and besides, work that she can call her own is always more important to her than work that someone else did.

The older your child gets, the more self-reliant she must be. Right from the beginning of school, help her get to know her strengths and weaknesses. Help her make good choices (like using a video recorder for her class report) and ask for help when she needs it (like having a classroom buddy to call on). She may need to find ways around her difficulties all her life, so right now is the time to prepare her and give her the confidence to do so.

Setting up homework management methods

All children do better homework when they establish an effective homework routine. This is doubly true for a dyslexic child because she has disadvantages to contend with. Not only are reading and writing hard for your dyslexic child, but she also may have trouble focusing on homework and remembering precisely what she's supposed to be doing. Help her manage the homework monster by trying out these strategies. (If you're already on top of them, give yourself a hearty slap on the back for being a regular smarty-pants.)

- ✔ **Getting set:** In the first week of a new school year, many schools send your child home with a homework survival list. You're supposed to buy everything on the list so that when your child announces that she must make a mobile using different colors of construction paper, some string, and several sticks, right now, you at least have everything but the sticks. Have your child's survival kit (of construction paper, glue, tape, pens, a ruler, an eraser, a hole puncher, a stapler, scissors, string, and anything else you think of) at the ready. Then you're one step ahead of the home-work monster (and he's pretty fast).

- ✔ **Planning:** A daily planner is part of your child's school equipment. Often the school has you buy a planner directly from it so that every child has the same one. The planner is really a diary in which your child is supposed to jot all homework reminders and which you, the parent, signs each day to verify that she did indeed complete all the day's homework.

  The reality about your dyslexic child's planner is that she may write illegibly in it and you may hastily sign it in the morning worrying more about whether you get peanut butter on it than whether it's actually working. Unless you schedule time for looking *properly* at your child's planner each day, it can feel like a daily burden. Help your child under-stand that short legible notes are best and that each one gets checked off *after* she's answered it. Try to muster up nice feelings about the plan-ner so that it really *is* a link between you and the teacher and a gauge of how well your child is keeping abreast of her daily obligations.

- ✔ **Prioritizing:** Your dyslexic child can easily become absorbed in her lizard poster when she should in fact be doing her fractions. Help her put first things first and establish the habit of referring to her planner every single day. Which things must be done immediately and which can wait? Does your child need special supplies (like modeling clay) within the next few days? Do some assignments warrant more attention than others because they earn her more credit?

- ✔ **Setting time limits:** Your dyslexic child may take longer with her assign-ments than you think she needs to. She may spend a long time fussing and complaining. Setting a time limit for each homework subject can help. If you link rewards (like TV viewing time) to your child completing a subject in, say 30 minutes, the system may work even better. Parents who enforce limits and carry through, even though they feel like army sergeants during the first few days, may find that this strategy ends up imposing relative calm on a previously homework-shocked household.

- ✔ **Studying from a guide:** A study guide is an at-a-glance summary of the main points of a topic or, like in algebra, the techniques. If your child has trouble figuring out the key concepts in a subject (and for that matter, you do too), you may find that a study guide helps you sort the wood from the trees.

✔ **Using hand-held devices:** Spell checkers/dictionaries and reading pens are low-tech, ultra-simple-to-use gadgets that can make your dyslexic child's homework go infinitely smoother. A simple spell checker, for about $25, looks a bit like a calculator. Your child types in her word, probably spelled phonetically, and sees the correct spelling displayed on the screen. For about $60 you can buy a spell checker that displays *and* speaks the words. A reading pen, for about $280, performs the same functions as a displaying/speaking spell checker, only your child just has to run the reading pen over a word (or sentence) to get it displayed and read out to her. To view a bunch of these nifty hand-held devices, check out www.franklin.com. See the next section for more info on technology.

✔ **Using software and online materials:** Your dyslexic child can do her homework much easier if she has access to a comprehensive encyclopedia. You can install an encyclopedia on her computer or sign up for online use. One popular encyclopedia available in both of those options is Encarta. To buy the CD-ROM or DVD (Windows), go to www.amazon.com/exec/obidos/tg/detail/-/B00027TJCG/002-2234208-1291230?v=glance. To subscribe for online use, go to www.encarta.msn.com. For software in special subjects, like foreign languages, search the "software" category at an online store like Amazon (www.amazon.com) using words like "children," "learn," and "French."

✔ **Replacing lost items:** At some point your child is going to lose something that she vows she can't live without. "I can't do my homework without it. I've looked everywhere. I'm gonna fail," she'll sob. Will you punish her? If she's lost a book, will you zip to an online bookstore (like Amazon at www.amazon.com) and buy her another? Will you make her buy another from her own money?

The point I'm making here is that you probably need to decide, in advance, on a strategy before you become exasperated and your child's homework (which she can't do without her book) mounts up.

Using technology

Kids who adeptly cruise the Internet and tap confidently on a keyboard have a big advantage over those who don't. You'd be hard pressed to find a child who's completely in the dark in these areas, but still, the more knowledge the better. You may find it humiliating to run to your 10-year-old every few minutes for help navigating the Web, but in the big picture, the benefits are worth it (easy for *me* to say huh?).

I don't delve into the benefits of the Internet in the following sections (all that pretty much speaks for itself), but I look at the simpler forms of technology (like word processors) that you may not be making full use of with homework and the alternative kinds of technology (like speech-recognition software) that you may have only heard of. Chapter 20 has more info on some of these tools.

All of the gadgets in the following sections can, of course, be useful for adult dyslexics too.

Word processing programs

Basic word processing know-how is pretty much a necessity for anyone who has to write stuff. But word processing can be especially beneficial for a dyslexic child for typing her homework:

- ✔ Her work looks legible.

- ✔ She can enlarge her letters and choose a clear font so she can more easily read what she writes.

- ✔ Typing can be easier on her hands than writing.

- ✔ Especially if she practices keyboarding skills, writing is quicker for her.

- ✔ She learns a skill and keeps abreast of current trends (not many kids use pen and paper for assignments these days, and after about grade 2, many teachers specify that homework assignments *must* be typed).

As soon as your child lays her fingers on the keyboard of her computer, have her use the spell check and thesaurus functions in whatever word processing program you use. The spell check can iron out a lot of her spelling mistakes, and the thesaurus can turn her little words into the bigger ones she knows but can't pull out of her brain.

The read-back feature that you can get on most computers these days is a great tool for dyslexics, too. When the computer reads back items your child has typed, she can hear the words she's written and any mistakes she's made. Your child should also get comfortable with the cut and paste features so she can jot down her first draft of an assignment, run the spell check and thesaurus over it, and then give it a final cleanup by rearranging the words if she wants.

You may not even realize (most people don't) that you have the text-to-voice function on your computer. Go to your help menu to find it. You get a mechanical sounding read-back of what you type, but it's still worth having. To buy text-to-voice software to install in your computer, check out Natural Reader at www.naturalreaders.com and Read Please at www.readplease.com. Natural Reader comes in a professional version for $39.50 and a free downloadable version, too. Read Please costs $35 and comes in a huge range of voices that you pick by gender, language, and accent (like Julia-US-Female). Both programs are for Windows operating systems.

If you're really savvy with computers, or have a friend who is, you can search the Internet and find free downloadable text-to-voice programs, including programs that read Internet pages out loud to you.

The following Web sites are full of info on software that can improve your child's word processing:

✔ For software to help your child get quicker at keyboarding, visit http://store.sunburst.com. You can get a free 30-day trial of "Type to Learn 3" and also order a new typing program in the fun Jump Start series (Jump Start Typing). Just click on Keyboarding and then on Activities.

✔ For reviews from parents of dyslexics of software that helps with spelling, go to www.dyslexia-parent.com/software.html.

✔ See a review of the award-winning "Read and Write" program (and useful links) at the dyslexia site, www.dyslexia-parent.com/mag31.html.

The organization TopTenReviews evaluates a bunch of kids' typing software at http://typing-for-kids-software-review.toptenreviews.com/.

Pocket spell checkers

Ever heard of a pocket spell checker? If not, you may want to visit these two Web sites: www.schwablearning.org/articles.asp?r=444&g=4 and www.dyslexia-parent.com/software.html. These nifty little gadgets are inexpensive and, according to many dyslexic students, particularly useful.

Tape recorders and books on tape

A sturdy tape recorder is a great investment for all kids, but especially for older kids. Your child can use it to tape lessons (ask the teacher's permission first) so she can listen to them later and fill in any gaps in her notes or understanding.

And don't forget the benefits of having your child listen to schoolbooks on tape either. If your child's panicking because she has to read *Charlotte's Web* in a week, or write a report on a book that has more than 300 pages, no problem. Get the book on tape. If you're really on the ball, get, in advance, a list of all the other books her class will be using over the year or semester so you can order your books on tape early and avoid being wait-listed.

Here are two options for recorded books:

✔ For a $65 registration fee and $35 annual membership, you can join Recording for the Blind and Dyslexic at www.rfbd.org, phone 800-221-4792. Its lending library has more than 98,000 titles in subjects ranging from literature and history to math and the sciences, at all

> levels, from kindergarten through professional. Chances are, if the book is in your child's curriculum, it's in the library. Anyone with a documented disability (in other words, your child's dyslexia assessment results) is eligible.

> ✔ Books on Tape at `www.booksontape.com` doesn't have a lending option, only buying. The books can be pretty expensive (ranging from $10 to $100 depending on the age and size of the book and whether you buy tapes or more expensive CDs), so you may want to think about lobbying your school to fork out for a school library copy. Books on Tape has lower rates for schools and libraries.

Photocopying and print-recognition software

People who have dyslexia read things over and over. When everyone else reads a passage once and gets the drift, someone with dyslexia needs to read and reread before she gets it. Distinguishing key concepts from secondary concepts is hard for a dyslexic, so she needs to mull over the text and use a highlighter pen on it.

Get comfortable with photocopiers and scanners so you can ask your child's teacher if you can sometimes photocopy his notes, or pages from books he refers to, for you and your child to read later on. Then, when your child has an important report to do, you get a better understanding of what's required and can be a bigger help to your child. Your child gets the opportunity to revisit material that may have escaped her in class.

Fancy print-recognition (or optical character recognition) software lets your child scan pages into her word processor so she can alter and add to the text. It may all sound puzzling for the technology scaredy-cats among us, but if you or someone in your family is good with computers, you may want to include it among your dyslexia-busting arsenal. It can save a lot of tears when your child wants to do something like scan her handwritten project into a Word document instead of rewriting it. TextBridge, published by ScanSoft Inc., is one program you may want to check out because it's available as a free demo download (for Windows operating systems) from `www.softlookup.com/display.asp?id=5585`.

Speech-recognition software

When I first tampered with speech-recognition software (also called speech-to-text software), which lets you talk into your computer and have your words appear on the screen, the technology was in its teething stage. Now it's much better and can chomp firmly down on bigger words and say them back to you in a more normal-sounding voice. Speech-to-text software is typically used by older kids when they do reports and other lengthy written assignments. Here's how it works:

1. **Buy the software (called names like Dragon Naturally Speaking, Kurzweil, and Via Voice) and install it on your computer.**

2. **Train your computer to recognize your voice by talking to it for many hours.**

   In the training process, the computer says words back to you so it can verify your words.

   The training takes a long time, and the playback sounds weird because the computer doesn't use the same inflections that you use in regular speech. After you get all this under your belt, however, you're set to go.

3. **Read out what you want to write.**

   The computer types it for you.

4. **Paste it into a word document for final editing.**

   Presto! You have a piece of written work anyone would be proud of.

Speech-recognition software has come so far now that a program may also perform the print-recognition functions that I discuss in the previous section.

And here are the benefits of voice-recognition software:

- ✔ All those words you could never get down on paper before are at last there to show the world that you're smart after all!

- ✔ The vocabulary you have in your head now shows up in your reports, and you get better grades.

- ✔ You have the confidence to do things you've never done before — like send a note to someone you like!

- ✔ You may get the feeling that your reading is improving.

- ✔ You consider going to college now that you can write well.

Speech-recognition technology overwhelms some people, so it's not the answer for everyone. But for those who use it, it's liberating. It's an equalizer, and people rely on it. And therein lies the cause of some controversy. Special education teachers are catching onto this technology, but regular classroom teachers can be less enthusiastic. Their concern is that this software prevents kids from learning for themselves, but so far, research shows the opposite. Children who use speech-recognition technology seem to be making gains in reading and spelling, and when you think about what's happening, you can see why. Multisensory techniques (see, hear, say, and do) work, and that's what this software gives. Say it, then see it on the screen, and then change the text (type; cut and paste) if you want. (Check out Chapter 14 for more about multisensory methods.)

To read an article about tests and comparisons of Dragon Naturally Speaking and Via Voice, check out the Dyslexic.com Web site at www.dyslexic.com/dictcomp.htm.

Steering clear of a math meltdown

Dyslexia is primarily a language disability, but it can have an impact on your child's performance in math. Your child may have trouble remembering sequences of numbers, like multiplication tables, and what specialized words like "product" and "reciprocal" mean. In addition, she may confuse written symbols, such as the division and multiplication symbols, and struggle with word problems. And she may have these problems even when she's a whiz with harder mathematical processes and concepts.

In the following sections, I cover easy methods for helping your dyslexic child with math at home.

Introducing simple math concepts

If math is a struggle for your younger child, here are a few simple things you can do at home to help:

- Use beans, counters, or coins to help your child see the four functions (adding, subtracting, multiplying, and dividing) in action.
- Bring fractions to life by cutting up cake, bread, or fruit.
- Demonstrate how your child can work out the area of your floor. Do the same thing with a tabletop and count the individual squares to check that the formula (length × width) really works.
- Help your child see small angles by having him open a door and tell you when she's made a right angle or a bigger or smaller angle.
- Explain place value with pennies and dimes (because ten pennies equals a dime and kids have familiarity with these small coins). For more activities to help your child with place value, check out www.mathcat.com/grownupcats/ideabankplacevalue.html.
- Help your child keep a home bankbook with deposit and withdrawal columns and figure out her running balance.

Tackling word problems

Math word problems can give anyone trouble, so in this section I give you handy tips that your dyslexic child is bound to find useful either for herself or when she helps friends with *their* math!

- ✔ Read the question at least twice. This advice is important for any child but especially for your dyslexic child. She needs to not only identify which word is key but that she has read it correctly in the first place.

- ✔ Highlight key words. For example, in a problem like "David has a discovered a number pattern that starts with 1, 4, 9, 16, 25. What are the next three numbers in this pattern?" the key words are "pattern" and "next three numbers."

- ✔ Draw a table. This method is good for questions like "Ashley saved $2 on Tuesday. Each day after that she saved twice as much as she saved the day before. If she keeps doing this, how much will she save on Friday? How much will she save in total?" The following table shows how to get the answer.

Day	*Amount Saved*
Tuesday	$2
Wednesday	$4
Thursday	$8
Friday	$16
TOTAL	$30

- ✔ Work backwards. This technique is for problems like "Trish walked from Wakefield to Reading. It took her 1 hour and 25 minutes to walk from Wakefield to North Reading. Then it took 25 minutes to walk from North Reading to Reading. She arrived in Reading at 2:45 p.m. At what time did she leave Wakefield?" Your child needs first to establish what she needs to find out (what time it was when Trish left) and then that the way to do it is to subtract times backwards from the time she arrived. Subtract 25 minutes from 2.45 (giving you 2.20) and then 1 hour and 25 minutes from that (giving you a leaving time of 12:55 p.m.).

- ✔ Guess and then verify. This works for a problem like "Jill and Liz sold 12 raffle tickets altogether. Jill sold 2 more tickets than Liz. How many tickets did each girl sell?" Your child must find two numbers that add up to make 12, with a difference of 2 between them. Guesses: 8 and 4; 9 and 3; 7 and 5 (bravo!).

For more information and sample word problems, go to www.math stories.com.

Chapter 10

Working Productively with Your Child's Teacher

*Y*our child's teacher is your greatest ally in helping your child handle dyslexia. Being in a partnership with your child's teacher is better than being at odds with her. Here's why:

✔ When you have a friendly relationship with your child's teacher, she's more likely to stay after class to quickly make sure your child knows what the homework is, jot you a note to let you know the tricky parts of the homework, and regularly touch base with you by phone or e-mail.

✔ When the teacher wants to help you out with stuff like assessments and therapy, she can make calls to people like psychologists so you get your scissors moving quicker on the red tape.

✔ When the teacher is comfortable with you, she can call you or leave a note in your child's bag so you get quick information. Otherwise, she may communicate with you via the school secretary and formal notes.

✔ When your child's teacher knows you won't question her judgment, she tries out different strategies with your child to make tasks easier for him.

✔ When you're on friendly terms with the teacher, she's likely to tell you about new books or programs she hears about.

And that's just the beginning! In this chapter, I tell you how to conduct successful meetings with your child's teacher, plan effective accommodations, and help your child avoid classroom pitfalls.

With the right instruction and accommodations, dyslexic children get better at reading (even becoming keen readers) and have pretty much the same experiences at school as anyone else. So let your child know that!

Requesting and Preparing for a Conference

On paper establishing a harmonious relationship with your child's teacher sounds easy. And in many cases it is. But when your child struggles in class, tells you how miserable he is, and cries a lot, you may feel that the teacher isn't doing enough to help or isn't doing the right kinds of things to help.

Even if you're calm and composed, and even if your child is generally happy and keeping up in class, you need to schedule a meeting with your child's teacher. Talking for a few hasty minutes after class or even writing notes or e-mails to the teacher isn't the same as getting scheduled, uninterrupted, personal time with her. The following sections give you the lowdown of successfully setting up and getting ready for a conference.

Don't go over the head of the teacher as a first response. Have a discussion with her first because she will understandably feel slighted if you bypass her, and you may never make up that lost ground. If she doesn't respond to your requests for a conference, is rude to you, or acts problematically in any other way, then you can justifiably approach the principal.

Asking the teacher to meet

Ask your child's teacher to meet you before or after school for about half an hour to discuss your child's progress. Ask her in person or via a note, an e-mail, or a phone call. If you can manage it, both parents (or guardians) should attend.

Parents are usually allotted two or three conferences a year at the time that report cards are given out. You can have a conference at other times too, so don't be afraid to ask. Remember, though, the teacher has a life and won't be happy staying after school to talk to you about trivial things. If Johnny always loses his school-to-home notes or doesn't want to sit next to Jane, you can probably work it out via notes. Conferences are for your bigger issues.

Assembling important info

What exactly do you want to happen as a result of the meeting? What points do you especially want to make? Do you already have practical ideas that you think may help your child keep up in class? You need to jot all this info down so you don't get sidetracked and waste any of your time with the teacher.

Keep a paper trail of everything you ask for or tell the teacher about because you never know when you might need it. Mistakes happen, and details get forgotten. If they do, your records and notes allow you to remind teachers what you explained or planned and bring you quickly back on track.

How does your paper trail relate to a conference? Before you meet with the teacher, jot down suggestions you have for dealing with general problems and get to the nitty-gritty of specific problems too. If your child is unhappy, how exactly do you know it? If his homework plunges him into despair, which particular assignments cause him the most grief? If a book is beyond him, what's its title and how much time does he have to read it? Jot down the details, including dates and conversations, so the teacher knows you're a person she can work with. If your child is going through weeks or months of being upset, jot down specific incidents and the dates they happened.

If you present this information to the teacher in an I-care way (rather than an I-blame-you way), you increase your chances of getting a great response from her. Who wouldn't want to join forces with a reasonable, organized, and caring parent (that's you, by the way!)?

You may want to share your sketched-out plan with the teacher before your meeting. By having a rough idea of the issues that parents want to address, teachers can reflect on them in advance and not feel like they're on the spot during the meeting. They can also bring work samples, future assignments, current grades, and so on if they know it would be helpful to you.

Determining whether to bring your child

Before the conference, you'll also want to decide whether you want your child to come to the meeting. If you think he can benefit from attending, you need to invite him to come and tell him what will happen, what kinds of things he may want to talk about, and how he should jot key points down so the meeting stays succinct and on track. Whether you do or don't invite your child, let the teacher know in advance.

Advantages of having your child attend the conference include the following:

- ✔ He gets practice at speaking up for himself.

- ✔ He finds out what happens during conferences so he's prepared to take a more active role in them as he gets older.

- ✔ He's heard immediately and, likewise, gets immediate feedback.

Possible disadvantages are that your child may have no interest in attending (he's a kid and he wants to play or hang out), and he may find it hard to talk openly to teachers. He may prefer that you relay his thoughts because he can tell them to you without feeling shy or disrespectful.

Keeping a Conference on Track and Following Up Smartly

You don't get a whole lot of time in a conference with your child's teacher, so you want to be sure of making all your points, sending out "I'm competent, concerned, and incredibly cool to work with" kinds of vibes, and pinning down outcomes you expect to see as a result of the conference. I walk you through all these topics and more in the following sections. For examples of accommodations that teachers can use in response to your child's issues, see the section "Coming Up with Cool Accommodations," later in this chapter.

Creating a positive mood

So how exactly do you project an I-care and I'm-competent tone during the meeting with your child's teacher? The trick is to be concise and positive. (That's why you write a list of points to cover — see the section "Assembling important info," earlier in this chapter, for details.) You want to focus on practical solutions, not blame, and your comments must tell the teacher that you're willing to collaborate and accept her professional judgment.

Your opening remarks should be positive and open. You should say something supportive to the teacher, like "I'm so glad to have this chance to talk to you," and then quickly ask for her impressions of (and concerns about) your child's schoolwork and behavior. You need to hear from her early on for two reasons.

- ✔ She feels more at ease. Like everyone else, the teacher likes to talk about things she's savvy on, and she likes to be listened to. When you give her this lead, she feels she's on safe and familiar ground.

- ✔ You get a chance to scope out the territory. You find out what the teacher believes about your child, and you can adjust your own remarks accordingly. For example, suppose that your child cries about his schoolwork most nights and says he's miserable in class, but the teacher seems to have no idea about his feelings. You can say something like "Johnny may be giving you the impression that everything's okay" rather than "I'm sure you know that Johnny's only barely coping."

Remember to show your appreciation of the good things, big *and* little, the teacher does for your child. The first rule for positive and effective work relations is to home in on a person's contributions so that she's motivated to make more.

Emphasizing your child's needs

The way to make sure that you avoid blaming the teacher for your child's difficulties and instead form an alliance with her is to focus on your child's needs (not what the teacher may or may not have done). If you talk in terms of your child's needs, you pinpoint *his* problems — not the teacher's — and set the stage for planning practical steps that address them.

Describe your child's problems in terms of his own learning style and personality traits rather than focusing on the teacher's actions. Lay out your points, making sure that your tone stays solutions based. To see exactly what I'm talking about, check out Table 10-1.

Table 10-1	Telling the Teacher about Your Child
It's Better to Say	*Rather Than*
Johnny doesn't want to go to school in the morning and feels that he's hardly managing to keep up in class.	You make him unhappy.
He spends at least three hours on homework every night, and it really worries me.	You give him too much homework.
I'm wondering what kinds of strategies I can use to help Johnny finish his work without missing out on recess.	You keep him in at recess.
Johnny's book seems to be frustrating. There are so many words in it that he can't figure out, and he feels overwhelmed.	You give him books that are way too hard for him.
How can I make the spelling list easier for Johnny? He tries so hard, but the copying activity, in its present form, really doesn't help him remember.	You give him spelling words that are way beyond his ability.

Pushing your points firmly

In real life your conference doesn't stick to a point-by-point format. You may want to disagree with the teacher. You may feel that she isn't doing anything to adjust classroom requirements to meet your child's needs. You may feel like you're not really being heard.

One strategy that can help is to revisit your list of main points. Stay calm, keep your voice at a normal tone, and repeat the points you think are key. As you make those points, have the following goals in the back of your mind:

- ✔ Focus on your child, not the teacher.
- ✔ Seek specific solutions, not blame
- ✔ Make suggestions, not demands.
- ✔ Project an all-around air of collaboration, not confrontation.

In Table 10-2, I give a few examples of how a teacher might respond to your concerns and how you can stick to your points in reply.

Table 10-2	Clarifying Your Main Points
What Your Child's Teacher Might Say	*How You Can Press Your Point*
Our reading program is excellent.	I'm sure the program is great, but it isn't meeting Johnny's needs.
All children must do homework.	With some minor accommodations, Johnny would be much more successful with homework.
All assignments must be handed in on time.	Advance notification of the semester's assignments would be a great help to Johnny.
Every child must give class presentations.	Because Johnny struggles with the written component of the presentation, can he make charts in place of some of the writing?
Your child must read three books each month.	Johnny has to read a book several times in order to understand it, so can we get the book list early on so we can order the books on tape too?
Your child is discourteous and disruptive.	Johnny's frustration comes out like this. What goals and strategies do you suggest we work on to improve this?

Adhering to the teacher's goals

When you speak with your child's teacher about solutions to problems, respect the fact that she's in charge of the class. Keep her goals in mind so that you're more likely to come to an agreement in which the goals that both of you have are maintained.

Your child's teacher may have plenty of good ideas for helping your child keep up with assignments and improve his language skills. If so, help her by monitoring your child's behavior at home and augmenting anything done in class. During your conference, you may want to offer the following:

- ✔ Working through a phonics program with your child at home, under the teacher's guidance (see Chapter 12 for more about phonics)

- ✔ Doing guided reading with your child at home, under the teacher's guidance (see Chapter 13 for time-tested reading strategies)

- ✔ Practicing spelling strategies that the teacher recommends

- ✔ Making copies of the teacher's notes or texts so your child is prepared for coming projects or can revisit information that was given in class

- ✔ Getting book lists from the teacher so you can reserve books on tape at your library or from programs that offer books for the blind and dyslexic (check this out in Appendix B)

Stay in the teacher's good graces by remembering that she's in charge. Ask for her help. Say that you may have forgotten this or misunderstood that. You may feel like you're eating a generous serving of humble pie, but that approach is easier than getting into a confrontation (by lashing out with statements like "You didn't give me this or properly explain that"). Don't be eager to second-guess every move the teacher makes, and don't immediately challenge the teacher's professionalism and skills.

Your child needs to use cooperative and constructive words with his teacher too. Teachers, like everyone else, prefer to deal with polite rather than impolite folks. By talking the right talk, your child practices the important life skill of showing respect for authority. Help him use terms like " It's better for me if" and "I like to" rather than "No" and "I won't."

Taking action after a conference

Immediately after a conference, update your paper trail with the details of what was said and promised. If you're good with computers, you may want to start a chart or database with headings like "date," "attendees," "points discussed," "goals," and "follow-up" (see Figure 10-1). Record everyone's contact details on your chart and (in point form) all the important things that were said. Determine the dates when you'll reassess your child's progress, and have some idea of behaviors or scores you're looking for to show whether your child is making headway. If your child has an Individualized Education Program (IEP), these details must be on it (I talk about IEPs in Chapter 8).

Date	Attendees	Points Discussed	Goals	Follow-up
10/4/05	T. Wood	TW asked for next semester's book list.	Get the booklist.	Call LC on 10/14/05 to check that goals are being reached.
	R. Richards	TW asked about a homework buddy.	Have LC and Jason choose a homework buddy.	
	L. Conley	LC said Jason needs to speak up.	Coach Jason to approach LC after class and explain what he needs.	

Figure 10-1:
Keep track of your conference notes with a handy chart.

Contact info for R. Richards: (123) 465-7890, extension 31; rrichards@meadowlea-school.com

Contact info for L. Conley: (123) 465-7890, extension 12; lconley@meadowlea-school.com

Coming Up with Cool Accommodations

By using the word "accommodations," you sound informed. It's written into laws that relate to children with dyslexia (see Chapter 8 for details), and it's what teachers and professionals talk about.

What, precisely, are *accommodations?* They're the big or small changes you make to your child's environment and to the tasks he does that enable him to perform better. When you and your child's teacher home in on your child's specific difficulties, you can probably think of dozens of accommodations. For some initial inspiration, take a look at the following sections.

Understanding oral instructions clearly

Your dyslexic child may have trouble understanding oral instructions because he can't keep a firm hold on sequences of information. He may forget parts of the sequences, moving for example from step one straight to step four, or he may muddle up the order of the steps. The following accommodations can help your child:

- ✔ Let the teacher know that your child sometimes struggles with lists of verbal instructions and ask her to speak clearly and in small bites of information to him. Also let her know that your child may sometimes ask her to reiterate things. The teacher may have a preference about whether she wants your child to do this in class or after class.

- ✔ Help your child have the confidence to speak up for himself, perhaps by role-playing the actual conversation. Your child may be nervous about asking for help even though to you it seems like a simple thing. Or he may want to ask and ask, so you can show him how to behave courteously and appropriately.

- ✔ Have the teacher find your child a buddy he can chat with to clarify what the teacher said.

- ✔ Encourage your child to makes notes and lists. At home, help your child improve his note-taking skills. I talk about this in detail in Chapter 16.

- ✔ Ask the teacher if she will write all assignments on the board, on a hand-out, on the Internet, or in Johnny's notebook.

Reading large amounts of text

Reading a lot of text at once usually presents problems for a dyslexic child because he ends up spending hours and hours on an assignment meant to be fairly short. You can do your part to help:

- ✔ When the teacher assigns books to read, borrow books on tape for your child. He can listen to the text on tape while following the written version.

- ✔ Read through homework text with him a few times (see Chapter 13 for tips on reading with your child effectively).

Comprehending text

A dyslexic child's text comprehension may not be strong because he loses the flow and gist of what he's reading when he takes a long time figuring words out. You can accommodate his needs in the following ways:

✔ Encourage your child to draw story maps and mind maps, highlight key words in text, and talk the text over with other students (maybe a buddy). (A story map is a pictorial depiction of events in a story, and a mind map is like a story map, only it depicts whatever it is you're learning. Have you ever seen people drawing bubbles that link to other bubbles? That's a mind map.)

✔ Help your child at home by drawing story maps and mind maps for assigned books and going over text with him until he understands key concepts and sequences of events.

Writing large amounts of text

Writing can give a dyslexic child trouble because he really has to think about most of the words he's jotting down. The following suggestions can help your child with writing:

✔ See that your child learns to touch-type. Touch typing is the art of typing without looking at the keyboard, and your child needs to get at least to the stage where he uses all his fingers on the keyboard and checks on them only intermittently.

✔ Type for your child while he dictates homework assignments to you.

✔ Buy speech-to-text software for your child and help him learn how to use it. He gets to dictate stuff to his computer and have it appear in a word processing document, thus saving him the hard work of writing.

As long as your child understands what he's dictating, this software doesn't make him lazy but helps him compete on an even field with classmates. In fact, some researchers say that speech-to-text software actually improves your child's spelling because he's saying the words, then seeing them appear on the screen, so his learning is multisensory. See Chapter 9 for more info.

Copying from the board with ease

A dyslexic child can have difficulty copying words from the board; by the time he shifts his eyes from the board to the paper, he's forgotten the image he just saw. You can find ways to make copying words easier for your child:

- ✔ Ask the teacher to make sure that your child sits close to the board.

- ✔ Ask the teacher to underline key words; your child can copy only these.

- ✔ Make sure your child has a buddy whose notes he can take home to copy (or maybe the teacher can photocopy them).

Spelling successfully

Spelling can be rough for your child because he has trouble matching letters to sounds and may have trouble facing individual letters the right way too. Consider these ways of accommodating his needs in this area:

- ✔ Help your child develop his phonemic and phonics skills when he does language homework by showing him word families like *might, sight, tight, slight,* and *right.* I talk about this in detail in Chapter 12.

- ✔ Help your child group spellings he brings home from class into families.

- ✔ Help your child sound out parts of his spelling words and highlight (to visually memorize) parts that don't sound out.

- ✔ Coach your child on the memorizing strategy: look, cover, write, check. First, he looks at the word, then covers it with his hand or paper or a book, writes it from memory, and, finally, checks what he's written against the original word and makes corrections. Your dyslexic child usually needs to write a word out several times before it sticks in his visual memory, and even then, he should check that it's still there a few hours later!

- ✔ Help your child to put each spelling word from a list on a small piece of paper so he can spread and overturn all the words in playing-card fashion. In Chapter 11 I describe how your child can keep ten words in an envelope and play a few games with them each day (for about five minutes) to help him remember them.

Finishing classroom work and homework on time

A dyslexic child's timing skills may be weak; it takes him longer than other students to complete tasks, and he may be more disorganized than the average child too. Here are ways to help your child finish his work on time:

✔ See that your child has a buddy to help him in ways the teacher specifies, like putting away supplies, so that he has fewer things on his plate and can focus on the more important tasks at hand.

✔ Help your child keep a calendar or pocket organizer and follow a time line to complete assignments.

✔ See that your child uses speech-to-text software, books on tape, a laptop, and other time-saving gadgets.

Avoiding Dyslexic Land Mines with a Teacher's Help

For dyslexic children, some things that typically go on in school are virtual land mines. Your dyslexic child dreads being graded and taking standardized tests, hates being timed or having to race the clock when he does spellings, and can never churn out facts and figures, like multiplication tables, that other children learn by rote in a few weeks. In the next sections, I give you advice on helping your child skirt around these land mines.

Being graded, tested, and (worst) retained

If your child goes to any school other than some alternative schools (see Chapter 7 for more on those), his teacher has to grade him. She generally grades his performance according to a list of given skills and can hold him back a grade if she feels he's not coping. Children also take plenty of standardized tests during their years in school.

Grades can embarrass and stress out your child, but retention (being held back a grade) is a lot worse. In the following sections, I give you advice on asking the teacher to be sensitive about grades and tackling standardized tests, and then give you the latest news on what researchers have found out about grade retention.

Making the grade

Your child may get Cs, Ds, or worse in his school grades no matter how hard he tries because grades primarily reflect his ranking (how he compares to classmates) rather than the effort he makes.

Can anything be done? Absolutely. You can ask for special consideration for your child, and this is where the good relationship you've cultivated with the teacher really comes in handy! (See the section "Keeping a Conference on Track and Following Up Smartly," earlier in this chapter, for details.) Ask your child's teacher to tweak her normal grading system to meet your child's extra needs.

Exactly what kind of tweaking helps? The kind that puts your child's effort into the frame. You want your child's grades to reflect his effort. So that everyone knows what counts as effort, you may want to collaborate with the teacher to draw up a bunch of identifiers that influence his grade. For example, you may want the list to indicate when your child accomplished the following:

- ✔ Wrote more than one page
- ✔ Answered every question
- ✔ Used periods and capital letters
- ✔ Wrote his name and the date
- ✔ Started each line against the margin
- ✔ Included diagrams, lists, or pictures

The teacher should have plenty of ideas about what to include as grading identifiers, and after the list is drafted, you may want to finalize it with your child. It's really his list because from it he can see that any effort he makes really pays off. He should understand how the system works and, as a result, feel motivated. Of course, encouraging comments, stars, and smiley faces on his work may count just as much to him too.

Surviving standardized tests

When all the parents in school are talking about achievement tests, and you get a note from the school saying that your child will be taking tests for two whole weeks and that only famine, disease, or pestilence should keep him from attending school at this important time — the pressure is on! This is the standardized, high-stakes testing that politicians assure us improves standards in our schools.

These tests are "standardized" because hundreds of children have taken them in order to get a *norm* (what most kids the same age can be expected to score) and a *range* (how far either side of that norm the rest of the kids usually score). Standardized tests have names like the California Achievement Test (CAT) and the Stanford Achievement Test (SAT).

These tests, predictably enough, are hard on your child for a few reasons:

- ✔ Your child may have trouble reading the questions.

- ✔ He may need more time than other children to answer the questions (because he reads more slowly).

- ✔ He may mark the wrong answer boxes in multiple choice tests because he confuses *b* and *d* or forgets which letter he was thinking of.

- ✔ He may be improving in class, but the test results don't show that.

- ✔ He may perform badly on tests because, knowing that he does badly on them, he's understandably nervous.

How can you (with the help of your child's teacher) help your child get through these tests and come out unscathed or even optimistic?

- ✔ If your child has an Individualized Education Program, or IEP (I talk about IEPs in Chapter 8), you need to use it to plan for tests. Decide how your child's teacher will prepare him for tests and what accommodations he can use during the test. Accommodations such as having extra time or a reader to read questions out loud to your child can make all the difference in his score.

- ✔ High-stakes testing, in which one test result determines huge things like whether your child advances to the next grade, is not impossible to get around. If you run into problems with the outcome of the testing, contact one of the big organizations I list in Appendix B. The International Dyslexia Association and the Learning Disabilities Association have experience with contesting school district decisions. The legal organizations I list can tell you about other families who have fought their cases in court. Before getting into battle though, consult the usual chain of command in your school (teacher, school counselor, principal, and superintendent). Your school doesn't really want to get into a dispute with you, and chances are, you can come to a happy resolution without working up a sweat.

In addition to speaking to your child's teacher about standardized tests, you can provide some help at home. Ask your child's guidance counselor or resource teacher about summer classes or if they have practice tests you can use. Your dyslexic child needs plenty of practice runs on these tests. Attack them in short blasts and have good things to eat. You want to prepare your child but not exhaust or terrify him.

Also, tutors can help your child prepare for tests and may offer test-preparation courses specifically for exams like the SAT that older kids take. I talk about tutoring in more detail in Chapter 9.

Staying back a grade

For the past few years, the trend has been for teachers to keep some children back a grade, especially in kindergarten and especially with boys. Grade retention is a real hot potato, however. Many parents and teachers believe that retention allows a child to mature and get extra practice in class, but many researchers say that the evidence just doesn't bear this out.

Based on studies of the way that retained children see themselves and perform on class tests, researchers say that retained children

- ✔ Feel ashamed or embarrassed in front of other kids because they're bigger and older than classmates.

- ✔ Get teased by classmates for being "dumb."

- ✔ Feel that their parents forced or misled them into staying back a grade.

- ✔ Don't make appreciable headway in the skills they initially lacked and often fall back even further (compared to struggling kids who were not retained).

- ✔ Are much more likely than nonretained children to drop out of school.

- ✔ Often say that being held back was the worst thing that ever happened to them.

Holding a child back is done with the best intentions, but it can have long-term dangers. Grade-retained children invariably report that being held back traumatized them, and some researchers link increased rates of substance abuse and depression in adolescence with grade retention in earlier years (for details, check out www.schwablearning.org/articles.asp?r=315).

Grade retention at the time of moving from one school to the next may work for your child. If, for example, he finds that he's entering a grade in which all the students are a year older than him (because he started school earlier in another place), then the school may give him the choice of whether to join that grade or start out a grade lower (with same-age children). The lower grade may be more attractive *if* your child chooses it himself.

Your child's teacher has a lot of say in whether your child is retained or promoted, but if you disagree with proposed retention, even if your child has scored low in tests, you should contest the proposal and say why your child should be promoted; for example, you can say that he can get private instruction in his weak areas, and research points to the damaging effects of retention. There are no hard-and-fast rules for retention, and some parents who have taken their objection to retention to court have succeeded in having their children promoted.

The best way to address your child's academic problems is to give him individualized instruction in his areas of weakness (if he has an IEP, this instruction is described in it). And if your child has dyslexia, the arguments against retention are especially pertinent. Research shows that a dyslexic child doesn't catch up to his peers by being given more of the same instruction. He catches up through multisensory instruction that takes him systematically through phonics. (I cover phonics in Chapter 12 and multisensory activities in Chapter 14.)

Learning in parrot fashion

Rote learning is the process by which your child learns isolated facts (like multiplication tables, dates of events, and names of cities) by parroting them out many times. Not many people are great at rote learning because it's hard to remember things without using memory joggers (like rhymes) or attaching meaning to them. But your dyslexic child may find rote learning even harder because his short-term recall of information is weak even *with* memory joggers (see Chapter 11 for more about these items). The added challenge of having to recite facts at a fast speed, which happens in most classrooms, can cause him major stress.

Strategies that can help your child join in activities like chanting multiplication tables include allowing him to use a calculator or a fact sheet. The teacher, together with your child, should probably explain this accommodation openly to the class first so that students realize the work isn't made easier for your child, just accessible.

Smoothly integrating children with disabilities into a classroom requires good communication. When other students can walk a few miles in the shoes of children with disabilities and see that they're not favored in class but rather included, integration has every chance of being successful.

Part IV

Taking Part in Your Child's Treatment

The 5th Wave   By Rich Tennant

In this part . . .

When your child has dyslexia, she struggles with phonics. In this part of the book, you get everything you need to know about phonics, including how to help your child sound out tricky words like *right* and *round*.

But of course, phonics isn't the whole picture. Your child needs to recognize "sight words," such as *who* and *they,* instantly, and she needs plenty of real reading and multi-sensory activity. And besides all of that, her dyslexia makes things, like following sequences of instructions, difficult, so she also needs help there. In this part, I give you practical advice on all of these topics.

Chapter 11

Putting Memorizing, Visualizing, and Rhyming to Good Use

In This Chapter

▶ Finding novel ways to remember single letters

▶ Using rhyme to read and spell whole bunches of words

▶ Making easy work of sight words

▶ Telling the difference between sound-alike words

▶ Getting a grip on tricky words

---

*E*verybody uses rhymes and memory joggers now and then. "*I* before *e* except after *c*" is probably etched on millions of minds, and think how handy "spring forward; fall back" is for helping you set your clock to a new hour twice a year!

When you're dealing with dyslexia, rhyming and visualizing can be virtual lifelines. In this chapter, you get the handiest memory joggers of all for helping your dyslexic child master many words that start off looking pretty formidable.

 Just about all the activities that I describe in this chapter (especially the ones related to spelling, sight words, sound-alike words, and mnemonics) are good for anybody, young or less young. After all, a few extra years don't suddenly make you want to avoid effective learning strategies, even if they *are* more fun than you were expecting!

One by One: Starting with Single Letters

Remembering 26 of anything can be hard, so you need to give your dyslexic child a lot of practice with the look and sound of each letter of the alphabet before she can remember all 26 letters.

You can run through the "a is for apple" type of activities and flip through alphabet books with her, and that's good, but an even better approach is to bring each letter alive. Draw sound-associated pictures into them, and make some of them into quirky characters. I'm beginning to sound ethereal now, so how about letting me give you practical examples of exactly what I mean in the following sections?

Drawing pictures into vowels

Looking at apples, alligators, and ants to learn about the letter *a* is a fairly complex business. In fact, when you think about it, it's amazing that children learn this way because, unless your child already knows the *a* sound of the letter *a*, how does she recall that *apple, alligator,* and *ant* are all *a* words?

A much easier way for a dyslexic child to learn the 26 letter sounds is to learn just 26 images. Help your child remember the letters by turning them into visual images or models she can feel.

Vowels are especially tricky for your dyslexic child because each vowel always has at least two sounds, short and long, and can make other sounds too (about 44 of them) when grouped together with other letters. In the following vowel activities, you do away with vowel names altogether and focus wholly on sounds and vowel-specific visual images.

✔ Help your child remember the sound of short *a* by having her draw the letter *a* from an apple. She holds the apple on paper and draws around it and then adds the vertical stick to make *a.* Have her make the *a* (like in *apple*) sound while she's holding and drawing.

✔ Help your child remember the sound of short *e* by having her draw a big *e* and nesting an egg (hard boiled!) in the semicircular part of the letter. Explain that no other letter has that nice shape that fits snuggly into that semicircular part, so when she sees the letter *e,* she can think of *egg* (the short *e* sound is like the *e* in *egg*).

✔ Help your child remember *i* for *ink* by having her hold down a pen and draw around it. Have her add the ink blob on top to make *i* and remember, *i* is for *ink* (say it out loud).

✔ Help your child remember the sound of short *o* by having her draw an octopus's legs coming off the letter *o.* Tell her that *o* is a round, smooth octopus that has its eight legs tucked under it when you see it as plain *o.* Remember to say *o* for *octopus.*

✔ Help your child remember *u* with a u-handled umbrella. *U* is for *umbrella.* If you don't have a u-handled umbrella, you can just turn *u* into a nice image. Add arrowheads to the two ends of the *u* (pointing upwards) and tell your child that *u* is for *up.* (She has to say it out loud, of course, to get the full multisensory complement!)

You may already have guessed this, but I'm not the first person to think of turning letters into characters. Many early learning and phonics programs draw characters into letters to help kids remember them. Two programs that are well worth looking at are Letterland and Zoo-Phonics. Both programs have books, flashcards, CD-ROMS, readers, and a whole mega bunch of goods, so if you want to start your child on letter sounds from scratch, check them out at www.letterland.com and www.zoophonics.com or flip to Chapter 4, where I tell you more about these products and give some prices.

Knocking b and d into shape

A dyslexic child typically has trouble facing her letters the right way, and the letters that cause her the most trouble are *b* and *d*. There are two good ways you can help your child get her *b*'s and *d*'s to behave, and they both involve visualizing cute images.

Batter up!

If your child's a baseball nut, you'll like this trick. Tell your child to think "bat and ball" and hear the *b* sound. Now have her draw a standing-up baseball bat (a cricket bat works too) and next to it, on the ground, a ball. You've made the letter *b,* and now you just have to remember that *d* faces the opposite way.

The one glitch with the bat and ball image is remembering which side to place the ball. I always tell kids to think of the reading and writing direction, or left to write. You write from left to right, and that's the direction to remember when you draw *first* the bat and next the ball.

Make your bed!

Here's a way to remember *b* and *d* together in one snuggly image. Take a look at Figure 11-1 and then read the instructions that follow to see what it's all about:

1. Explain to your child that the bed picture can help her remember which way *b* and *d* face.

2. Draw this simple shape: l__l

   Have your child do the same.

3. Draw a pillow and blanket on top of yours and have your child do the same with her picture.

4. Write the word *bed* in the bed picture, using the sides of the bed as the vertical lines in your *b* and *d,* and sound it out so that your child hears the *b* and *d* sounds. Have her do the same on her picture.

5. Tell her that when she can't remember *b* ("buh") or *d* ("duh"), she can just make her bed! Be sure that nothing is sticking out — that's the big secret. (If letters face the wrong way, they stick out and someone may trip over them.)

6. Explain that she's making a big bouncy bed as a quick way of remembering the orientation of *b* and *d*.

Figure 11-1: You can help your child remember a cozy image for *b* and *d*.

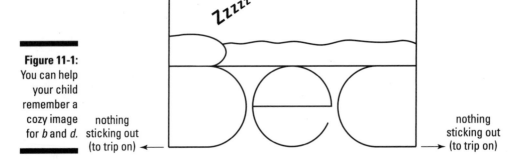

nothing sticking out (to trip on) ←

→ nothing sticking out (to trip on)

You can also show your child how to make her bed with her hands. Figure 11-2 shows you how. Just have your child touch the tips of her thumb and forefinger together on each hand (making a circle), then point her remaining fingers straight up together (making a *b* shape with the left hand and a *d* shape with the right).

Figure 11-2: Making a bed with your hands is a fun and easy way to remember *b* and *d*.

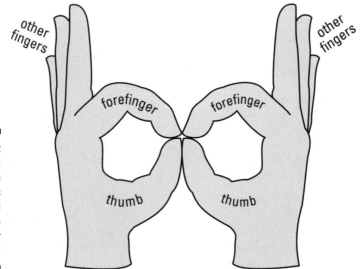

TIP

Putting P in its place

Some dyslexic kids have trouble distinguishing between the number 9 and the letter *P*. Here's a way to iron it out:

1. Ask your child which direction she reads and writes in. Get the answer "left to right" from her and have her point to the right.

2. Ask her to tell you a name that begins with *P*, like Peter, Paul, or Polly.

3. Tell her to draw a face onto the circle part of *P*, the nose pointing in the reading and writing direction.

4. Ask your child to add features like hair, a cap, and glasses and write the person's name above him.

5. Tell your child that whenever she's not sure about P, she can draw her character, facing in the reading and writing direction. You can see a sample *P* drawing in Figure 11-3.

Polly

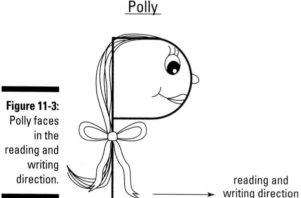

Figure 11-3:
Polly faces
in the
reading and
writing
direction.

reading and
writing direction

Letters Joining Forces: Getting on Top of a Few Good Spelling Rules

When letters band together, they can retain their individual sounds but still blend smoothly together, or they can make new sounds that you just have to get to know afresh, like *ch* and *ir*. Luckily, some of the most common letter clusters are governed by nifty and easy-to-remember rules. Dyslexic kids especially need to have a few rules up their sleeves so they can impose order on letters that otherwise make no sense to them.

In the next sections, I show you blatantly *Bossy e,* friendly vowels that conform to the adage "opposites attract," and the timeless rhyme "*i* before *e* except after *c.*"

Get full use from the tables I provide in the following sections by having your child go through plenty of re-readings, spot spelling rules, and write words out for herself. This kind of repetition and *consolidation* (firming up understanding) is really helpful to dyslexic children, so to make sure you cover it, have your child do the following:

- ✔ Read all the words, first to last.
- ✔ Read all the words, last to first.
- ✔ Read words in random order as you point to them.
- ✔ Read every second or third or fifth word.
- ✔ Find words as you call them out.
- ✔ Highlight each family (*a-e* words, *e-e* words, *i-e* words, *o-e* words, and *u-e* words) in a different color.
- ✔ Write out words that you dictate.

Blatantly Bossy e

Have you ever noticed the pattern in words like *pin* and *pine, hop* and *hope, mad* and *made?* This simple rule explains it: When you add *e* onto the end of small words like *pin,* or to word-parts like *lak,* the *e* bosses the earlier vowel into shouting out its name. *Pin* becomes *pine* (hear the change in the vowel sound), *lak* becomes *lake,* and all the while the surreptitiously *Bossy e* stays silent itself.

The long sound of a vowel is the same as its name, like in *ay, ee, eye, oh,* and *you.* I say that the vowel shouts its name in response to *Bossy e* because that concept tends to be easier for a child to remember than telling her that the vowel makes its long sound.

The *Bossy e* rule helps your dyslexic child read and write hundreds of words, but if you're the creative type and have a younger child, you may prefer the *Magic e* version of the same rule:

> *Magic e* is a special letter. When it sits on the end of a word, it throws its magic dust out. The dust floats over the neighboring letter but sticks to the vowel. The vowel feels so special that it shouts out its name.

With this rule, you get to grab some glitter or glitter pens (magic dust) and draw posters of *Magic e* doing its thing. It looks cute and helps to plant the rule firmly in your child's mind. Wands and cloaks add even more magic.

Now that you know the rule, you're probably wondering about the hundreds of words that use it. I said that *Bossy e* enables your child to read and write oodles of words, so here, to put the truth to my claim, is Table 11-1, which lists at least some of those *Bossy e* words.

Table 11-1	*Bossy e* Words	
ape	graze	tale
bake	lake	tape
base	lane	wake
blade	late	wave
blame	made	dive
brave	mane	drive
cake	mate	file
came	name	fine
cane	pale	five
cape	pane	hide
case	plate	hike
crate	rake	nine
chase	sale	bone
date	save	broke
fade	scrape	code
fake	shade	cone
flake	shake	hole
flame	shape	home
game	skate	hope
gate	snake	cute
gave	state	fume
grade	stale	mule
grape	take	rule

Your child likes to show off to you. Let her read and write words for you and be appreciative of her effort. Soup up the writing part by providing her with a book-sized whiteboard and colored markers. Have your own too so you can write her messages or join in the activity with her.

Extroverted and introverted vowels

All vowels can make a short sound (like in *apple, egg, ink, octopus,* and *up*) or a long sound (which is the same as saying the names of the letters). The rule that I give you now helps your dyslexic child distinguish which sound (short or long) a vowel is making in a word. Prepare to smile, because this rule is such a cute rhyme that it's easy to remember:

"When two vowels go walking, the first one does the talking."

How does it work? Your child sees four particular pairs of vowels, side by side in words, time and time again. They're the buddies, *ee, ea, ai,* and *oa,* and they're special because when they go walking only the first one does the talking. The second vowel is the quiet type and says nothing. The first vowel is the loud type and it shouts, I'm sure you'll be surprised to hear, its name.

Your child only has to remember the four pairs of friends (each comprised of an extrovert and an introvert), and like before, hundreds of new words become clear to her. In Table 11-2, you get plenty to try out. Go through the reading, finding, highlighting, and writing activities that I gave earlier in this chapter, and your child will soon be feeling comfortable with the walking vowels.

Table 11-2	Words with Two Vowels That Go Walking	
bee	bleed	cheer
creek	creep	deep
feel	feet	free
green	jeep	heel
keep	meet	need
see	seed	seen
sleep	speech	speed
steel	steep	sweet
tree	week	bead
beak	bean	beat

cheap	cheat	clear
deal	dream	each
ear	east	eat
fear	feast	hear
heat	meal	mean
meat	neat	reach
read	real	scream
seal	seat	sneak
speak	steal	steam
stream	teach	team
braid	brain	chain
drain	fail	mail
main	pain	train
sail	tail	train
wait	boast	boat
coat	float	goat
road	roast	soap
throat	toad	toast

The groups your child highlights for this rule are *ee, ea, ai,* and *oa* words (the four most common walking partners). Ask your child which groups are the biggest and smallest so she can see how often *ee* and *ea* crop up.

An old favorite: "i before e except after c"

Here's the old-timer of spelling rules. Just about everyone has heard of it, including parents and grandparents, and it's handy because it helps your dyslexic child tame some pretty ferocious spellings, like *receive, perceive,* and *receipt,* and *neighbor* and *eight* too. Here's the full verse:

> "*i* ('eye') before *e* ('ee') except after *c* ('see') unless you hear 'ay' (like in *neighbor* and *weigh*)"

Table 11-3 has some spellings that demonstrate that rule.

In compliance: Most words follow the "i before e" rule

Words like *believe* and *weigh* follow the *"i before e except after c unless you hear ay"* rule so nicely that I feel I'm about to spoil the mood. You see a lot of words don't follow the rule, leading people to say downright peevish things like "Is this rule useful at all?" Well, at the risk of incurring the wrath of those of you who can think of half a zillion words that don't give a hoot about *"i before e,"* I have to say I shall remain a fan.

And what's more, I just happen to have found someone who likes counting words and has investigated just how often, or not, the *"i before e"* rule works. At www.usingenglish.com/weblog/archives/000021.html, you can find a discussion about the efficacy of the *"i before e"* rule that ends by saying that the rule, when taught properly, works approximately 90 percent of the time. The "properly" part means that you should tell your child not just *"i before e except after c unless you hear 'ay' (like in *neighbor* and *weigh*)."* Your child also needs to know this rule:

> *"i* before *e* except after *c* unless you hear 'ay' (like in *neighbor* and *weigh*) or when *cie* makes a 'shuh' sound (like in *ancient, proficient,* and *deficient*)"

Phew, have I blinded you with science yet? If not, and you rather enjoy a debate, you can find a nice discussion of the "this rule is useless" side of the argument, and a whole bunch of rule-breakers (which may in fact work if you follow the "or when *cie* makes a 'shuh' sound" addition to the rule!) at www.alt-usage-english.org/I_before_E.html.

Table 11-3	i before e	
believe	brief	ceiling
conceit	deceive	field
niece	perceive	piece
priest	receipt	receive
shield	thief	veil
vein	weight	yield

I Know You! Having Fun with Sight Words

Some words in our language crop up a lot more often than others. Take, for example, the word *they*. You see *they* time and time again, so it's a word that your dyslexic child must get to know early on and thoroughly. Luckily, a guy named Edward W. Dolch counted the frequency of commonly used words back in the 1950s and came up with a list of 220 of the most common words of all. Ever since then, teachers have used this list, or others like it, to help children get "sight" recognition of those most common words. You hear teachers call them "most common" or "frequently used" words, or "sight" words. I call them "sight" words because I want you to know that the significant thing about them is that your child needs to have instant (or sight) recognition of them.

Your child needs instant recognition of all 220 of the sight words in order to be a fluent reader. Without this, she is a stop-start, "I'll get it in a minute" kind of reader, which is frustrating for her and everyone else.

In Table 11-4, I list Mr. Dolch's 220 sight words.

Table 11-4				220 Sight Words		
a	call	funny	just	only	small	use
about	came	gave	keep	open	so	very
after	can	get	kind	or	some	walk
again	carry	give	know	our	soon	want
all	clean	go	laugh	out	start	warm
always	cold	goes	let	over	stop	was
am	come	going	light	own	take	wash
an	could	good	like	pick	tell	we
and	cut	got	little	play	ten	well
any	did	green	live	please	thank	went
are	do	grow	long	pretty	that	were
around	does	had	look	pull	the	what
as	don't	has	made	put	their	when
ask	done	have	make	ran	them	where
at	down	he	many	read	then	which
ate	draw	help	may	red	there	white
away	drink	her	me	ride	these	who
be	eat	here	much	right	they	why
because	eight	him	must	round	think	will

(continued)

Table 17-1 (continued)

been	every	his	my	run	this	wish
before	fall	hold	myself	said	those	with
best	far	hot	never	saw	three	work
better	fast	how	new	say	to	would
big	find	hurt	no	see	today	write
black	first	I	not	seven	together	yellow
blue	five	if	now	shall	too	yes
both	fly	in	of	she	try	you
bring	for	into	off	show	two	your
brown	found	is	old	sing	under	
but	four	it	on	sit	up	
buy	from	its	once	six	upon	
by	full	jump	one	sleep	us	

The more practice you give your child with sight words, the better she remembers them. That said, the following sections are devoted to simple and fun activities you can do with your child to really bring those words home.

Ten at a time

The simplest way for your child to learn to read or write a new word is to read and/or write it plenty of times. Have her do this by running her though these activities using ten sight words at a time:

1. Write ten sight words on ten pieces of paper. Have your child spread them out face down and then ask her to turn each word over, read it, and then, without referring back to it, write it on her paper.

2. Have your child put the ten words into a stack and ask her to turn each one over, read it, and then write it down.

3. Holding the words in a fan facing you, ask your child to pick a word, read it, and write it down.

4. Holding the ten words in a fan facing you, ask her to select but not look at a word and then take three guesses at which word she's selected. If she guesses correctly, she reads it and writes it down. If not, it goes back into the fan. Keep going until she's done all ten words.

These activities take only five or ten minutes. Have your child put her ten words into an envelope and do any or all of the activities every day for a week (breakfast or bedtime are great times). By the end of a week, she'll be right at home with the words. If not, pop any words she still struggles with back into the envelope to comprise part of her next ten words.

Use fewer than ten words if you think that works better for your dyslexic child, but don't use more than ten words. Your child can't remember more than ten, and getting a solid grasp of ten words is better than a tenuous grasp of twenty.

Picture this

Dyslexic children remember graphic images far better than written words, so it makes perfect sense for them to turn words into images whenever they can (so they remember them better). Sight words like *jump, walk,* and *eat* are ideal for this. Your child can make letters jump out of *jump,* add a pair of feet to the bottom of the *k* in *walk,* and put *eat* on a plate.

For inspiration, check out www.picturemereading.com. Then grab some markers and a snack and settle down with your child for some cartoon fun. If your child is a great artist and you're not, she'll especially enjoy sympathizing over your indistinct doodles while being a paragon of modesty about her own masterpieces.

Bang!

Here's a noisy game for a few players that provides lots of laughs. Write 32 sight words on individual pieces of paper and write the word "bang" on 8 pieces of paper. Place all the pieces of paper into a box or can. Player number one takes a word and reads it out. If she is correct, she keeps the card, and play goes to the next player. Players keep taking one card and reading out the word until a player pulls out a "bang" card. She shouts out "bang" and puts *all* her cards back. The winner is the person left holding the most cards.

Playing the numbers (and name) game

Dyslexic kids not only have trouble with reading and spelling words; they can have a hard time with numbers and names too. You can help your child remember stuff like who to call and how with a few handy tips:

✔ Have your child remember phone numbers in chunks of numbers rather than in single numbers. It's easier to remember 782-22-33-240 than 7-8-2-2-2-3-3-2-4-0. Even better, attach meaning to the chunks: "7 ate (munch, munch) 2"; 22 (my aunt's age); 33 (one digit up from 22); 240 (two was regurgitated, then doubled, and then zeroed out!).

✔ Have your child remember people's names by visualizing them in different poses, clothes, or whatever, or by remembering who else has that name. I once had to remember the name "Verpee" and could only do it by starting off with "verb." Names like Mr. Hill, Mr. Mountain, and Mr. Wood (all topographical) go together nicely, and Tanya can have a tan, Ashley can smoke, and Kelly can be smelly!

Word roll

For this group game, you need three pieces of colored paper, a dice, and three boxes. Cut each piece of colored paper into 20 ticket-sized pieces and write a different sight word on each ticket. Put each color into a separate box. Player number one rolls the dice and takes from any box the number of words that corresponds to the number she rolled. She reads the word, and if she is correct, play goes to the next player. If she misreads any word, all her words go back into the box. The winner is the player with the most words when all the boxes are empty.

Soup this game up by having number 1 on the dice mean "miss a turn" and number 6 mean "you win an extra roll."

Five up

This is a card game for two or more players. The size of your card deck depends on how many people play. For two players, you need a pack of 30 cards comprised of 15 pairs of identical sight words.

Deal four cards to each player, face up in a row. Deal five face-up cards in the middle of the table. Place the remainder of the pack face down in the middle of the table. Player number one checks her cards against the five center cards to see if she has a match. If she does, she takes the card or cards that match, keeps her pairs, and draws cards to rebuild her hand and the five center cards. Play moves to the next player and so on until all the cards are paired. The winner is the player with the most pairs.

Bingo

Smaller children like playing bingo, and prizes like packets of markers and candy bars can add incentive. You need bingo-type cards divided into 25 squares (5 rows x 5 rows), a list of 100 sight words, scissors, a pen, and coins to use as markers.

Write a different arrangement of words from the list of a hundred onto each bingo card. Have players take a bingo card and a bunch of coins and let one person be the caller. The caller cuts up the 100 words and put them into a calling box. The caller pulls words out of the calling box, one at a time, and calls them out. She jots down each called word too so she can check the winner's words at the end of play. Each player places a coin over any called word she has on her card until someone gets a row of five. That player calls out "bingo," and if the caller finds her words were indeed all called out, that player wins.

Have your child help write the 100 words and the bingo cards. Let the players take turns at being caller too because all of this practice with words helps a dyslexic child memorize them.

Do You See the Sea? Distinguishing between Sound-Alike Words

Plenty of words sound the same but are spelled differently, which may confuse your dyslexic child to no end. Sound-alike words are called either "homonyms" or "homophones." You may hear the word "homographs" too. Here's a quick explanation of all three terms:

- ✔ **Homonyms:** A general term for words that are the same in sound but not in spelling (like *son* and *sun*), in spelling but not sound (like *bow* in your hair and *bow* of a ship), or in both spelling *and* sound (like *grave* in a cemetery and *grave* as in serious). Homographs and homophones are subsets of the bigger, general term "homonyms."

- ✔ **Homophones:** These words sound the same but are spelled differently, such as *you* are nice and the farmer has a *ewe*.

- ✔ **Homographs:** Words that are spelled the same but are pronounced differently, like *bow* in your hair and *bow* to the king.

Table 11-5 lists some common pairs of sound-alike words.

Table 11-5	Common Pairs of Sound-Alike Words	
aloud/allowed	pain/pane	son/sun
ate/eight	pair/pear	steal/steel
blue/blew	passed/past	straight/strait
board/bored	patience/patients	symbol/cymbal
break/brake	peace/piece	tail/tale
buy/by	plain/plane	there/they're/their
cereal/serial	principal/principle	threw/through
deer/dear	rain/reign/rein	thrown/throne
for/four	real/reel	tide/tied
groan/grown	rode/road/rowed	to/too/two
hair/hare	sale/sail	wear/where
hear/here	scene/seen	week/weak
hole/whole	scent/sent/cent	whether/weather
knot/not	seam/seem	who's/whose
lead/led	see/sea	witch/which
meet/meat	sew/so/sow	write/right
naval/navel	sight/site/cite	
no/know	some/sum	

How can you help your child read and spell the common pairs of sound-alike words, like *seen* and *scene,* that bother even nondyslexics? You can do the following:

✔ Help her put words in "families." A family is a set of words with the same ending, like in *light, bright, tight, sight,* and *might.* Your child remembers one written pattern and, from it, generates a whole bunch of words. Anytime you see a family, show it to your child so you give her a quick hoist up the spelling ladder.

✔ Be sure she understands what each word in a pair means and, if it's appropriate, which word is more common. Pairs of words in which one word of the pair is much more commonly used than the other include *seem* and *seam; where* and *wear;* and *not* and *knot.* When your child learns the common spelling first, she at least knows which situations it doesn't apply to. To find the more unusual spelling after that, she can try a few drafts of possible spellings to see which one looks right.

✔ Help your child mark parts of words that don't sound out, or sound out in unusual ways, so she learns them by their visual appearance. Colored highlighter pens are good for this, but circling or underlining the letters works too. The words to have your child mark are words like *br<u>ea</u>k* (the *ea* is unexpected), *al<u>low</u>ed* (two *l*'s and the *ow* spelling), and *<u>sc</u>ene* (pronounce it to help remember its spelling). Mark away! Encourage your child to mark any word in any way that helps her remember the look of it.

Looking for a great book of word lists? *The Reading Teacher's Book of Lists,* by Edward Fry, PhD (published by Jossey-Bass), has a great collection of homographs and homophones and all sorts of other great stuff.

The Hard Stuff: Remembering Especially Tricky Words

Oh my gosh, how much fun can a person stand? In this section I give you a whole bunch of cute *mnemonics* (memory joggers) that teachers (the cool ones) show their students (especially the dyslexic ones) to help them with words that always trip people up. You get sayings that help your child do the following:

✔ Sort out the *cause* part of *because.*

✔ Choose wisely between *stationery* and *stationary.*

✔ Organize every incarnation of *to (to, too,* and *two).*

And that's only the half of it!

Rhymes and other mnemonics that help you order letters inside a word are particularly useful for your dyslexic child because poor visual recall (which letter goes where) can be a big part of her dyslexia. Show your child any mnemonic you know and help her come up with some of her own, too. Start with the ones in Table 11-6. Fix them in her mind by singing, saying, and using them often. If it helps to repeat them ten times straight or write them down, do that, too.

Table 11-6	Mnemonics for Remembering Tricky Spellings
Tricky Spelling	*Helpful Mnemonic*
because	"**Big** **e**lephants **c**an **a**lways **u**nderstand **s**mall **e**lephants."
stationery/stationary	"There's an **e**nvelope in station**e**ry."
to/too/two	In "too much" you see too many *o*'s.
	"**Two** twins."
necessary	"Wear one **c**ap, two **s**ocks."
friend	"**Fri**e**nd**ship never ends."
they	"There's no 'hay' in they" (it's not "**thay**").
principal/principle	"The princi**pal** is your pal."
here, there, where	"There" and "where" both have "here" in them because they're both about positions.
bought/thought	"**O**nly **u**gly **g**irls **h**ate **t**oothpaste."
four/fourteen/forty	"If **u** bet, **u** should stay in for four and fourteen dollars but not for forty."
beautiful	"**B**are **e**legant **a**rms are **u**sually beautiful."
business	"Catch the bus to your **bus**iness."
secretary	"The secretary keeps **secret**s."
rhythm	"**R**hythm **h**elps **y**our **t**wo **h**ips **m**ove."

The *ight* spelling is an important one for your child to remember because several common words use it *(light, right, bright, tight, sight,* and *might)*. How on earth will your dyslexic child remember the order of all those unexpected letters? I haven't come across a really great mnemonic yet, but here are two that are better than nothing!

"**I**ndian **g**irls **h**ave **t**oys."

"**I**sabel **g**oes **h**ome **t**oday."

I warned you that they weren't great! Maybe you and your child can think up something infinitely better, and for that matter, change any of the suggestions I give you into things you think will stick better.

Chapter 12

Playing with Phonics

. . . .

In This Chapter

▶ Starting with single letters

▶ Meeting word families

▶ Discovering blends and digraphs

▶ Working out difficult vowel sounds

▶ Taking control of challenging consonants

. . . .

*W*hen you take a look at what happens in dyslexia programs, phonics is key. *Phonics* is the teaching method in which you show your child that single letters and chunks of letters represent the sounds he hears inside words. Phonics is pretty much the backbone of learning to read (and the thing that catches dyslexics out the most), so of course it's important that you lead your child through it systematically and thoroughly. Luckily, teachers have taught phonics for decades and figured out great strategies, so all you really have to do is learn to recognize them and run through a few at home.

In this chapter, I explain how you can make sure your child gets the structured, sequential instruction in phonics that experts recommend. I show you how to give your child the scoop on single letters, make sure he's friendly with word families, help him with blends and digraphs, and get on top of tricky vowel and consonant sounds.

You can help your child get a strong handle on letters and spelling with the use of memorization, visualization, and rhyming tricks. Chapter 11 has the full scoop. (For more tips about spelling, check out my book *Teaching Kids to Spell For Dummies,* published by Wiley.) To find out just how much your child already knows, you can run him through the quick tests I provide in Appendix A.

Emphasizing Single Letters

When you lead your dyslexic child through phonics, start by making sure he knows the sound of each letter of the alphabet. If he knows the letter names already, tell him to forget them for the time being and instead talk of "a" (like in *apple*), "buh" (like in *big*) and "cuh" (like in *cup*). Once your child can sound out a few consonants and the short sounds of the five vowels, he's ready for sliding them together into three-letter words (see the section "Building Three-Letter Words in Word Families," later in this chapter).

Cozying up with consonants

A great way to help your child learn the consonant sounds is to draw features into each letter that turn it into a memorable individual character that behaves in its own distinctive ways. Great idea, huh? I'd like to take all the credit for it, but a few people have come up with this idea before me and produced whole programs based around it. In Chapter 4, I give you details on Letterland and Zoo-Phonics, two programs that you may want to buy bits and pieces of or at least get ideas from. For more immediate ideas, here is a list of consonant-learning activities teachers typically use.

✔ Teach your child only the "hard" sounds of the consonants *c* and *g* ("cuh" and "guh") to start with. See the section "Sounding out the softies," later in this chapter, to get a few details about the soft "see" and "jee" sounds that these letters also make.

✔ Focus on one letter a week and talk every day about things that start with that letter, like milk, medicine, mud, melon, mops, moss, and mom.

✔ Get library books (from the picture books or first readers sections) that focus on your letter and read them together, paying special attention to your letter sound. If the letter is written on the pages, point it out to your child and, if it's written big enough, have him trace over it with his finger while saying the sound (like "mmmuh").

✔ Make posters adorned with pictures or magazine cutouts of items that start with your letter. Say each picture's name.

✔ Eat foods whose names start with your letter and make the letter out of breadsticks, pasta, chocolate sauce, and anything else that can be arranged or squeezed into shape. Say the sound as you go.

✔ Draw the letter for your child to trace over and glue things onto. Finger-paint your letter and have your child draw over your letter in rainbow colors. Draw the letter in chalk on your sidewalk. Make the letter's sound.

✔ Sing songs and listen to alphabet tapes and CD-ROMS.

Multisensory learning, which I talk more about in Chapter 14, is a great way for your dyslexic child to learn. In fact, just about anyone who knows anything about dyslexia says that multisensory learning is the very best way for a dyslexic child to go. When your child sees a letter, says it, and traces it, he's engaging in multisensory learning — he's using a few senses at pretty much the same time, so information comes to him from different angles and therefore sticks in his memory better. That's why I'm always encouraging you to have your child say the sound out loud when he sees or draws a letter or an object whose name begins with that letter.

Taking a long look at short vowels

Vowels are especially important because there's a vowel in almost every word (the exceptions being words like *my* that have *y* in them, making a vowel sound — in this case, long *i*). Since all vowels make at least two sounds, they're especially tricky to learn.

When your child learns the vowel sounds, start by teaching him only the short sounds: *a* like in *apple*, *e* like in *egg*, *i* like in *ink*, *o* like in *octopus*, *u* like in *up*. He learns the long vowel sounds (like in *ape*, *eagle*, *ice*, *open*, and *uniform*) later, along with other vowel combinations like *er* and *ei*. (Check out the section "Opening up to long vowels," later in this chapter, for details.)

Show your child the vowel sounds by going through the routines I describe in the earlier section on consonants. For children younger than about grade 2, you can also add this next game to your repertoire of activities. It's fun, so your child will want to play, and the more practice he gets with vowels, the better. Here's how to prepare and play the game:

1. **Cut up a sheet (or two) of paper into 20 pieces, each about 1 x 2 inches in size.**

2. **Write a vowel on each card (a mixed bunch of vowels), leaving four cards blank.**

3. **Draw a smiley face on each of these blanks.**

4. **Have your child hold the cards in a face-down pack and overturn them, one at a time, telling you each letter sound as he turns it over.**

5. **If he turns over a smiley face, he claps three times and runs to the door and knocks on it.**

    You can make the smiley face mean any kind of action, depending on the age of your child and the available space.

Before you start this game with your child, he can pencil drawings (like an apple in the *a*, an egg inside the *e*, an ink spot for the dot on the *i*, an octopus in the *o*, and arrows on top of the vertical lines of the *u* to signify "up") into the letters if it helps him recall the sounds.

Introducing letters by name

What about letter names? Your dyslexic child has probably watched a few episodes of *Sesame Street* or other TV shows for preschoolers and young children, and that's good. These shows are jam-packed with instructions about the alphabet, so chances are your child has learned the names of one or two letters from them. Songs are another great way of getting letter names into your child's memory. Have your child sing the ABC song as often as you can stand so that the rhythm and sheer fun make letters stick in his mind.

The ABC song is the one you hear all over the place. Your child sings the letter names to the tune of "Twinkle Twinkle Little Star." Because they're catchy, songs, more than just about any other activity, help your child learn the letter names.

It's great if your child knows the letter names early on, but it's much more important for him to learn the letter sounds. After he establishes a firm grip on letter sounds and can read words like *sat* and *flat,* that are made of single letter sounds joined together, then he can take a look at letter names. You can show him that in words like *ape* and *eve* the long vowel sound is the same thing as the vowel name. Ta-da, vowel names now become relevant! (And he's probably learned the other letter names along the way anyway.)

Building Three-Letter Words in Word Families

The first words your child sounds out by himself are usually short-vowel, phonetically regular words like *hat, hen, hit, hot,* and *hut* that sound out just the way your child expects them to. But how do you help him move smoothly from single letter sounds ("a," "buh," "cuh") to reading these complete words? By starting with the word *at* and building up from there.

You can start your child off with *it* or *ot* if you want, but *at* is best because it's easy to pronounce, it's a word in itself, and from it your child can build a lot more new words.

Good readers read words in chunks. They get to know common chunks like *at* and read them quickly without laboring over each single letter's sound. That's why teaching your child to read chunks like *at, an,* and *in* very early on is a terrific reading strategy.

In the following sections, I show you how to start your child off with the word *at* and from it build the *at* word family *(at, sat, fat, mat,* and *bat)*. Then I give you a few more word families for extra practice.

A *word family* is a group of words that follow a spelling and sound pattern. Using word families early on is a great idea because it's easier for your child to recall a group of words that share a pattern than it is for him to recall each word separately and without the pattern-cue. There are plenty of families (like *fight, light, tight,* and *sight; round, sound, pound,* and *found*) for him to learn.

Putting together "at"

The best way for your dyslexic child to read *at* is to physically discover for himself, by sliding letter cards (or tiles) together, how *a* and *t* can be joined. Find a quiet time to do the activity that I give next and spend a few minutes on it until your child feels comfortable with *at.*

In the following game, by sliding *a* and saying its name, and then sliding on *t* and saying its name, your child is doing a multisensory activity. I talk at length about multisensory learning in Chapter 14.

Take an index card and cut it in half. Write *a* on one half of the card and *t* on the other (calling them "ah" and "tuh") and give them to your child. Now here's what to do:

1. **Have him tell you their sounds.**

2. **Ask him to put down the *a* (pronounced like in *apple*) and slide *tuh* next to it, saying each sound as he moves it.**

3. **Have him do this a few times until he hears the word *at* and gets the very core of reading — that letters represent the sounds that join together to make words.**

When you make the letter cards in this activity, use lowercase letters. In school, your child is taught that capitals are only for names and the beginnings of sentences, so you help him by sticking to those rules at home.

Moving on up with "bat," "cat," "fat," and more

After your child is well acquainted with *at,* he's ready to meet members of the whole *at* word family. The next activity shows you how to have your child build the eight words — *bat, cat, fat, hat, mat, pat, rat,* and *sat* — by joining letters onto *at.*

Have *at* written on one whole index card. Cut four other index cards in half and write the single letters *b, c, f, h, m, p, r,* and *s,* one on each of the eight halves of card. Give all the cards to your child and ask him to put *at* down in front of him. Have him slide each single letter in front of *at* and read the words he makes.

Now is a great time to have your child make a set of flashcards. Have him write each of the *at* words *(bat, cat, fat, hat, mat, pat, rat,* and *sat)* on a separate index card and read them to defenseless family members and friends.

Running through additional word families

In Table 12-1 you get more word families, so your child can practice the same activities he just did in the previous sections (with *at* words) on a whole new bunch of words. Show your child the chunks *an, ap, ug, in,* and *ip* and then let him read you the words. He'll start feeling like this reading thing isn't so bad after all!

Table 12-1		First Word Families		
an	*ap*	*ug*	*in*	*ip*
an	cap	bug	bin	dip
ban	gap	dug	din	hip
can	lap	hug	fin	lip
fan	map	jug	in	nip
man	nap	mug	pin	rip
pan	rap	rug	tin	sip
ran	sap	tug	win	tip
tan	tap			zip
van				

Mixing It Up with Blended Consonants

After your child reads words like *cat* and *fat,* he's ready to read consonant blends like *st, str,* and *bl* in phonetically regular words like *stand, strap,* and *blink.*

The term *blending* describes how your child blends letters (like *a* and *t*) together to read whole words (like *at*), but the consonant blends I'm talking about here are chunks of two or three consonants, like *st* and *str.*

In the following sections, I cover blended consonants at the start and at the end of words.

Blends at the beginning

By the time your child has mastered the easier words in Table 12-1 he's probably eager to flex his newly developing reading muscles. Table 12-2 gives him words that look impressive but are in fact fairly easy to sound out. Initially, your child needs to say and hear the blend in the first column, but that done, he can whiz through the words in the second column. Your child may want to read the table in two or three separate sessions, but if not, he can blast through them all in one go. Whichever of these options you take, you need to do plenty of re-reads. An easy routine to use for this and other tables is to choose whether to use all the table or just a few rows and then have your child do the following:

✔ Read out the table words top to bottom.

✔ Read out the table words bottom to top.

✔ Read out random words as you point to them.

✔ Find words that you call out.

✔ Write ten words that you dictate.

Words like *draft, crisp,* and *trend* can be particularly challenging for your child at first because they have double blends (at the beginning *and* end). You may want to write them out larger for your child so he can underline each blend before tackling them.

Table 12-2	Easy Words with Blends
Blend	*Examples*
bl	black, blast, blimp, blink, blocks, blot
br	Brad, brag, brick, bring
cl	clamp, clap, clasp, cliff, clip, clock
cr	crab, craft, crest, crisp, crust
dr	draft, drink, drop, drum
fl	flag, flan, flash, flick, flip, flood

(continued)

Table 12-2 *(continued)*

Blend	Examples
fr	Fred, fresh, frog, frost, fry
gl	glad, glen, gloss
gr	grand, grass, grin, grip, grub
pl	plan, plant, plod, plug
pr	prick, print, prod
sk	sketch, skin, skip, skunk
sl	slant, slim, slip
sm	smack, smell
sn	snap, snip
sp	spank, spell, spill, spin
spl	splash, split
spr	spring, sprint
st	stack, stand, stand, stem, stink, stop
str	string, strip
sw	swell, swill, swim, swing
tr	trap, trend, trip
tw	twig, twin, twist

Blends at the end

Your child can get to grips with blends at the ends of words in the same ways that he can master blends at the beginning, except that a couple of ending blends may need special attention. Walk your child through Table 12-3, taking extra care over words ending in *nk* and *ng*. Sometimes these blends can be harder to distinguish than other blends. If your child needs extra practice, grab paper or a whiteboard and have him write the relevant words, underlining the blends. Reading these words is easier for him when tricky letters are highlighted so he can give them extra thought.

Table 12-3	Easy Words with Blends on the End
Blend	***Examples***
ct	fact, insect, inspect, pact
lk	bulk, milk, silk, sulk
mp	bump, cramp, hump, lump, jump, lamp, limp, stamp, stump
nd	band, bend, end, fend, hand, land, lend, pond, stand, spend, trend
ng	bang, bring, clang, fling, hang, long, lung, ring, sing, song, sting, tang, wing
nk	blink, bunk, chunk, mink, sink, skunk, think, trunk, wink
nt	bent, blunt, sent, spent, tent
sk	ask, mask, risk, task, tusk
st	best, cost, dust, frost, last, list, mast, mist, nest, past, pest, test, trust

Delving into Digraphs

Earlier in this chapter I tell you that your child needs to know chunks of speech sounds and how those chunks are written, or in other words, phonics. I say that he needs to move forward systematically so that he first learns simple words like *hat* and then harder words like *last*.

But here's the thing. When your child looks at books, he finds that all sorts of easy and hard words are in there together. How do you help him deal with that? Pretty much at the same time as you lead him from easy to harder word families, you show him (a few at a time) new sounds, like *ch, sh,* and *th*. These sounds are called *digraphs*.

A *digraph* is a sound/spelling chunk made by two letters that join to make their own distinctive sound (that's not like their two individual sounds blended together). The consonant digraphs are *ch, sh, th,* and *ph,* and *wh* can be considered a digraph, too.

In Table 12-4 is a bunch of easy *ch, sh,* and *th* words for you to launch your child straight into. Your child needs to be comfortable with *ph* and *wh,* but I focus on the other consonant digraphs *(ch, sh,* and *th)* because *ch, sh,* and *th* words are much more common.

Move through the table, having your child read and say the words, and write some as you dictate them; then for variety, read out the next quiz questions and ask your child to write the answers.

1. **A turtle and a crab both have this (shell)**
2. **A board game with a castle, a queen, and a knight in it (chess)**
3. **Another name for a talk (chat)**
4. **The bottom front part of your leg (shin)**
5. **A baby chicken (chick)**
6. **The part of your face below your mouth (chin)**
7. **Opposite of fat (thin)**
8. **A large boat (ship)**
9. **Opposite of "this" (that)**
10. **The short word for "chimpanzee"**

Table 12-4	Words with *ch*, *sh*, and *th*	
ch	*sh*	*th*
champ	shack	than
chap	shall	thank
chat	shelf	that
check	shell	them
chess	shift	then
chest	shin	theft
chick	ship	thick
chill	shock	thin
chimp	shot	thing
chin		think
chip		this
chomp		thrash
chop		thrill
chum		thrush
chunk		thump

You may want to tell your child that *th* has two sounds: one for words like *thank* and *thin* and one for words like *this* and *then*.

A number of *sight words* (words that are so common that they should be learned to a level of automatic recognition) include digraphs and may be a little tricky for your dyslexic child to sound out. However, it's really worth it for your child to memorize sight words because they're used so often in the English language. For tips on committing sight words to memory, see Chapter 11.

Mastering Tricky Vowel Sounds

Vowels represent two sounds, called short and long sounds, and can join together with other letters to make a few more sounds besides. *Short vowel sounds* are the vowel sounds you hear in *apple, egg, ink, octopus,* and *up; long vowel sounds* are the sounds you hear in *ape, eve, ice, open,* and *uniform.* Long vowel sounds are also the sounds you hear when you say the letter names.

In this section I show you the different ways that long vowels are written and the simple rules that help your child recognize them. I show you how the letter *y* can take the place of a vowel in words like *my* and *by.* Finally I show you how vowels can appear next to other letters to make special new sounds that can trip up a dyslexic child if he's not primed to watch out for them.

Opening up to long vowels

Your child needs to hear the different vowel sounds in words like *met* and *meet* so she can read and spell them for herself. A gazillion words (like *meet, pain, road,* and *cute*) have long vowel sounds in them, but luckily two easy phonics rules apply to most of these.

In Chapter 11, I give you the complete ins and outs of the *Bossy e* and when-two-vowels-go-walking rules, but here's a lightning summary:

✔ To help your child read and spell words such as *bake, like,* and *cute,* show him the *Bossy e* rule. When *Bossy e* sits on the end of short words, such as *cut,* or word chunks, such as *bak,* it bosses the vowel into making its long sound. *Cut* becomes *cute,* and *bak* becomes *bake.*

✔ To help your child read and spell words like *meet, road,* and *rain,* show him the rule that says "when two vowels go walking, the first one does the talking." When he sees the vowel pairs *ee, ea, oa,* and *ai,* they nearly always work as a partnership in which the first vowel shouts its name while the second stays silent.

Hearing "y" sound like a vowel

One special letter you'll want to point out to your child is *y*. In words such as *yellow* and *yam*, *y* makes its simple alphabet sound, but in words such as *merry, mystery,* and *my,* it makes the sounds usually made by long *e*, and short and long *i*.

The tables in the following sections give you easy words for practicing the *y* sounds. Have your child read through them, saying, hearing, and seeing how *y* can make long and short *e* and *i* sounds.

When "y" acts like a long "e"

On the ends of words with more than one syllable, y usually sounds like long *e*. Table 12-5 gives example words that your child can easily read so that this long e pattern becomes clear. Have your child highlight the *y* in each word, saying the "ee" sound as he goes, and then have him mark and say other long vowels, in *creepy, bravely, breezily,* and *really.* Lastly, have him read out the words, choosing his own order. He can read columns or rows until he has read all 40 words or he can save some words for another time.

Your dyslexic child can easily become tired or disheartened, so gauge the amount of work he does, and the time he takes, to make sure he stays motivated and on track. It's better to have your dyslexic child work slowly on tasks and repeat them so he gets a firm understanding than it is to let him move forward more quickly but less surely. He needs frequent short breaks, too, so he can concentrate better after he's refreshed (just like the rest of us).

Table 12-5		*y* Sounding Like Long *e*		
baby	chilly	funny	lumpy	simply
berry	copy	happy	marry	skinny
body	creepy	helpfully	merry	sorry
bravely	dizzy	holly	milky	spotty
breezily	empty	hurry	nanny	sunny
bumpy	enemy	jolly	plenty	ugly
bunny	entry	lanky	really	very
cherry	family	lucky	silly	windy

When "y" acts like a short "i"

The letter *y* turns up in the middle (or near the middle) of quite a few words. Tell your child to watch out for this. It means that an *i* sound, short or long but more often short, is being made. The best way for your child to work out what sound *y* is making is to try out the short *i* sound first. Table 12-6 gives you some words to get started on. Have your child mark each *y* in the words and then figure out whether the *y* is on the end (in which case a long "ee" sound is made), or in the middle (in which case the sound is short or long *i*).

When *y* comes after *c* or *g,* it makes those letters make their soft ("ss" and "juh") sounds.

Table 12-6	*y* Sounding Like Short *i*	
crypt	gypsy	symbol
cryptic	hymn	system
cymbal	mystery	
gymnastics	myth	

When "y" acts like a long "i"

In a few short one-syllable words, *y,* when it's the last letter in the word, sounds like long *i*. Table 12-7 gives you this small group of fairly common words so your child can whiz through them a few times and mentally file them under "got it!"

Table 12-7	*y* Sounding Like Long *i*	
by	cry	dry
fly	fry	my
pry	shy	sky
sly	try	why

Teaching your child spelling patterns can be an ongoing process. If your child gets quickly on top of the words in Table 12-7, you may want to show him another bunch of words that have the same *"y acting like long i"* pattern, only with the *y* in the middle (not the end) of the word. Longer words like *style, type,* and *python* fit into this group, and so do the words *cycle* and *cyclone*. The rule for "cy" words is that when *c* is followed by *y,* it makes its soft sound ("s"), while the *y* can make either a long *i* sound (like in *cyclist*) or a short *i* sound (like in *cyst*). How should your child remember words like *style, type,* and *python?* By taking a good look at them, saying them out loud, and jotting them down a few times. There are no hard and fast rules for spelling them, but bunching them together (in the *"y* acting as short or long *i"* word family) helps.

A strategy that can help your child remember a group of words like *style, type,* and *python* is to keep a personal dictionary. Your child writes groups of words in it, adding new group members (like *dynamite, typhoon,* and *hype*) as he comes across them.

Surveying schwa vowels

When your child says words like *ago* and *around,* he pronounces the first *a* as "uh." This "uh" sound is called a *schwa,* and you need to tell your child about it so that he doesn't spell the words *ugo* and *uround.* You don't have to mention the technical schwa stuff though; just say that sometimes the letter *a* has an indistinct "uh" sound.

Schwa is technically an unstressed vowel sound. It's easiest to hear in the vowel *a* (like in *ago, again, above,* and *about*), but other vowels can be schwa sounds, too (like the *o* in *melon*). Because this is a tricky concept, and an even trickier thing to hear, especially because your dialect affects your pronunciation (and stressing) of vowels, I don't go into it too deeply. Your child learns about schwa better in context (and without mention of the technical term *schwa*) than in a theoretical explanation.

The best way for your child to read these fuzzy sounds is to pronounce them phonetically and then correct himself ("a-go," uh-oh, that's really "uhgo"). One good tip though: The names of many countries end with a schwa, including Argentina, Australia, Austria, Canada, China, Cuba, Uganda, and Venezuela. Names of many U.S. states end with a schwa, too, including Arizona, California, Georgia, and Pennsylvania.

Singling out sound-alike chunks featuring vowels

Reading teachers show your child plenty of sound/spelling chunks. In the following sections, I give you spelling chunks that any teacher worth his salt shows to his students so they can push forward with harder, livelier text. Here you get the tricky, but well-worth-knowing, chunks *oy/oi, ow/ou,* and *aw/au.* Take your time showing them to your child and coming up with words of your own that follow each spelling pattern.

Practice one spelling (like *oy*) of each sound with your child before telling him about the second spelling (like *oi*). He needs a lot of exposure to one spelling before he can comfortably assimilate the other spelling or he gets overwhelmed.

The best way to turn your child off reading and make him think he'll never get this nut cracked is to overload him. Anytime you show him a new spelling chunk, like *oy*, take a slow and sure approach. Have him read, say, and write plenty of words that fit the spelling pattern, such as *boy, toy, coy, joy,* and *soy.* Then when he's really sure of that spelling, slowly introduce a new one, like *oi.*

Oy and oi

In Table 12-8, I give you some *oy* and *oi* words for your child to sink his teeth into. Make a copy and have your child highlight (or circle or underline) the *oy* or *oi* part of each word, saying the sound as he goes. Point out that *oy* shows up on the ends of words (like in *toy*) or at the end of the first syllable of a word (like in *royal*), whereas *oi* features at the beginning or middle of words (like in *oil* and *soil*). After your child has marked the words and is comfortable with the positioning of the two different spellings, have him read the words in the table out loud to you and then dictate them for him to write. Warn him of other special spelling features if you want, like the *s* in noise (sounds like *z* but is spelled with *s*), the two *n*'s in annoy and the *al* in *royal* (it sounds like it could be *al* or *le,* or even another combination a dyslexic might use, like *el, ul,* or *il*).

Table 12-8	*oy* and *oi* Words
oy	*oi*
annoy	boil
boy	moist
employ	noise
joy	oil
Roy	soil
royal	spoil
toy	toil

Ow and ou

The *ou* sound is my favorite. Show it to your child by explaining that whenever he sees either *ow,* like in *cow,* or *ou,* like in *out,* he needs to make the sound he would make if you pinched him. After that, have him highlight the digraphs *(ow* and *ou)* in Table 12-9 while he makes the sound, and then have him read the words to you. Then he can write a few you dictate to him. Ways to prompt him along include the following:

- ✔ Give him several soft and timely pinches when he reads *ow* and *ou!*

- ✔ Have him jot down the two versions of a word (like *brown* and *broun*) when he's spelling them, to see if he can spot the right one.

- ✔ Tell him which digraph to use when he's struggling to spell a word.

- ✔ Have him draw his own two-column table and randomly dictate words from Table 12-9 for him to fit into it.

Table 12-9	*ow* and *ou* Words
ow	*ou*
bow	around
brown	bound
cow	cloud
crown	found
down	house
drown	loud
frown	mound
growl	mouse
how	noun
now	pound
scowl	proud
sow	round
town	sound

Aw and au

The digraphs *aw* and *au* are pretty tricky, so here's what you can do to show them to your child in a slow and sure way:

- ✔ Show your child the *aw* spellings first. He's seen the word *saw* plenty of times, so start with that. Have him write and say the word *saw* five times. Now ask him to change the *s* in *saw* to an *l*.

- ✔ Have him change the *s* in *saw* to *dr.*

- ✔ Have him write the three words *saw, law,* and *draw.*

- When he's happy with *saw, law,* and *draw,* show him the words in the *aw* column of Table 12-10.

- Have him highlight the *aw* digraph in each word and then read the words to you, top to bottom, bottom to top, and then randomly as you point a pencil at a few words.

- Have him write the *aw* words as you dictate them.

- When your child has a firm understanding of *aw,* you can drop the bombshell about there being another *aw* sound, spelled *au,* and repeat the same procedure.

Table 12-10	*aw* and *au* **Words**
aw	*au*
awning	applaud
caw	auto
claw	author
crawl	fraud
dawn	haul
draw	laundry
fawn	maul
jaw	sauce
law	taut
lawn	
prawn	
saw	
straw	
yawn	

When your child comes across spellings like *aunty* that have a different *au* sound, just explain that words often fall outside a rule. It doesn't mean that the rule isn't useful; it's just that there are some outsiders or rule breakers they'll have to get to know eventually.

Partnering vowels with "r"

If you've been skimming through these phonics tips up until now, this may be a good time to slow down. Your child needs a firm grip on the vowel + *r* spelling that I tell you about here because it crops up often and its sound is never the straightforward blended sound of its two letters.

Quickly tell your child that a vowel + *r* spelling makes its own new sound and then have him look at Table 12-11. Ask him to cover the first two columns and look only at the last three columns, *er, ir,* and *ur*. When he reads a few words (you can help him do this) from each column, what does he notice? Be sure to have your child discover, or point out to him, that *er, ir,* and *ur* all sound the same. Once your child appreciates the sound that these three digraphs make, have him highlight the digraphs in each word, sounding them out as he goes, and then read the words to you (top to bottom and so on like you did in the previous sections). Have your child write the words out from your dictation. If he gets stuck writing a word, have him jot down the possibilities (like *her, hir,* or *hur*) to see whether he can spot the right-looking spelling. If he can't see the right one, tell him the spelling and have him jot it down a few more times.

Table 12-11		The Five Vowels + *r*		
or	*ar*	*er*	*ir*	*ur*
corn	art	her	bird	burn
for	barn	herd	dirt	curl
fork	car	nerve	firm	curse
horse	dart	perch	first	hurl
north	far	person	flirt	hurt
or	farm	serve	girl	nurse
storm	hard	stern	shirt	purse
torn	large		sir	surf
worn	marsh		stir	turn
	star		third	

When you dictate a few words to your child, doing so helps him consolidate what he's already practiced. Your dyslexic child needs to read, say, and write words he's already gone over, so give him as much repetition as you can, within reasonable boundaries of bribery and coercion!

After your child feels happy with *er, ir,* and *ur* words, you can show him the *or* and *ar* columns of Table 12-11. Go through the reading, marking, and writing routine that you did with the other columns and then, if you're both feeling creative and energetic, have your child jot all the words down on small pieces of paper and spread them, face down, in front of him. Can he turn over and read out loud all of the words? Can he spell each one if he turns each card over, takes a quick peek, and then jots it down? Can he spell each one if you dictate it and he doesn't get to take a take a helpful peek? When your child is done with the word cards, have him keep them. After a few days, have him run through a shortened version of these activities to see how well he recalls all the words. Keep any words that slipped through the net. Pin them on a wall and have your child read them to you and jot them down a few more times over the next week.

Lopping vowels off the ends of words

Like many children, your dyslexic child may have trouble reading and spelling words like *riding*. Should he write *rideing* or *riding,* and how can he remember in future?

The easy rule for sorting out *ing* words is drop the *e* (pronounced "ee") when you add *i-n-g* (pronounced "eye-en-gee"). Want practice with it? Check out Table 12-12.

Terrific tips for handling any difficult words

As soon as your child starts to read, he comes across words like *they* and *was* that don't sound out regularly. How can you help him with these kinds of words? Where do you start? In addition to the activities I provide in the rest of this chapter, here are some general strategies that can make those words seem easier.

✔ Notice the shape of the word. Draw an outline around the word to show tall and short letters and the length of the whole word.

✔ Circle, or mark with a highlighter pen, the tricky parts of words. In *words,* for example, the *or* is tricky (because it sounds like "er").

✔ Have your child tape words onto walls where he will often see them. Bathrooms and bedrooms are good.

✔ Run your child through the look, say, cover, write routine: He looks at the word he wants to learn, says it out loud, covers it over, and writes it from memory.

✔ Use the word envelope routine I describe in Chapter 11. Your child puts up to 10 words, each one written on a small piece of paper, in an envelope. Every day for a week he takes them out of the envelope and plays games that help him fix the words in his memory with them.

Show your child how the *e* gets dropped. Dictate the base words (the ones without the *ing* added on) for him to write down. If you need to revise the "Bossy e" rule that all these words follow, flip to Chapter 11. Have your child add the *ing* ending to his base words, saying the "Drop the *e* when you add *i-n-g*" rule as he goes.

Have your child verbalize what he's doing because sounding out or saying rules out loud is a helpful multisensory learning strategy. Seeing, saying, and writing, just about together, is a more effective way to learn than any of those three things done alone.

Table 12-12	Adding *i-n-g* to Words Ending with *e*
bake – baking	ride - riding
bite – biting	shake - shaking
drive – driving	skate - skating
fake – faking	slide - sliding
glide – gliding	smile - smiling
hide – hiding	take – taking
hike – hiking	time – timing
make – making	wave - waving

Bringing Consonants under Control

You need to show your child the quirky but common sounds that consonants can make when they get together with certain other consonants or vowels. Otherwise, stuff like the *z* sound that *s* makes on the end of *friends,* and the soft sounds that *c* and *g* can make, may throw him into confusion. In the following sections, I deal with those spellings and others that can be similarly troublesome.

Unmasking consonants in disguise

This is where I talk about innocent-looking letters that make sneaky little sounds. Here you take a look at *s* sounding like *z* in words like *dogs* and find out how to deal with the three sounds of *ed.* The ones you never even noticed until now!

When "s" sounds like "z"

A single letter you may want to alert your child to is *s*. In words like *friends, hands, loves,* and *dogs,* your child hears the sound of *z* but sees the letter *s*. A quick heads up from you may save him from feeling that words are put together pretty randomly.

In words like *foxes, horses,* and *boxes,* your child sees *es,* but actually hears a sort of "iz" sound.

When your dyslexic child comes across a word that doesn't follow the rule, have him consider it a rogue, pretty much an all-by-itself word, or see whether he can find a few other words like it and make it into a whole rogue word family. For example, take the word *friend*. It doesn't follow the usual *ie* pronunciation, like in *field, piece,* and *believe,* and there aren't several common words like it, so it's easiest to brand it as a loner renegade word to watch out for. A word like *love* however, is a renegade, but not a loner. Show your child that it breaks the usual "Bossy e" rule but does so in good company. Its word family includes the words *dove, glove,* and *above.*

When "ed" sounds like "t" or "duh"

If your child *hopped, skipped,* and *jumped,* he did three things ending with the "t" sound spelled as *ed.* Tell your child that the *ed* ending can sound like "ed" as in *chatted,* "duh" like in *smiled,* or "tuh" like in *hopped.* And so that he gets to see this for himself, have him read out loud the words in Table 12-13. As usual, writing down the words as you dictate them helps him fix the words in his mind, and reminding him to say the word as he writes it helps too.

Table 12-13	The Three Sounds of *ed*	
"ed" Sound	*"t" Sound*	*"duh" Sound*
batted	hopped	dreamed
chatted	jumped	planned
shifted	skipped	smiled
shouted	stripped	waved

Sounding out the softies

When your child learns that *c* and *g* make the soft sounds "see" and "jee," he may start switching between hard and soft sounds pretty erratically.

Here's a rule that can help your child. Briefly explain it and then have him read the words in Table 12-14 so he makes his own hands-on discovery. The rule is, "Soft *c* and *g* are followed by *i, y,* or *e,*" as in *city, cyst,* and *cent*.

Here are some general help-him-with-reading tips:

- ✔ **Break words into syllables.** It doesn't much matter whether your child puts his break in exactly the right spot as long as he hears the distinctly separate parts of a word. For example, the word *city* is made from the two syllables — ci-ty — but your child might choose to break it up into cit-y. The break that he puts for himself is probably the most useful to him because he remembers his own creation better than someone else's.

- ✔ **Highlight tricky parts.** In the word *peace,* for example, your child might highlight *ea* and/or *ce* (because *ea* and *ce* are next to each other, he might mark them in different colors, or circle one and underline the other).

- ✔ **Look for spelling rules,** like "Bossy e" and "When two vowels go walking, the first one does the talking," and in this case, of course, "Soft *c* and *g* are followed by *i, y,* or *e.*"

Here are some general help-him-with-writing tips:

- ✔ **Sound out the word** (out loud, not just in your head), from beginning to end, and in syllables if your word has more than one syllable.

- ✔ **Jot down possible spellings of a sound** (like *ase, ayse, ayce,* or *ace*) before you commit to one.

- ✔ **Encourage your child to jot down the spelling possibilities he thinks of** even if you know some of them are impossible. His own discoveries stick better in his mind than your instructions, and the more spelling discoveries he makes, the better he gets at making future spelling guesses.

- ✔ **Exaggerate pronunciation if it helps.** For example, you can pronounce the word *bandage* as "band-age," not the usual "band-ige" of normal people-talk.

- ✔ **Listen for short and long vowel sounds** so you can use spelling rules ("Bossy e" and "When two vowels go walking the first one does the talking").

Table 12-14	Soft *c* and *g*
Soft *c*	Soft *g*
ace	age
cell	average
cent	bandage

Soft *c*	Soft *g*
center	bulge
chance	cabbage
city	cage
dance	gem
dice	general
face	gin
fancy	gym
fence	hostage
France	huge
glance	luggage
grace	page
ice	plunge
lace	rage
lice	stage
mice	wage
nice	
pace	
peace	
place	
price	
prince	
race	
rice	
since	
slice	
space	
twice	
wince	

Spotting the silent types

Silent letters are a challenge for just about everyone, but for your dyslexic child, they may be especially tricky. To help your child remember where these letters pop up, have him read through Table 12-15 and try these strategies:

- ✔ Get the right spelling of these words by pronouncing the silent letters. (For example, it's okay for your child to say "k-nife" every time he spells *knife,* until after plenty of this overpronouncing, he remembers the spelling *without* the weird talk!)

- ✔ Remember words with silent letters like *balm, calm,* and *palm* in their families (see the section "Building Three-Letter Words in Word Families," earlier in this chapter, for details about this concept).

- ✔ Devise mnemonics (such as "**I** g**e**t **h**ot **t**oes") for remembering letter combinations like *ight.*

- ✔ Sound out the parts of words that can be sounded out and highlight other silent (or otherwise tricky) parts so you remember the look of them.

Table 12-15				Silent Letters		
k	*b*	*l*	*gh*	*w*	*t*	*g*
knack	bomb	balm	blight	wrap	bristle	align
knead	climb	calm	bought	wreath	bustle	campaign
knee	comb	could	bright	wreck	castle	champagne
kneel	crumb	embalm	brought	wren	gristle	diaphragm
knew	debt	folk	delight	wrench	hustle	design
knick	doubt	palm	fight	wrestle	rustle	sign
knife	lamb	should	flight	wretch	thistle	resign
knight	limb	would	fought	wriggle	whistle	
knit	plumber	yolk	fright	wring		
knob	thumb		high	wrinkle		
knock	tomb		light	wrist		
knoll	womb		might	write		
knot			night	writhe		

k	b	l	gh	w	t	g
know			ought	wrong		
knowledge			plight			
knuckle			right			
			sight			
			slight			
			sought			
			thigh			
			thought			
			tight			
			light			

Doubling up

When I was a child, I had a lot of trouble spelling *written* and *writing*. Should I use one *t* or two? Then I learned the rule that I'm about to give you now (and I got a computer spell checker for all the other words I can't spell!).

Here's the rule that helps me with *written* and *writing* and can help your child with words like *pinned* and *pined*, *hopped* and *hoped*, *bitten* and *biting*. When your child reads or writes a short word with an ending added onto it (like *written* and *bitten*), the rule is "double the letter to keep the vowel short." The double letter in words like *pinned* and *hopped* prevents you from mistakenly musing about things you *pined* and *hoped* for (like sweethearts or chocolate).

Make a copy of the words in Table 12-16 and have your child read them out loud to you. Let him use his pen to identify the double letters, and after he's marked them all, dictate several for him to write. Have him say each word out loud as he writes it so he hears that short sound.

The "double the letter to keep the vowel short" rule works on short words like *hop* and longer words like *drip* that have a blend (in this case *dr*) at the front. But if there's a blend at the end of a short word (like in *sing*), forget this rule. It doesn't work on blend-at-the-end words or on blend-on-both-ends words, like *stamp*.

Table 12-16	Adding *ing* and *ed* to Short Words
Base Word	*"ing" or "ed" Added*
clap	clapping, clapped
dot	dotting, dotted
drip	dripping, dripped
drop	dropping, dropped
flip	flipping, flipped
flop	flopping, flopped
hop	hopping, hopped
hug	hugging, hugged
jot	jotting, jotted
mop	mopping, mopped
nod	nodding, nodded
prod	prodding, prodded
rob	robbing, robbed
rub	rubbing, rubbed
skip	skipping, skipped
slip	slipping, slipped
slop	slopping, slopped
sob	sobbing, sobbed
spot	spotting, spotted
step	stepping, stepped
stop	stopping, stopped
top	topping, topped
trot	trotting, trotted

Chapter 13

Sprinting Ahead with Reading Basics and Practice

*W*hen you read out loud to your child, she's a picture of happiness, but when you ask her to read out loud to you, she dissolves into tears. That's the way it is for kids who have dyslexia. This chapter shows you what your child must learn in order to be a good reader, how you can help her get those skills under her belt with a reading routine, and which reading strategies really work. I also show you how to gently but effectively handle your child's reading errors and difficulties.

See Jane Read: Looking at Reading Fundamentals

You can read an awful lot of theory about how kids learn to read if you want to, or you can take it from me (someone who has read a stack of theory and spent over 20 years helping kids read): In order to read, your child needs to do the following:

✔ Automatically recognize the most common words, or *sight words*, like *the, was,* and *they* (because these words crop up so often).

✔ Be able to sound out or have phonics under control. "But the English language is so irregular," I hear you say. Ah yes, some words definitely defy sounding out, but more than half, and some people say almost all, can be sounded out as long as you know which letters, and clusters of letters, make which sounds. *Phonics* means matching written letters, and groups of letters, to their corresponding sounds.

✔ Get a lot of reading practice by having someone (that's you!) help her read books that are at the right level for her. (Too hard is overwhelming, and too easy is dull.) This reading practice shows your child that all the work she does on sight words and phonics leads to a great end, gives her on-the-job practice of sight words and phonics (rather than learning through isolated practice tasks), and improves her comprehension (the fancy word for understanding). The more reading she does, the more familiar she becomes with typical plot elements, style, and grammar, and if she talks text over with you, even better.

An acronym I use to remember these three reading essentials is SPRint. Help your child regularly and systematically with the following:

✔ Sight words

✔ Phonics

✔ Reading practice

If you do, you'll see her SPRint forward! And that, in a nutshell, is what you need to know about how basic word reading works. I could talk about grammar, tenses, and punctuation if you like, but I'm guessing that if you wanted that extra jazz, you'd have picked up a book about English usage.

In the rest of this chapter, I discuss the reading (or R) part of SPRint. Before that, though, I give you the basics on sight words, a lightning rundown of sounding out, and a quick explanation of what "comprehension" means in the following sections.

Being quick to recognize sight words

Your dyslexic child won't be able to read fluently without having instant or "sight" recognition of sight words because these words are so common that 220 of them comprise about 70 percent of all text. Did I just say "all text"? That's right. Pick up a regular book, comic, or flyer, and you see sight words all through it.

In Chapter 11, I give you the list of 220 sight words and a bunch of nifty ways to help your child get the instant recognition she needs.

Feeling good about phonics

When your child learns phonics, she learns how letters and bunches of letters represent the sounds inside words. She starts off by learning single letter sounds, like "a" (as in "apple"), "buh," and "cuh"; progresses to sounds like "st," "cl," and "ch"; and much farther down the line, learns about tricky sounds like "ough." Particularly for struggling dyslexic readers, mastery of phonics is, well, huge!

Most people use the words *phonetic, phonological,* and *phonemic* interchangeably to mean sounding out. You may encounter the odd person (and you can interpret "odd" any way you like here) who tells you I'm oversimplifying, but we could both be here a long and fairly boring time if I got into the fine distinctions.

Phonics means matching written letters, and groups of letters, to their corresponding sounds. It's been around a long time, and teachers know how to do it well. They know that structured and sequential phonics instruction is best and that learning letter-sound associations is easier when you group them in word families or bunches of words that all have the same chunk of sound in them.

In practical terms you need to teach your child the following things, in roughly this order:

- ✔ Each single letter represents a sound and sometimes more than one sound.
- ✔ Vowels always represent at least two sounds (usually called short and long sounds).
- ✔ Every word has a vowel, but *y* can take the place of a vowel and be a pretend vowel (like in *my* and *by*).
- ✔ You need to know all the common sound-chunks, like "ch," "ea," and "ow."
- ✔ The best way to remember sound-chunks is to put them into word families, like *pain, rain, drain,* and *brain.*

Check out Chapter 12 for more details on dealing with phonics.

Understanding about comprehension

If you worry that your child reads and then has no idea what she's just read, this section, all about comprehension, is for you.

Comprehension means understanding. If your child comprehends something, she gets it. Whatever she reads, she gets the point and understands who did what and why. If she doesn't have good comprehension, she just doesn't get it, can't remember who did what, and hasn't a hope of fathoming why.

Things that cause or signify lack of comprehension include the following:

✔ Your child reads so slowly that she loses the point along the way. By the time she gets to the end of the text, she's forgotten what the beginning was.

✔ Your child makes so many mistakes that the meaning of the text is muddled or lost on her.

✔ Your child doesn't care what the text says. It's boring.

✔ Your child has trouble remembering names and keeping a sequence of events in its right order.

✔ Your child doesn't know some of the vocabulary in the text. She may have missed or struggled with so much reading in class that she never got the chance to read and reread new vocabulary.

✔ Your child misunderstands the inferences and unstated parts of a text. She grasps only the concrete, openly stated parts, so things like implied jealousy, love, or scheming are lost on her.

You can take the following steps to improve your child's reading comprehension:

✔ Bring your child's recognition of sight words and phonics skills up to par so she reads more fluently. (I cover this in Chapters 11 and 12.)

✔ Listen to your child read manageable and fun text often.

✔ Help your child figure out words by starting at the beginning and moving forward, chunk by chunk. Children often misread words because they focus on just one chunk of a word and then guess the rest.

Technically the chunks I talk about are syllables, digraphs, phonemes, and morphemes.

• A *syllable* is a word-chunk that has a vowel in it (or vowel equivalent like the *y* in the single-syllable word *my*).

• A *digraph* is two or more letters that together make a common word chunk, such as *ai, oa, ch,* and *ing.*

• A *phoneme* is the smallest unit of sound in a word, such that it can be just one letter, like in *c-a-t.*

• A *morpheme* is the minimum meaningful element in a word, so it includes suffixes like *tion* that make *act* mean something different from *action.*

There can be overlap with these classifications; for example, *action* is made both of two syllables and two morphemes. Your child gets to know all the chunks inside words, no matter what you call them, through saying, reading, and writing them a lot.

✔ Aim to read often. Let your child read material she wants to read, including comics and joke books, so that she reads more often and gets the practice she needs. It's better for your child to willingly read three easy books than for her to struggle through one harder book and become disheartened and angry. See the section "Choosing the right books," later in this chapter, for more about selecting great reading material.

✔ Teach your child to distinguish between main and secondary points in a text. To help her with this task, have her jot down words as she reads so she ends up with a list of words that roughly describes what she's reading.

✔ Encourage your child to draw diagrams of the book's plot and jot down the names of key characters.

✔ Read some of your child's homework to her (otherwise, she can't get through it all) and explain new vocabulary. Ask her to use new words in context so she remembers them. Older children who don't read as much as classmates can fall a long way behind with subject-specific vocabulary. I cover teen dyslexia issues in more detail in Chapter 16.

✔ Talk about what's happening in stories and fiction and ask your child questions about the plot. What's openly said and what's implied? What feelings, motives, and undercurrents can you detect? Could the reader face surprises up ahead?

In the Habit: Establishing a Happy Reading Routine

You should regularly read with your child. Did I forget that you have other obligations (such as meal preparation, a job, and a mammoth pile of laundry)? No, but the thing is, I'm compelled to drive you. I have to push the issue of reading with your child (every day, no rain checks) because right now, this very day, is the best time to help your child.

The sooner and more often you help your child read, the easier it is on both of you. Older kids and adults have more catching up to do because all through school they've missed years of reading. The sooner you help your child and the more help you give her, the better. I cover specific techniques that you can use in the next section.

Older kids and adults who are dyslexic can always learn to read. It takes a lot of time and effort, but the feeling of accomplishment is big, too! Don't be set back by feeling guilty that you didn't help your child sooner or never learned to read yourself; instead, establish a manageable routine of learning a repertoire of sight words and phonics and doing some daily reading. Reading out loud is a useful strategy for any age because the act of looking at words and saying them out loud helps you get the multisensory learning that works best. Find out more about multisensory methods in Chapter 14.

What kind of things can ease your way on the path to reading regularly with your child? Here are some practical tips to help your child enjoy reading and help you save time and energy (yours, that is — I won't be asking you to turn off the heat or lights).

✔ Choose books that your child wants rather than books you think she should read. Comics are fine, and so are joke books or any other kind of book with short blasts of print. Get plenty of easy books rather than one book that's too hard, which is likely to turn your child off. See the section "Choosing the right books," later in this chapter, to get started.

✔ Set a regular time for reading, ideally 20 minutes each day, and stick to it. Bedtime suits most families, but some early birds like to read at the breakfast table.

✔ If you occasionally miss out on a day of reading, it's okay, but don't let those times sneak up on you until you miss more sessions than you make.

✔ Have a record-keeping system. Your child likes to know how she's doing. Just like everyone else, she feels good when she knows she's making progress and has checked a few things off her list. Help her keep a record of the books she reads, something like the one in Figure 13-1.

The chart you use to record books read should include columns with:

• The name of the book

• Categories for bad, average, and good books — just mark the column that applies to a given book

• The date that your child finished the book

✔ Establish a reward system. A good reason for rewarding your child is that she's doing something she wasn't keen on in the first place, and another reason for rewarding her is that she likes rewards!

But maybe rewarding isn't for you. Older kids can be all rewarded-out, and besides, you may want to stick with intrinsic rewards. The fact that your child gets through those books can be reward in itself.

Whether you give extrinsic rewards (like extra TV, extra play, or a later bedtime on weekends) or not, always give your child your attention. A simple smile, hug, or "good job" sometimes may work better than all the other hoopla.

Book	Bad?	Average?	Good?	Date
Hop on Pop			▓▓▓	June 24
Fat Cat		▓▓▓		June 27
Happy Family			▓▓▓	June 30
Cat Chocolate				
Green Fingers				

Figure 13-1: A chart can help you reward your dyslexic child for finishing books.

 Another way to help encourage your child to look forward to reading as a pleasurable activity and want to make it part of her daily routine is to let her see that you and your spouse are avid readers. In that way, you model reading for your child, and she has even more incentive to head to the bookshelf.

Page after Page: Using Special Strategies for Reading Success

You want your child to read interesting and fun books early on so she can see what all the fuss is about and feels motivated to keep going. But even with the best intentions, many parents find great ways to switch their child right off reading! They ask their children to read books that are too hard for them or don't manage to get into a happy reading-out-loud routine. In the following sections, I show you how to select the best books for your child, and I provide you with some proven reading strategies.

 You can very easily turn your child off when it comes to reading with just a few impatient words at the wrong time. So no losing your patience, heavy sighing, or saying things like "You just saw that word already!" If you feel your patience being tested, take a break, change books (this one may be too hard), and refocus (remind yourself that everyone learns by making mistakes). See the section "Nice and Gentle: Handling Your Child's Difficulties with Kindness," later in this chapter, for more tips.

Your child may tell you that reading is boring, stupid, or just not for her. Don't believe her. Not everyone loves reading, of course, but everyone at least wants to be able to do it. It's normal for struggling dyslexic readers to pretend they don't want to read; otherwise, they'd have to admit that they can't read and that's too crushing. Let her whining wash over you, and persevere. With carefully chosen books, sensitivity, and commitment, you can help your child (no matter what age) make progress.

I'm not the only one who makes a big deal out of reading out loud. The 2002 "Teaching Children to Read Report" (U.S. government funded and involving years of study and heaps of experts) states that guided reading out loud is one of the most effective strategies you can use to help your child read better. And you don't get a much higher source than the government and all its experts!

Choosing the right books

To make sure that your child can read out loud to you smoothly and with just a few errors, you need to carefully choose the books she reads. She can choose her own books for browsing later on, but you need to select her first reading-all-by-herself books. To achieve the perfect choice, forget about levels and about titles with "beginner" in them (I see plenty of so-called beginner books with words that are too hard in them) and look instead for books that are phonetically controlled and/or pass the one-hand rule (which I explain later in this section).

Phonetically controlled books have titles like *Fat Cat* and *Jake and the Snake* and follow two guidelines:

- ✔ They are written with a phonetic rule in mind, like using short *a,* and use mostly words that follow that rule ("a fat cat sat on a mat").

- ✔ Other words that they use are either words your child learned in earlier books in the series or newly introduced words that the author lists in the front or back pages (only a few new words are introduced in each book).

With phonetically controlled books, you know what you're getting. You won't find words like "enough" and "furious" thrown in with "cat" and "fat," so you won't have to wonder what on earth to do about it. When reading these books, you show your child the new words (listed at the front or back), remind her about the phonetic rule (short *a*), and off you go. (Check out Chapter 12 for more about phonics.) Ta-da, your child can read the book pretty much all by herself, and everyone's happy.

My shelves are stocked with series of phonetically controlled books, and I wouldn't dream of helping a struggling reader without using them. They work. Even if you think to yourself that they're boring, your child won't think that way. She wants to read by herself, and these kinds of books do the trick.

Leveled books and books with controlled vocabulary aren't the same thing as phonetically controlled books.

✔ Leveling, or controlling the vocabulary in a book, means that a book is classified (usually as Level 1, 2, 3 or A, B, C) by degree of difficulty based on how many hard words are in it. The hard words are selected and counted by using one of several methods (like Reading Recovery or Guided Reading) that ask things like whether a word is easy to spell and whether its meaning is clear.

✔ Phonetically controlled books are classified by difficulty, too, but the classification is according to the phonological difficulty of the words in the book.

What this all means in practice is that a leveled or controlled vocabulary book can have mixed text in it with all kinds of spellings, as long as they're within the level. A phonetically controlled book sticks to a phonics rule or two, so its content is repetitive; for example, all the words may be from the *at* word family, with only two or three other words, like *the* and *was*.

Flip through the pages of a book before buying. The best books for beginners are phonetically controlled books that list new words that are hard to sound out (like *the*, *was*, and *who*) before or after the main text. You can walk your child through the list of new words and avoid nasty surprises in the middle of reading, and all other words sound out in a predictable way.

Your child's comfort level for reading any book is when only 5 percent of what she reads (5 words in every 100) poses a challenge. To find this just-right text, give your child a page of 100 words to read (or a few pages that together make up 100 words) and tell her to close one finger on the same hand every time she reaches a word she doesn't know. If she runs out of fingers on one hand before she finishes the words, the book is too hard. That's the "one-hand rule."

To find series of phonetically controlled books, head to your library or ask at school. If you want to buy, check out these series (roughly in order from easy to more advanced):

✔ **Bob Books:** Published by Scholastic. Small books in a box, 12 books per boxed set. There are three levels — A, B, and C — and more than one box set per level. Available everywhere in the United States and Canada. Find out more at www.bobbooks.com.

- ✔ **Primary Phonics:** Published by Educators Publishing Service. In this series, you get five sets of books with ten books per set. View and buy the books at www.epsbooks.com or phone 800-435-7728 or 617-547-6706.

- ✔ **The Alphabet Series:** Published by Educators Publishing Service. In this series, you get two volumes with eighteen books per set. View and buy the books at www.epsbooks.com or phone 800-435-7728 or 617-547-6706.

- ✔ **Fitzroy Readers:** Distributed by Fitzroy Programs. If you want something your child has never seen before (unless you live in Australia) and won't feel embarrassed using, look at this series. Written by teachers in an Australian alternative school, these books come in boxed sets and are easy to buy online. Check them out at www.fitzprog.com.au.

- ✔ **Read with Ladybird:** "Ladybird" makes a great book series, but my favorite is the Ladybird Learning to Read series. You get small hardback books with short stories (children often like these better than long stories) that are perfect after your child has easier books, like Level A Bob Books, under her belt and needs slightly harder books. Originally a British product (watch out for words like "mum" and "trousers," which means pants), you can now get these books online wherever you live. Go to www.penguin.com and then search. Book 1, Set 1 is "Happy Family" by Shirley Jackson.

- ✔ **Solo books:** To edge your child slowly forward from beginning books (like the Ladybird books), here's the perfect series. The Solo series contains 44 books, originally published by Scholastic Australia. To see the list of 44 titles, go to www.scholastic.com.au/schools/curriculum/ solo/booklist.asp and then find a description of the books and buy them at Amazon.com or ask at your local bookstore. Two books to start your search off are *What a Mess, Fang Fang!* by Sally Rippin and *Smart Dad* by Amanda Graham.

- ✔ **See More Readers:** Published by SeaStar Books. The books in this series, by author Seymour Simon, aren't phonetically controlled, but they're categorized by reading level, so stick to Level 1. The books feature science and nature themes and fantastic photos. You can get them in shops and online at www.amazon.com. Be sure to check out *Incredible Sharks*.

- ✔ **Reading Rainbow Readers:** Published by SeaStar Books. These books aren't phonetically controlled either, but they don't go overboard with tricky words. Each book has a theme and short stories by various authors. Titles include *Family Stories* and *Friendship Stories,* and they're available in bookstores and at www.amazon.com.

Don't make your child stick exclusively with phonetically controlled books that confine the text to sentences like "Dan can fan" — that's so boring. Let her pick plenty of her own books (about things like basketball, ocean life, and pets) for browsing. That way, she gets to have books she's really interested in (the whole point!), and as long as you have her read phonetically controlled books, too, it doesn't matter if the text is beyond her reading skills.

When your child has flipped through plenty of phonetically controlled reading books and is ready to move to harder text (but not too much harder), you may want to stock up on favorite, but fairly simple, book series. Finding books in a series is easier than searching randomly, so here are my suggestions for book series that appeal to nearly all kids:

- ✔ Captain Underpants by Dav Pilkey (published by Blue Sky Press). Available at all good bookstores.

- ✔ Magic Tree House by Mary Pope Osborne (published by Random House). Available at all good bookstores.

- ✔ The Secrets of Droon by Tony Abbott (published by Scholastic). Available at all good bookstores.

- ✔ Woodland Mysteries by various authors (published by the Wright Group). Get these books at www.wrightgroup.com (click on "Wright Group" and then "Chapter Books/Independent Reading").

For reading books for adult dyslexics, check out Avanti Books at www.avantibooks.com.

Reading to your child first

To prime your child (at any age) for reading a book, read it through to her first. This gives her the sense of the text so that, when she reads alone, she's better able to use contextual and grammatical cues to figure words out more easily.

- ✔ Contextual cues are indirect clues you get from diagrams, headings, and a general understanding of the topic. If, for example, you see the word "horse" in a heading and a diagram of a currycomb, you can guess that the text is about horse care.

- ✔ You get grammatical cues from understanding how words fit together in sentences. For example, if you read, "they wants to gets swimming," you know you've misread because the words don't flow together and the sentence is grammatically incorrect.

I cover these concepts in more detail in the section "Helping your child find contextual cues," later in this chapter.

Pairing up to read

If you leave your dyslexic child alone with a book and expect her to read it, you'll be disappointed. Her reading is slow and labored, so she gets no pleasure from it — only frustration. The solution is to read along with her. You can choose from a few great ways to do "paired reading," and in the next sections, I take you through them step by step.

Have your child read out loud to you regularly because it's one of the best ways to help her become more fluent. Psyche yourself up to do a good job of listening to her. She's a beginner, so she'll make mistakes and you have to gently help her through them. The most important thing that your beginning reader needs to get from reading out loud to you is the feeling that she's moving forward and making you happy.

Choral reading

Choral reading means reading out loud with your child, the same text at the same time. You read together, in unison, and your child gets to hear your voice, guiding and supporting, all the while. When she's not sure of a word she can listen to you. When she's reading smoothly without having to use your cues, she still has you right there joining in the fun. Because it's so easy to do, choral reading is especially good for re-engaging a child who's avoided reading for a long time. As you get in tune with one another, try reading very slightly after your child says the words. You get to hear her better, and she still gets to listen to your voice when she needs to.

A nice modification of choral reading, when you really get into the swing of it, is the tap-or-nudge routine. Decide upon a signal, like a tap or nudge, that your child gives you when she wants you to stop reading. She taps for you to stop reading and then taps again when she wants you to read again. The tap can be on your arm or on the table, and the nudge pretty much speaks for itself. Try it; after you get a rhythm going, it's easy. This modification gives your child more control, which in turn makes her a more confident reader.

Taking turns

Taking turns reading out loud together from the same book is a nice step up from choral reading (for when your child is a little more independent), but start small. If you tell your child to read a page to you, she may balk, so ask her to read just a sentence (or even a word) on each page to start with. Gradually ask her to read more and let her choose the sentence or paragraph she reads. If she's reluctant, don't get annoyed, but don't give up either. Make deals. You'll read an extra three pages if she reads three sentences per page.

As always, a terrific book does half the work for you. Your child soon gets hooked into the story (or science or mechanics) and wants to know what happens next, so she keeps reading.

Interrupted reading

Interrupted reading is a great way to take advantage of engrossing stories. If you want your child to try reading all by herself, read to her at bedtime and then stop reading at a crucial point in the story. Excuse yourself by saying you have to let the dog out, clean the kitchen, or tuck her sister in. Then graciously allow her a few more minutes of reading time on her own if she wants it (*if* she wants it — are you kidding me?). Usually she'll get several more pages under her belt.

For interrupted reading to work, you should be well into the book (so your child is completely familiar with the characters and plot), and your child should be feeling confident about reading.

Running through multiple readings

Reading a book several times makes your child faster and more fluent at reading it and, as a result, more confident to tackle new books. A lot of reading programs include repeated readings as one of their regular activities, and schools buy whole kits of books and charts designed especially for lessons in repeated reading.

The Read Naturally program is popular among resource teachers who are in charge of helping dyslexic students. Children read a story, listen to it on tape, practice reading it to themselves, and then read it again, timed this time. You can check out the program at www.readnaturally.com, where you can also find home products for parents.

You can easily do repeated reading at home without spending a lot of money. All you have to do is get a book that's not too hard for your child and have her read a small section of 100 words from it to you three to five times (whatever suits you both best) against a stopwatch. Draw a chart or graph to plot her progress (see Figure 13-2). Record the number of words read correctly (out of the 100) on one page of a book and the time she takes. She usually improves with each reading and gets even better on the next book excerpt. Read about ten successive excerpts like this between the other regular reading you do. Your child gets a quick boost in skill and confidence, and then before the routine gets boring, it's over. After a break of a few weeks, start up another ten-excerpt booster program if you want.

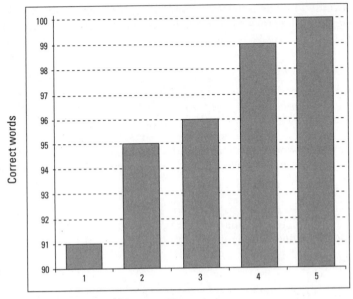

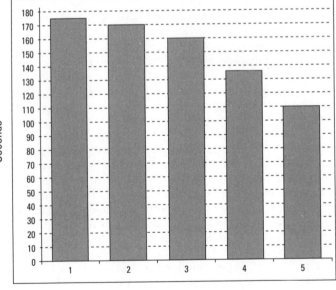

Figure 13-2:
Graphs can
help you
track your
child's
reading
progress.

If your child hates being timed, do without the timing part of this activity. You still get good results, and your child doesn't get stressed or overwhelmed.

Nice and Gentle: Handling Your Child's Difficulties with Kindness

When your child reads out loud to you and makes mistakes, which ones should you let pass and which should you correct? Do you simply tell her the word and move on, or should you have her sound out the words? Should you have her jot down the problem words to look at later? In the next sections I give you the answers.

Helping children who have dyslexia is all about modifying their environment and accommodating their needs rather than forcing things upon them. If your child is struggling with a book, find another book, empathize, and find ways (like taking breaks and reading out loud with her) to make things easier.

Knowing when to give a quick answer

When your child is reading out loud to you and gets stuck on the word "through," give her the answer straight away and continue reading. Hard words aren't worth battling. Your child will get to know them by reading them often, and meanwhile you can help by having her write them down on paper and read them back to you every day for several days. Post them on your walls too.

Don't interrupt the flow of your child's reading to try to get her to figure all the hard words out. If a word sounds out easily, like "problem," have her sound it out, but don't interrupt her every time she stumbles. She's likely to lose the drift if you do. When you let the reading flow, your child has the chance to understand the text and to feel that she is a reader.

To make headway with reading, your child must feel secure. To appreciate what it's like for someone with dyslexia, imagine getting a thing wrong time and time again. Imagine someone leaning over you and correcting you every few minutes. You can see why you must limit your interruptions.

Having your child figure a word out when the time is right

When you're reading with your child, here's when it's fine to take time out and have her figure out words she gets stuck on:

✔ The interruption doesn't make her forget what's going on in the text.

✔ You know she can sound out the word as long as you prompt her. If she's stuck on "remain," you can prompt her if she already learned the "ai" digraph. A digraph is a two-letter sound/spelling chunk. The two letters (like *ai*) make one sound.

✔ You haven't stopped to figure out words a dozen times already (in which case your child is close to burn-out).

✔ Your child is receptive. If she's had enough, tell her the words! You can always have her re-read the text later.

Knowing when to have your child figure out a word for herself is fairly easy, but what's the best way to tell her to do it? You want to avoid tears, furious exits (hers or yours), and damage to her fragile ego with a misplaced word or insensitive demand, but how exactly? Table 13-1 gives you a few do's and don'ts for earning your child's cooperation.

Table 13-1	Asking Your Child to Figure Out Words
Don't Say	*Do Say*
Look at it! You've already seen this word!	I think we just saw this word.
That's not right. Sound it out!	Take this word bit by bit.
That's wrong.	That doesn't sound quite right.
No, it can't say that!	Hmm, does that make sense?
Don't just guess!	Almost. Try that one more time.

Helping your child find contextual cues

Contextual cues are clues your child gets about the meaning of text and the words she may expect to find from subheadings, diagrams, and key words. Here are some suggestions on how you can be sure you're using all those helpful cues:

✔ **Cover blurb:** You may use the cover blurb to help you decide what books you want to read. Make sure your child knows that this material is a way to find out what's inside and doesn't skip it. (You and I think it's obvious that the blurb is there to be read first, but it may not be obvious to your child. Many things look different to your dyslexic child.)

✔ **Table of contents:** If your child is about to read a whole book, she should first check out the table of contents in the front of the book. She usually can get a rough idea of what's coming from the chapter headings.

✔ **Introduction:** If a book or document has an introduction, have your child read it. Dyslexics need as much of this kind of priming as they can get because reading text cold is so hard for them.

✔ **Subtitles:** If your child sees words like "boy" or "horse," she knows the text is more likely to be about a boy doing stuff with a horse than a woman getting robbed!

✔ **Pictures and diagrams:** Any illustrations your child can find in text are helpful to her. Help her get into the habit of glancing at these anytime they appear.

✔ **Key words:** When words repeat themselves in text, they're probably important. After your child has read factual text for the first time (she probably needs several readings), have her check for nouns that appear often. If she gets words like "reflection" and "refraction" in her mind before she reads through a page about light for the second time, she's already won half the comprehension battle.

✔ **Grammar:** Your child can use grammatical cues when she's in the middle of reading. If she reads something like "They was went to school," she can hear that she needs to read the sentence again. It doesn't sound right at all — it's grammatically incorrect — so she must have misread.

I don't get caught up in grammatical rules in this book, but I do have one point to make. If you make sure that your child talks properly (saying, for example, "we were" and not "we was"), you help with her reading. She knows which words go together and that, if she reads things like "they is" and "you'd going next," she needs to reread.

Using contextual cues is a secondary reading skill. If your child relies too much on contextual cues and forgets to sound out, her reading is all over the place.

Chapter 14

Taking Advantage of Multisensory Methods

Multisensory learning is big in the world of dyslexia. Some people have written whole books about it, so it's only right that I devote a chapter to it now. This chapter tells you, in a nutshell, what you must do to be multisensory, why it matters for dyslexics, and how to fit a good supply of multisensory tools in your house without having to remodel.

Bringing the Term "Multisensory" Down to Earth

Fancy terminology can sometimes be more trouble than it's worth. But the word "multisensory" is really very handy because once you feel comfortable using it, you get to cut out a long-winded explanation of what you mean. Without "multisensory," you'd have to say something like this:

> The stuff good teachers have always done. Putting hands-on practice into teaching and learning. Adding talk, movement, and touch to reading and writing. Being an active, engaging instructor rather than a person who drones on and on and then tells your child to copy things down.

The following sections describe multisensory teaching, explain how it's different from traditional teaching methods, and detail its importance to dyslexics.

Distinguishing multisensory teaching from traditional methods

Multisensory teaching (and learning) is pretty much everything that old-fashioned chalk-and-talk teaching isn't. What happens in chalk-and-talk teaching is simply that the teacher talks about a subject, writes information on the board, and asks kids to copy it. Every teacher does chalk-and-talk teaching sometimes (we're only human), but too much of it is bad news for dyslexics. Chalk-and-talk teaching requires students to mostly use just two senses, hearing (or auditory) and vision, and dyslexics happen to be conspicuously poor in both.

Dyslexics struggle with auditory memory or processing. They have trouble recalling words and how they're pronounced (saying things like "pasghetti" instead of "spaghetti") and don't hear parts of words well (was it a dairy farm or a dirty farm?). A dyslexic child may also be weak at *visual tracking* (following words one after the other along lines on a page) and *visual processing,* or *visual discrimination* (seeing the difference between different letters and letters facing in different ways). Check out Chapter 3 for more details on signs of dyslexia.

When you give your child tasks that use just his hearing and vision, without drawing upon his other senses, you put him at a disadvantage.

Teaching in a *multisensory* way means helping a child learn through the use of more than two of his senses. It especially means adding touch (the tactile sense) and movement (the kinetic sense) to his activities so that his brain has information that it reads better and so that he has more to hang onto. If you teach your child things in a multisensory way, he won't be merely sitting down copying words — he'll be doing things like making 3D words from modeling clay and acting out phrases. Adding multisensory teaching will feel less like a one-way exchange, from you to your child, and more like a cooperative. It should also be fun.

Researchers know that multisensory learning works because they've done studies that prove it. In rough terms, they know that people learn equally well by seeing or hearing a thing, they do a bit better when they talk a thing through, they do better still by doing a thing, and they learn best of all by seeing, hearing, saying, *and* doing that thing. So you can take away a couple of messages from the research:

✔ Creative play is really important because when your child plays, he does *all* this fancy learning quite naturally (and it's *so* cute when you see he is constructing and creating and happily talking to himself all the while too!).

✔ To maximize your dyslexic child's learning potential, ask him to see it, say it, hear it, and do it!

Multisensory learning was started by Dr. Samuel Orton and his colleagues back in the 1920s at a mobile mental health clinic in Iowa. Orton had children trace, copy, and write letters while saying their corresponding sounds and called this method "kinesthetic-tactile reinforcement of visual and auditory associations." Now his multisensory method is called the Orton-Gillingham method (Gillingham was Orton's colleague), and it's hugely popular among educators. Teachers can be specially trained in Orton-Gillingham methods, and Orton-Gillingham is mentioned in just about every place where people talk about how to address reading problems.

 The notion of visual, auditory, or kinesthetic learning styles is popular these days. Most people who know anything about dyslexia warn that even though you hear terms like "a kinesthetic learner" all the time, identifying an individual in this way is simplistic because people learn from all of their senses, especially in combo (also known as multisensory). That said, if you're interested in taking a free online test to see whether you have a dominant visual, auditory, or kinesthetic learning style, go to www.ldpride.net. The test is good for adults, too, and the idea is that if you know your dominant learning style, you can try to use it most but also get more practice in your weaker styles so you improve them, too.

Fitting together "multisensory" and "structured and sequential" teaching

Right now, multisensory learning is hot, so any reading instructor you talk to uses the word "multisensory" somewhere. When you hear it, chances are you also hear a whole bunch of stuff about "structured and sequential" learning. When a teacher puts explicit instruction of phonics rules into a program (instead of teaching them as they crop up in stories and other text), he has a structured approach. Teaching those phonics rules in a logical order makes the teaching also sequential. (Chapter 12 gives you the full scoop on phonics.)

On the subject of using a multisensory and structured, sequential approach, the International Dyslexia Association says that dyslexic students don't need more of the same instruction in class but a different type of instruction. They need to learn basic language sounds and the letters that make them, starting from the very beginning and moving forward in a gradual step-by-step, thorough way. And to help pull all of that together through their own discovery, they must use their eyes, ears, voices, and hands.

Setting the Stage for Multisensory Success

Before you can start helping your child with multisensory learning, you need to assume the role of facilitator or partner. When you model activities, replenish dwindling supplies of materials, and join in the fun but take a facilitating rather than a lead role, your child has ownership and control of a task and feels more inclined to get right into it (eyes, ears, voice, hands, and all!). Here are some ways you can let him assume ownership of his own learning so he can then get multisensory:

✔ Let your child hold his pen, paper, and book. He should feel that his work really *is* his work and not something you want him to do. Small acts like holding his book or peering over his shoulder make him feel that you're taking over, so hands off!

✔ Have a schedule and remind your child to follow it. Say things like "It's 5:00 now, time for homework" and calmly turn off the TV if you have to. Don't overtalk and get into monologues like "Turn off that TV. You never turn it off when you're supposed to. It's homework time, you know that. Go get your homework. Where have you put it? Have you got your pens? Have you been keeping your pencils sharp?"

✔ Offer your help in small doses as needed. Say things like "I'm here if you need me" or "Call me if you get stuck." You probably don't need to sit with your child the whole time, but if you do, stop giving your help as soon as you can and give it again only when it's needed.

✔ Have your child take responsibility for the things he is capable of doing, like putting his books away, sharpening his pencil, and bringing his journal to you to sign.

✔ Give your child small responsibilities at home so he can feel valuable and independent.

✔ Praise your child for doing what he's supposed to do and getting on with things independently.

✔ Teach your child to ask for help in normal, polite tones. If he whines and acts rudely, tell him calmly that you're happy to help and sympathize with his frustration, but remind him that he needs to ask you courteously.

Helping your child plug into multisensory mode at home is important for two reasons:

✔ He may get a lot of traditional chalk-and-talk instruction at school and not much hands-on stuff, so you can compensate for this at home.

✔ Much of what you do rubs off on your child, so taking stock of what you do makes sense. Are you stepping back and allowing him to try out new things for himself? Do you typically model a skill and then give him plenty of practice? Are you more of a doer than an armchair expert?

Making Homework Multisensory

Good teachers help kids apply what they learn in concrete ways. They take information that seems abstract (like a foreign language) and show students that it actually does count in the real world ("Here's a French magazine with Orlando Bloom in it. See! French is used by kids like you!"). You can help your child at home by doing the same thing with his homework. In this section I tell you how to set up and then surge forward.

Setting up a happier homework environment

The traditional idea of kids' doing homework at a desk in a quiet and brightly lit spot may not be right for your dyslexic child. Experiment with different ways of doing things and, as always, if something isn't working, don't force it on your child. Instead, try doing it a different way. You may want to give these simple, practical strategies a whirl.

✔ Let your child stand or alternate between standing and sitting to do his work if he wants. He may feel more comfortable switching positions than sitting for a long time, and in any case, movement helps his wandering thoughts refocus.

✔ Let him chew gum or nibble on a snack while he works. Even really small movements like these can help his mind stay on track.

✔ Let him sip from a water bottle. Again he gets the benefit of small movement, and of course he's hydrating, too.

✔ Many dyslexics are easily distracted by background noise, so you need to experiment. The same thing applies to light; some dyslexics find that an open or closed curtain makes a lot of difference in their ability to concentrate.

✔ Give him brightly colored highlighter pens and help him mark key words. Highlighting can be a nice change from writing or keyboarding, it draws his attention to small bites of important stuff, and it makes his page look cheerful.

✔ Give him a bookmark to keep track of how far he has read. Otherwise he wastes time searching for his place and probably gets irritated in the process.

✔ Give him something, like a set of beads or a squishy ball, to manipulate in his hand. Many dyslexic children have trouble being still, so things that allow your child some slight movement can be really helpful. You may even want to ask an occupational therapist about the range of devices, like squishy seat cushions and wobbly foot rests, you can buy.

✔ Let him take short breaks. At best, most children have an attention span of about 20 minutes, and the same goes for adults. Frequent quick breaks give a person a learning advantage.

✔ Help him represent information in diagrams and pictures. A few paragraphs of text can look infinitely clearer when your child summarizes them in simple bubbles and arrows.

Adult dyslexics need to find their preferred learning environment and routine, too. Take rest breaks and experiment with background noise, lighting, and things like gum and squishy hand devices that help you get a little movement.

Helping your child understand new information

Back in my schooldays, I had to study Shakespeare's *Henry V.* The teacher had my class read the play word for old-fashioned word, though no one understood it. The whole course was horribly tedious, and needless to say, I failed my exam. To this day I've never read any original Shakespeare, only modern kids' versions.

What I'm getting at here is that you can't easily learn a thing by starting from unknown territory. You need familiar ground to get a footing, which in the case of *Henry V* would have been a modern-day explanation (Who was that Henry dude? Who did he argue with? What kind of schoolyard scenario would be similar?).

To help your child with schoolwork or new information that seems foreign to him, link it to something he already knows, and do so in a multisensory way. How exactly? Here are some practical pointers:

✔ Put historical information into a current context that he knows ("Imagine if I made you walk to the gas station. That's how far the children had to walk to get water.")

✔ Use new words in a familiar context ("How many *fearsome* people do you know?").

✔ Act out and discuss new words.

✔ Make models, pictures, and diagrams when you can (like drawings of fearsome and tranquil scenes).

Having Practical Stuff for Playing at Your Fingertips

It's time to home in on the materials that teachers use to add the multisensory element to kids' reading, writing, and spelling activities. You won't be surprised to see modeling clay featuring first off, but did you ever see a teacher use sandpaper as an aid to literacy? In this section I talk about these and other materials that teachers use to give their students educational, feel-good (inside and out!) play.

Modeling clay

A lot of people feel that dyslexic children learn to read better if they see 3D models of letters and words, so modeling clay is a favorite medium. To make your own soft modeling clay, see the recipe in the nearby sidebar.

Gummy mixtures

If you want to have your dyslexic remember letter shapes through drawing them in mediums that give him all sorts of soft or tasty sensations, make him some gluggy, gooey, gummy mixtures to run his fingers through. For delicious mixes, try chocolate pudding, colored sugar, or whipped cream, or get dirty with sand, play cement, or good old garden mud. Another option is "gloop," a gooey, stretchy mix made from soapy stuff, which always feels nice to kids (see the recipe for it in the nearby sidebar). Have your child finger-write letters with these concoctions. Hopefully, he'll lick his fingers only after using the edible mixes!

Mixing up some modeling clay

If you're like me and have recipes jotted on bits of paper all over the house, and good intentions of one day collating them, you're sure to want to keep this "recipe" handy as an easy "treat" for your dyslexic child.

Easy (and edible) modeling clay

You need the following ingredients:

- ✔ 2½ cups flour

- ✔ ½ cup salt

- ✔ 3 tablespoons cooking oil

- ✔ ¼ teaspoon food coloring

- ✔ 2 cups boiling water

Mix the flour, salt, oil, and food coloring in a bowl. Add the boiling water. Mix well and then knead until smooth. (Use the kneading hook on your food mixer if you have one.) This dough will keep for several months in a plastic bag, but don't freeze it.

No food coloring? Try mixing JELL-O gelatin or fruit-drink powder into the boiling water instead.

Sandpaper

When your child uses modeling clay, he gets to squeeze, mold, and pull apart the nice soft dough, using his whole hands. When he feels sandpaper letters, his tactile sensations are fine-tuned further down to his fingertips, and through them he feels, literally, letter shapes. Cut letters out of fine sandpaper so your child can run his fingers over them to help fix the shapes in his brain. In Montessori schools, this activity is regarded so highly that you can always find it being used somewhere in every classroom. (I talk about Montessori schools in Chapter 7.)

To create other textured surfaces, have your child glue things on top of letters you write on paper. Use items like dried beans, rice, yarn, buttons, pencil shavings, and pasta shells.

Laminate

A roll of adhesive, clear book covering is a great investment. Write letters and words on regular paper and then stick this covering over them. Your child can trace over the letters with his fingers or use whiteboard pens and then reuse the sheets after a quick wipe. He gets plenty of hands-on practice of writing on a nice smooth surface, you can make big and small copies of the same letter, and erasing and starting over is a breeze. If you want the deluxe version of the same thing, take your letter sheets to an office supplies store to be laminated.

Gloop, wonderful gloop

Children love to run their hands through gloop, which you can make with the following ingredients:

- ✔ 1 cup white glue (Elmer's works best)

- ✔ 1 cup water

- ✔ Powder paint or food coloring

- ✔ 1½ teaspoons borax (find this in the detergent aisle at the grocery store)

- ✔ 1 cup warm water

Mix together the glue, water, and coloring. In a separate cup, dissolve the borax in 1 cup of warm water. Add the dissolved borax to the other ingredients and stir rapidly for about 2 minutes.

Teach your little child to write in stages with laminate:

1. **Have you child practice tracing over the letters of the alphabet**

2. **Have him write the letters by joining dots (that you already made for him.**

3. **Have him copy the letters, while looking at the originals, on a separate sheet of paper.**

4. **Have him write the letters without any props at all.**

Scissors

Scissors are a handy thing for your child to have so he can cut up lists of words and end up with a pile of single words to move around. By grouping the words (*rain, pain,* and *main,* for example) and using them like flashcards (see the following section), he gives himself a more interesting way to learn them than by just studying the list. For more games you can play with cut-out words, flip to Chapter 12.

Flashcards

Flashcards should come with a warning saying something like "WARNING: These cards are pointless and tedious unless basic procedures are followed." Here's an incident that happened in my family a few years ago that perfectly illustrates my point.

I arrived home from work one day and found my sister, Lyn, helping my kindergarten child, Lauren, with sight words. Lyn had found a pack of my flashcards (100 individual sight words) and my willing child, so thought she'd do a good deed. Now she sat in front of my daughter and held each of the 100 flashcards in front of her face, one at a time.

"When," said Lyn, holding up the card.

"When," repeated Lauren obligingly.

"Come," said Lyn.

"Come," repeated Lauren.

"Who."

"Who."

"Saw."

"Saw."

Was my sister giving Lauren a head start with reading? No. Lauren simply could not learn 100 words, all at one time, by seeing and reciting each one after my sister. The task was too enormous, and all she'd probably remember was the nice experience of having her aunt interact with her.

In the right hands flashcards are a terrific tool for children, especially dyslexic children, because they give small pieces of clear information that you can control. For example, you can use just ten cards for a few weeks before adding more, and you can go as slowly and with as much repetition as your child needs. But never just buy a pack of 100 words and flash every one in front of your child in the hope that some of the information will stick. Exactly how can you get things right for your dyslexic child on your first try?

- ✔ **Give information in small bites.** You should select five to ten cards. Most of us can retain only between five and ten pieces of new information at any one time.

- ✔ **Use only cards that your child's already primed for** (like *bug, hut,* and *luck* and not *bug, promise,* and *treat*) and progress to the other cards only when you've shown your child their spelling pattern (like *cheese, peel,* and *deep*).

- ✔ **Allow your child ownership.** So that Lauren feels in charge of her learning, my sister should invite her to choose the words for herself.

- ✔ **Have a hands-off policy.** Your child should handle the cards herself and put away the remaining cards herself. When you handle the cards, the paper, the book, or whatever is in front of your child, you take over.

LD Online: www.ldonline.com
This nice, easy site features forums, ask the experts, and in-depth information or FAQs. Use the top menu bar to navigate and check out "First person essays" to see what it's like to be dyslexic. (My favorite essay is "Upside down in a right sided world" by W. Sumner Davis, Ph.D, on page 1.)

Schwab Learning (part of the Charles and Helen Schwab Foundation):
www.schwablearning.org
Voice mail: 650-655-2410
Charles Schwab, business mogul and dyslexic, funds this site. Easy to use, it has some of the best, plain-talking articles I've read, covers summer camps and workshops, and includes message boards and everything else.

Smart Kids with Learning Disabilities: www.smartkidswithld.org
Another nice, easy-to-read, uplifting place to start finding stuff out. This site features, among other stuff, Ask the Experts, Teacher's Corner, and a Winner's Circle of personal accounts from successful adults with learning disabilities.

Five big organizations

For information on just about anything to do with dyslexia, consult the big shots. The organizations I list here have big reputations, big databases, and plenty of connections. They'll have answers for you, and if not, they'll connect you to someone who does.

International Dyslexia Association: www.interdys.org
The aspect of this site that I like is the network of local branches (see the next section).

LDA (Learning Disabilities Association of America): www.ldanatl.org
Voice mail: 888-300-6710, 412-341-1515
Call and leave your name and address to get an information package. The site offers an online parent course on advocacy and IDEA '97.

NCLD (National Center for Learning Disabilities): www.ld.org
Voice mail: 212-545-7510
Call and leave your name, address, and specific question to get information sent to you. You can also request info by clicking on your area on the map on the Web site and filling out the form.

NICHCY (National Dissemination Center for Children with Disabilities):
www.nichcy.org
Voice mail: 800-695-0285, 202-884-8200
Leave your name and address to get an information package sent to you

Appendix B

Contacts and Resources

• •

*T*he great thing about finding information on dyslexia is that every kind of help and advice you'll ever need is within reach. I've delved deeply into the Internet and run up a fearsome phone bill to give you exactly the right contacts. Here they are then, links and numbers that really do work.

If you don't see a phone number in the resources in this chapter, there isn't one. You have to get information (usually including an e-mail address), or your local phone number, from the Web site.

Getting General Information Online or by Voice Mail

The contacts in the following sections give you info on just about everything you would ever need to know about dyslexia (definitions, advocacy, parent courses, technology, legislature, local branches, ask the experts, FAQs, and chat rooms). I tell you what I think are each one's special strengths.

Five general Web sites to start you off

This appendix is so chock-full of Web sites that you may be wondering where on earth to start. Start here. The Web sites in this section are easy to navigate, friendly in tone, and really helpful (or I wouldn't have included them!).

Dyslexia Parents Resource: www.dyslexia-parent.com
This is such a terrific site! It has information for parents in any country, but especially for those in the United States and the United Kingdom. It includes sections for teenagers and college students and, well, everything you need, in attractive, simple terms.

Hello Friend: www.hellofriend.org
Hello Friend is a great feel-good place to start finding stuff out. Funded by actor Bill Cosby, it's dedicated to his late son, Ennis, who was dyslexic and is the home of the nonprofit Hello Friend Foundation that awards grants and books to classrooms and schools.

(allow seven to ten days). The organization offers free downloadable publications on grants, IDEA, research, and many other subjects, in English or Spanish.

The Dyslexia Institute (United Kingdom): www.dyslexia-inst.org.uk
Voice mail: 01784 2223000
The Web site is easy to navigate (you won't get lost, I promise) and offers brief, to-the-point information.

Talking to Someone Directly

Sometimes a Web site isn't what you want, and a recorded telephone message isn't the answer either. You need to talk to a real live person in the here and now. You can forgo technology for a while and get that simple human touch by contacting the groups in this section.

IDA (International Dyslexia Association): Want to talk to someone who isn't part of a government organization? Need to unload your concerns or meet other parents? Check out your local branch of the International Dyslexia Association. Go to www.interdys.org and click on IDA Branches/Affiliates, then IDA Branches, and lastly your state. You get phone numbers to call and if someone doesn't immediately answer, a person will call you back soon.

I called three branches to see how quickly I got to talk to someone and was called within the hour by Northern California (wow, David!), within the day by Massachusetts (well done, Pam!), and the next day by Ontario (go Ontario!)

National Crisis Helpline: For 24/7 telephone contact, call 800-999-9999. To find help lines outside the United States, do an Internet search for "help line." Older dyslexics can use this number in an emergency.

PTI (Parent Training and Information) centers: To talk to someone right now, call your Parent Training and Information Center. It's one of a network of centers all over the United States where you get disability-related advice (on practically any issue, like testing, finding a therapist, and advocating for your child in school), referrals, and even legal representation if it turns out you need it — all for free (it's federally funded)! When I called, I immediately got a real-life, cheerful person on the other end, and she called me right back when my line went crackly.

To find your center, call the Minnesota main office (also called the Parent Advocacy Coalition for Educational Rights) at 952-838-9000 or 888-248-0822 toll-free nationwide, or go to www.taalliance.org/centers/index.htm and click on your geographical zone.

Checking Your Child's Eyes, Ears, and Mouth

You want to be sure that your child's dyslexia isn't being made worse by speech, hearing, or vision problems. The Web sites in the following list provide direction on where you can get this important stuff checked out. See Chapter 4 for details on the importance of watching for vision, hearing, and speech problems at an early age.

  ✔ **Optometrists:** For information on vision problems and a directory of optometrists, log on to the Optometrists Network at www.children-special-needs.org.

  ✔ **Overlays and lenses:** To read about colored lenses and overlays, check out the Irlen Syndrome site at www.irlen.com/sss_main.htm and Howtolearn.com at www.howtolearn.com/filters.html (both are commercial sites) and Dyslexia Research Trust at www.dyslexic.org.uk/va_news.htm.

  ✔ **Speech therapy:** For information on language problems and speech therapy, log on to Speechville Express at www.speechville.com, the American Speech-Language-Hearing Association at www.asha.org/default.htm, and the Childhood Apraxia of Speech Association at www.apraxia-kids.org.

  ✔ **Treatments via the ears:** To read about dyslexia treatments that involve playing filtered sounds to your child through earphones, visit www.mozartcenter.com, where you can find out more about "The Sounds of Wellness," and Audiblox at www.audiblox2000.com/dyslexia_dyslexic/dyslexia.htm — both are commercial Web sites.

Surveying Self-Tests

When you have your child assessed for dyslexia, you typically work with a specialist within the local public school district or an independent tester. However, if you want to get reading and dyslexia tests for yourself, here are your connections. You can have your child take tests online, or you can download a test so she takes it the paper and pen way. Either way, you might get the basic information you want without paying the high fees that psychologists charge. See Chapter 6 for full details on the assessment process.

  ✔ **Burt Reading Test:** For the (British) Burt Reading Test, log on to the Reading Reform Foundation at www.rrf.org.uk.

  ✔ **Mail-in dyslexia tests:** For (worldwide) tests that purport to measure dyslexia, log on to www.dyslexia-test.com.

- ✔ **Online Learning Style Tests:** Take a free online test to see whether you have a dominant visual, auditory, or kinesthetic learning style at `www.ldpride.net`.

- ✔ **Read Aloud Tests of Reading:** For (Australian) read-aloud tests and spelling tests, log on to `www.literacytesting.com`.

- ✔ **Schonell Tests:** For the (British) Schonell Reading Test, log on to `http://members.tripod.com/~gleigh/readtst.htm`. For the (British) Schonell Spelling Test, log on to the Reading Reform Foundation at `www.rrf.org.uk`.

School districts may not accept the results of these self-tests on their own as reliable indicators that your child needs a dyslexia assessment or special accommodations in class.

Focusing on Alternative Schooling and School Reading Programs

Alternative schools offer programs that you may not find in a public school, but that doesn't mean they necessarily provide special help for dyslexic children. See Chapter 7 for details on selecting the best school for your child and then find your nearest schools by visiting the sites listed here. (Chapter 7 also has info on home schooling, including resources and materials.)

Schools

This section lets you search outside the lines. Here you're put in touch with private schools that might offer just the kind of curriculum you're thinking of for your child.

Charter schools near you
Web site: `www.uscharterschools.org`

Magnet schools of North America
Web site: `www.magnet.edu`
Phone: 202-824-0672

Montessori schools
Web site: `www.montessori.org`

NAPSEC (National Association of Private Special Education Centers)
Web site: `www.napsec.com`
Voice mail: 202-408-3338

Schools especially for children with dyslexia
Web site: `www.ldresources.org`

Waldorf Schools of North America
Web site: `www.awsna.org`
Phone: 916-961-0927

School reading programs

A traditional public school usually has a reading program in place. Get the full picture about a school reading program at the Web site or get a quick summary by phone. Either way, it can be well worth your while finding out how these programs work and whether you can get support materials to use at home.

Orton-Gillingham, Lindamood-Bell, Slingerland, and Spalding are well respected and widely used programs. They are school-based programs, but independent therapists and tutors also use these methods. I cover other therapists and tutors later in this appendix.

Academy of Orton-Gillingham Practitioners and Educators
Web site: www.ortonacademy.org
Phone: 845-373-8919

Alphabetic Phonics
Web site: www.epsbooks.com
(click on Dyslexia Materials)
Phone: 800-225-5750

Corrective Reading (also called SRA, Distar, and Direct Instruction)
Web site: www.sraonline.com
Phone: 888-772–4543

Davis Learning Strategies
Web site: www.davislearn.com
Phone: 650-692-7141 or 888-999-3324
(curriculum materials)

Early Intervention in Reading
Web site: www.earlyintervention
inreading.com
Phone: 763-785-0701

LANGUAGE!
Web site: www.language-usa.net/
default.html
Phone: 800-547-6747, ext. 266

Lexia Herman Method (also called Herman Method)
Web site: www.hermanmethod.com
Phone: 800-435-3942 or 781-259-8752

Lindamood-Bell Programs
Web site: www.lblp.com
Phone: 800-233-1819

Project Read
Web site: www.projectread.com
Phone: 800-450-0343

Read Naturally
Web site: www.readnaturally.com
Phone: 800-788-4085

Reading Recovery
Web site: www.reading
recovery.com
Phone: 614-310-7323

Recipe for Reading
Web site: www.epsbooks.com
(click on Dyslexia Materials)
Phone: 800-225-5750

Slingerland
Web site: www.slingerland.org
Phone: 425-453-1190

Spalding
Web site: www.spalding.org
Phone: 602-866-7801

Success for All (SFA)
Web site: www.successforall.net
Phone: 1-800-548-4998

Wilson Language Program
Web site: www.wilsonlanguage.com
Phone: 800-782-3766

Laying Down the Law

Legal jargon and legal forms are heavy stuff. In this section you get places you can go for legal advice and advocates you can call on to help you translate all the legal hoopla and IEP procedure into regular language. See Chapter 8 for more about your legal rights (and your child's).

Council of Parent Attorneys and Advocates: www.copaa.net
For a list of advocates and attorneys in your state, visit the site and click on Find an Attorney/Advocate. Advocates can go with you to IEP meetings and advise you on your rights, and attorneys can tell you the precise letter of the law if you run into difficulties.

Disability Law Centers: www.protectionandadvocacy.com
Phone: 202-408-9514
E-mail: napas@earthlink.net
Your Disability Law Center (part of a country-wide network) is a terrific place for getting free legal advice (for both kids and adults) and legal representation if you need it. The hub of this network is the National Association of Protection and Advocacy Systems in Washington, D.C. Call to get referred to your local center.

Wright's Law: www.wrightslaw.com
Attorney Pete Wright and psychotherapist Pam Wright maintain this comprehensive site that offers you everything from advocacy training and legal representation to tips for working with teachers and principals.

Finding Independent Programs, Therapists, and Learning Centers

Many of the places in the following sections have phone numbers and someone who answers them (not voice mail)! Call, talk, and get local contacts — as easily as that! When it comes to securing help outside school for your dyslexic child, your hardest task will be narrowing down your options (whether to go to a clinic, therapist, or tutor and whether you like the programs they use) rather than finding them in the first place. Check out Chapter 9 for additional information about securing independent help.

Dyslexia treatments

Intrigued by what you read about these programs in Chapter 20? Check out the following independent treatments with a quick call or Web surf. You'll probably have to call to get prices (they're usually not on the Web site), and even then you may have to persevere. If you're told, "It's different for each child," hang in there. You'll get to the cold figures in the end.

All Kinds of Minds
Web site: www.allkinds ofminds.org
Phone: 919-442-1033 or 646-775-6677

Audiblox
Web site: www.audiblox2000.com
Phone: 701-260-2777 (for orders)

Auditory Integration Training (AIT)
Web site: www.auditory integration.net
Phone: 828-683-6900 (North Carolina), 203-655-1091(Connecticut)

Balametrics
Web site: www.balametrics.com
Phone: 800-894-3187

Brain Gym
Web site: www.braingym.org
Phone: 800-356-2109 or 805-658-7942

Davis Dyslexia Correction
Web site: www.dyslexiahelp.com

DORE Program
Web site: www.dorecenters.com
Phone: 866-784-4377

Fast ForWord
Web site: www.scilearn.com
Phone: 888-358-0212 (United States and Canada), 701-298-6376 (international)

Feingold Program
Web site: www.feingold.org
Phone: 800-321-3287 (United States only), 631-369–9340 (international)

Irlen Method
Web site: www.irlen.com

Levinson Medical Centers
Web site: www.levinson medical.com
Phone: 516-482-2888, 800-334–READ (7323), 800-8-PHOBIA (746242)

Processing and Cognitive Enhancement (PACE)
Web site: www.brainskills.com
Phone: 866-679-1569

Tomatis
Web site: www.tomatis.com

Therapists and tutors

The term "therapist" or "consultant" usually signifies that the person using it is qualified and experienced. A "tutor" is probably a more modest deal in these areas, but you must check qualifications, experience, and all-round niceness on an individual basis.

ALTA (Academic Language Therapy Association)
Web site: www.altaread.org
Phone: 866-283-7133 or 972-233-9107, ext. 201

Association of Educational Therapists
Web site: www.aetonline.org
Phone: 818-843-1183

ASHA (American Speech-Language-Hearing Association)
Web site: www.asha.org
Phone: 800-638-TALK (8255)

Independent Educational Consultant Association
Web site: www.educational consulting.org
Phone: 800-808-IECA (4322) or 703-591-4850

Parents Active for Vision Education (PAVE)
Web site: www.pavevision.org/
Phone: 619-287-0081 or 800-PAVE (7283)-988

Professional Tutors of America
Web site: www.professional tutors.com
Phone: 800-TEACHUS (8322487)

Dyslexia clinics

A local dyslexia clinic can be an option for supplementing your child's education in school.

32º Masonic Learning Centers
Web site: www.childrenslearningcenters.org
Phone: 877-861-0528 or 781-862-8518

Dyslexia Institutes of America
Web site: www.dyslexiainstitutes.com
Phone: 217-235-0045 (home office)

General learning centers

If you're thinking of taking your child to a general learning center, a quick call to the numbers I list here can save you a lot of time. The people who work in these centers are always happy to tell you about their programs, but remember that as good as these centers sound, they are for everyone and *don't* focus solely on instruction for dyslexics.

Huntington Learning Centers
Web site: www.huntington
learning.com
Phone: 800-CAN-LEARN (226-53276)

Kumon Math and Reading Centers
Web site: www.kumon.com
Phone: 877-586-6673 (United States),
800-222-6284 (Canada)

Oxford Learning Centers
Web site: www.oxfordlearning.com
Phone: Find your nearest center's
number on the Web site

Score Educational Centers
Web site: www.escore.com
Phone: 866-65-SCORE (72673)

Sylvan Learning Center
Web site: www.educate.com
Phone: 888-EDUCATE (3382283)

Trying Technology

Are you stepping over CD-ROMS that your child used a few times and then
threw aside with her karaoke machine and Gameboy (it's six months old but
technologically speaking, obsolete)? Here are a few technical gizmos that, in
technical life spans, have longevity. Chapter 9 has additional info on other
gadgets that can help your dyslexic child.

- **Books on tape:** Get books on tape by visiting the Web site for Recording
  for the Blind and Dyslexic at www.rfbd.org or by calling 866-732-3585.
  You can also find them at www.booksontape.com.

- **CD-ROMs:** For a CD-ROM that's designed to fine-tune your child's auditory discrimination and phonemic awareness, check out Earobics at
  www.earobics.com.

  For a fun CD-ROM that helps your child with sounds and words,
  check out *Baileys Book House* at www.learningcompany.com
  (click on 4-5 Preschool) or call 800-395-0277.

  Get Smart Draw software at www.smartdraw.com or by calling
  858-225-3300. For Kidspiration and Inspiration software, visit
  www.kidspiration.com or call 503-297-3004.

- **Computers:** To buy used or reconditioned computers, check out
  www.dell.com, www.compaqfactoryoutlet.com, www.recycled
  goods.com, and www.ganc.com.

- **Print recognition software:** TextBridge, published by ScanSoft Inc., is a
  program you may want to check out because it's available as a free demo
  download (for Windows operating systems) from www.softlookup.com/
  display.asp?id=5585.

- ✔ **Spell checkers:** To find out about spell checkers, visit `www.schwab learning.org/articles.asp?r=444&g=4` and `www.dyslexia-parent.com/software.html`.

- ✔ **Typing:** Check out Typing Pal Junior at `www.demarque.com` or call 888-458-9143.

- ✔ **Speech-to-text software:** For comparisons of Dragon NaturallySpeaking and Via Voice, go to `www.dyslexic.com/dictcomp.htm`.

Lending a Hand to Teens, College Students, and Adults

Plenty of information is available about college and finances and other grown-up matters. The info can be overwhelming, so in this section I give you a handful of easy-to-understand resources. See Chapters 16, 17, and 18 for more about helping teens, college students, and adults.

College entrance exams and other tests

If terms such as SAT, GED, and ACT are unfamiliar to you, they can sound like alphabet soup. To get the dish on these tests, sample these wholesome Web sites:

- ✔ To find out about ACT testing, go to `www.actstudent.org`.

- ✔ For a description of the GED, visit `www.acenet.edu/`.

- ✔ To read about the SAT and other testing (like AP, GMAT, GRE, PRAXIS, and TOEFL), check out Educational Testing Service (ETS) at `www.ets.org` (click on Test Takers with Disabilities).

College and general education information

Whether you're learning to read and write from scratch or want to know which college can train you in law but make allowances for your dyslexia, here are some helpful contacts.

- ✔ **Courses:** Find online college and university courses at these Web sites:

  - `www.passGED.com`

  - `www.adultlearn.com`

  - `www.educationforadults.com`

- ✔ **Disabilities:** The HEATH Center of George Washington University is a clearinghouse of postsecondary education information for individuals with disabilities. Check out its main Web page at www.heath.gwu.edu or phone 800-544-3284 or 202-973-0904.

- ✔ **Dyslexia-friendly colleges:** For lists of dyslexia-friendly colleges, visit www.dyslexia-adults.com/a16.html and www.ldresources.org. For a list of colleges of excellence and answers to college-related questions, visit www.collegesofdistinction.com.

- ✔ **General:** Check out World of Dyslexia at www.dyslexia-college.com or www.dyslexia-adults.com.

- ✔ **Literacy:** For learn-to-read programs, check out America's Literacy Directory at www.literacydirectory.org or call 800-228-8813.

- ✔ **Test-free colleges:** The National Center for Fair and Open Testing lists colleges that don't ask your dyslexic child to submit test results. Check it out at www.fairtest.org.

Financial aid and scholarships

College costs money — no surprise there. Here are a few places that can give you advice about how to pay for it or even how to reduce your costs.

- ✔ **Awards and scholarships:** For information on the Marion Huber Learning through Listening Awards, go to www.rfbd.org or call 800-221-4792.

  For details on the Anne Ford Scholarship, go to www.ld.org/awards/afscholarinfo.cfm or use voice mail, 212-545-7510.

- ✔ **Books:** Octameron Associates is a higher education publishing and consulting firm. Check it out at www.octameron.com or call 703-836-5480.

- ✔ **Financial aid and loans:** Apply for federal student grants, work-study aid, and loans from the Department of Education at www.fafsa.ed.gov.

  Get more information about loans and financial plans at www.studentaid.ed.gov.

  For information about financial aid, including aid for families of veterans and students interested in careers in the military, and aid for people who have given community service (like volunteering in AmeriCorps), visit www.finaid.org.

- ✔ **Tax deductions:** You can claim tax deductions for your child's specialized tutoring and schooling. For the fine details, read IRS Publication 502 (Medical and Dental Expenses), downloadable from www.irs.gov/publications/p502/ (click on Forms and Publications and then Download Forms and Publications by: Publication Number).

Jobs and other life skills

Here's a quick section about jobs and cars. If you're out of work and need help getting back into the groove, your local vocational rehabilitation (VR) office can help. If you need a lot of practice for your driving test, you can take courses and get practice questions. Here are your starting points.

- ✔ **Advocacy:** Client Assistance Program (CAP) offices give you advice and advocacy (but not direct services). Call your nearest office if you're having trouble getting VR services: www.jan.wvu.edu/SBSES/VOCREHAB.HTM.

- ✔ **Driving:** Find your nearest Department of Motor Vehicles office at www.dmv.org.

- ✔ **Job training:** VR offices give job-training and job-finding services to people with disabilities. Find your nearest office at www.jan.wvu.edu/sbses/vocrehab.htm.

At-home dyslexia programs

Adult dyslexics can improve their reading skills at home by working through any one of the following programs. The best approach is to have a calm and constructive friend to guide you, but you can choose to work alone if you prefer or can't find a willing ally. To make the right choice of program, read my brief comment and then visit the sites you're interested in.

Alpha Phonics
Web site: www.howtotutor.com
Phone: 208-322-4440
This attractive, easy book has been around a long time and is inexpensive, too! The book costs $29.95, and for Windows computer users who wish to work by themselves, there's a CD-ROM that costs $39.95. Get a sneak preview of the first four lessons by using the online demo.

Language Tune-Up Kit
Web site: www.jwor.com
Phone: 888-431-6310 or 614-784-8710
This straightforward CD-ROM (Windows only) has easy-to-follow instructions (for all-by-yourself use) and a systematic progression of lessons. You get plenty of chances to practice new skills, and the site includes a progress chart. The adult's program, Language Tune-Up At Home, costs $159. (The Language Tune-Up Kit For Kids costs $69.)

Rush Reading Clinic
Web site: www.rushreadingclinic.com
Phone: 603-880-0125
This set of five videotapes is meant for your unassisted home use. Your first instruction is to go off and learn a bunch of sound-spellings by yourself.

You're shown the letters and told the sounds, but that's it; at this stage you get no explanation of sounding out. After you learn those sounds though, you get instruction about adding them to other sounds to build whole words. You are led through a series of phonics skills, and the familiar instruction to go off and learn new sounds crops up intermittently. Each videotape costs about $40.

We All Can Read

Web site: `www.weallcanread.com`

Phone: 404-310-2839

This fat book (third grade to adult) of large print exercises is handy if you have someone to guide you. The lessons progress systematically with plenty of repetition of new sounds, but you have to flip between student and instructor pages, and some of the concepts are best understood by someone with some previous experience in teaching reading. The book costs $33.

Index

• E •

• M •

• N •

• O •

• R •

• S •

• *Y* •

• *Z* •

BUSINESS, CAREERS & PERSONAL FINANCE

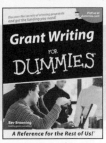

0-7645-5307-0

0-7645-5331-3 *†

Also available:
- Accounting For Dummies †
  0-7645-5314-3
- Business Plans Kit For Dummies †
  0-7645-5365-8
- Cover Letters For Dummies
  0-7645-5224-4
- Frugal Living For Dummies
  0-7645-5403-4
- Leadership For Dummies
  0-7645-5176-0
- Managing For Dummies
  0-7645-1771-6

- Marketing For Dummies
  0-7645-5600-2
- Personal Finance For Dummies *
  0-7645-2590-5
- Project Management For Dummies
  0-7645-5283-X
- Resumes For Dummies †
  0-7645-5471-9
- Selling For Dummies
  0-7645-5363-1
- Small Business Kit For Dummies *†
  0-7645-5093-4

HOME & BUSINESS COMPUTER BASICS

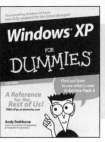

0-7645-4074-2

0-7645-3758-X

Also available:
- ACT! 6 For Dummies
  0-7645-2645-6
- iLife '04 All-in-One Desk Reference
  For Dummies
  0-7645-7347-0
- iPAQ For Dummies
  0-7645-6769-1
- Mac OS X Panther Timesaving
  Techniques For Dummies
  0-7645-5812-9
- Macs For Dummies
  0-7645-5656-8

- Microsoft Money 2004 For Dummies
  0-7645-4195-1
- Office 2003 All-in-One Desk Reference
  For Dummies
  0-7645-3883-7
- Outlook 2003 For Dummies
  0-7645-3759-8
- PCs For Dummies
  0-7645-4074-2
- TiVo For Dummies
  0-7645-6923-6
- Upgrading and Fixing PCs For Dummies
  0-7645-1665-5
- Windows XP Timesaving Techniques
  For Dummies
  0-7645-3748-2

FOOD, HOME, GARDEN, HOBBIES, MUSIC & PETS

0-7645-5295-3

0-7645-5232-5

Also available:
- Bass Guitar For Dummies
  0-7645-2487-9
- Diabetes Cookbook For Dummies
  0-7645-5230-9
- Gardening For Dummies *
  0-7645-5130-2
- Guitar For Dummies
  0-7645-5106-X
- Holiday Decorating For Dummies
  0-7645-2570-0
- Home Improvement All-in-One
  For Dummies
  0-7645-5680-0

- Knitting For Dummies
  0-7645-5395-X
- Piano For Dummies
  0-7645-5105-1
- Puppies For Dummies
  0-7645-5255-4
- Scrapbooking For Dummies
  0-7645-7208-3
- Senior Dogs For Dummies
  0-7645-5818-8
- Singing For Dummies
  0-7645-2475-5
- 30-Minute Meals For Dummies
  0-7645-2589-1

INTERNET & DIGITAL MEDIA

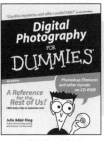

0-7645-1664-7

0-7645-6924-4

Also available:
- 2005 Online Shopping Directory
  For Dummies
  0-7645-7495-7
- CD & DVD Recording For Dummies
  0-7645-5956-7
- eBay For Dummies
  0-7645-5654-1
- Fighting Spam For Dummies
  0-7645-5965-6
- Genealogy Online For Dummies
  0-7645-5964-8
- Google For Dummies
  0-7645-4420-9

- Home Recording For Musicians
  For Dummies
  0-7645-1634-5
- The Internet For Dummies
  0-7645-4173-0
- iPod & iTunes For Dummies
  0-7645-7772-7
- Preventing Identity Theft For Dummies
  0-7645-7336-5
- Pro Tools All-in-One Desk Reference
  For Dummies
  0-7645-5714-9
- Roxio Easy Media Creator For Dummies
  0-7645-7131-1

* Separate Canadian edition also available
† Separate U.K. edition also available

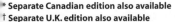

SPORTS, FITNESS, PARENTING, RELIGION & SPIRITUALITY

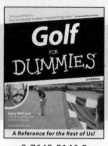

0-7645-5146-9

0-7645-5418-2

Also available:
- Adoption For Dummies
  0-7645-5488-3
- Basketball For Dummies
  0-7645-5248-1
- The Bible For Dummies
  0-7645-5296-1
- Buddhism For Dummies
  0-7645-5359-3
- Catholicism For Dummies
  0-7645-5391-7
- Hockey For Dummies
  0-7645-5228-7

- Judaism For Dummies
  0-7645-5299-6
- Martial Arts For Dummies
  0-7645-5358-5
- Pilates For Dummies
  0-7645-5397-6
- Religion For Dummies
  0-7645-5264-3
- Teaching Kids to Read For Dummies
  0-7645-4043-2
- Weight Training For Dummies
  0-7645-5168-X
- Yoga For Dummies
  0-7645-5117-5

TRAVEL

0-7645-5438-7

0-7645-5453-0

Also available:
- Alaska For Dummies
  0-7645-1761-9
- Arizona For Dummies
  0-7645-6938-4
- Cancún and the Yucatán For Dummies
  0-7645-2437-2
- Cruise Vacations For Dummies
  0-7645-6941-4
- Europe For Dummies
  0-7645-5456-5
- Ireland For Dummies
  0-7645-5455-7

- Las Vegas For Dummies
  0-7645-5448-4
- London For Dummies
  0-7645-4277-X
- New York City For Dummies
  0-7645-6945-7
- Paris For Dummies
  0-7645-5494-8
- RV Vacations For Dummies
  0-7645-5443-3
- Walt Disney World & Orlando For Dummies
  0-7645-6943-0

GRAPHICS, DESIGN & WEB DEVELOPMENT

0-7645-4345-8

0-7645-5589-8

Also available:
- Adobe Acrobat 6 PDF For Dummies
  0-7645-3760-1
- Building a Web Site For Dummies
  0-7645-7144-3
- Dreamweaver MX 2004 For Dummies
  0-7645-4342-3
- FrontPage 2003 For Dummies
  0-7645-3882-9
- HTML 4 For Dummies
  0-7645-1995-6
- Illustrator CS For Dummies
  0-7645-4084-X

- Macromedia Flash MX 2004 For Dummies
  0-7645-4358-X
- Photoshop 7 All-in-One Desk Reference For Dummies
  0-7645-1667-1
- Photoshop CS Timesaving Techniques For Dummies
  0-7645-6782-9
- PHP 5 For Dummies
  0-7645-4166-8
- PowerPoint 2003 For Dummies
  0-7645-3908-6
- QuarkXPress 6 For Dummies
  0-7645-2593-X

NETWORKING, SECURITY, PROGRAMMING & DATABASES

0-7645-6852-3

0-7645-5784-X

Also available:
- A+ Certification For Dummies
  0-7645-4187-0
- Access 2003 All-in-One Desk Reference For Dummies
  0-7645-3988-4
- Beginning Programming For Dummies
  0-7645-4997-9
- C For Dummies
  0-7645-7068-4
- Firewalls For Dummies
  0-7645-4048-3
- Home Networking For Dummies
  0-7645-42796

- Network Security For Dummies
  0-7645-1679-5
- Networking For Dummies
  0-7645-1677-9
- TCP/IP For Dummies
  0-7645-1760-0
- VBA For Dummies
  0-7645-3989-2
- Wireless All In-One Desk Reference For Dummies
  0-7645-7496-5
- Wireless Home Networking For Dummies
  0-7645-3910-8